This is a methods book that is easy to use. It includes all the practicalities relevant to the student, even the ones that are usually forgotten (e.g. how to work with the supervisor) – but without ever losing sight of the theoretical and philosophical embeddedness of the research process. Highly recommendable!
– Søren Askegaard, University of Southern Denmark

It is rare to find a qualitative research book that is both user-friendly and sophisticated. Chris Hackley's book speaks equally well to novices and experts. It covers the basics of how and why to do an interpretative research project and yet introduces advanced topics like introspection, literary analysis, phenomenology and discourse analysis.
– Russell Belk, Distinguished Research Professor and Kraft Foods Canada Chair in Marketing at Schulich School of Business, York University, Canada

Chris Hackley is the best in the business. And this book is Chris at his best. It's clear, concise, compelling and chock-full of clever ideas. If you have a dissertation to write, this is the book for you.
– Stephen Brown, Professor of Marketing Research at Ulster University, UK

In this important text, Chris covers the key aspects of interpretive research – including the collection of qualitative data, the phenomenological underpinnings, (auto)ethnography, literary criticism, semiotics and hermeneutics. Every serious student of marketing and management should take the opportunity to review this valuable introduction to a topic of great relevance to studies in the business area.
– Morris B. Holbrook, W. T. Dillard Professor Emeritus, Graduate School of Business, Columbia University, USA

I am delighted that an accessible, comprehensive and engaging text on qualitative research within an interpretative approach has finally been written! It deals with everything a novice researcher needs to know and is an ideal jumping off point for those involved with more advanced studies. I have already recommended it to my undergraduate, masters and doctoral students!
– Professor Lisa O'Malley, University of Limerick, Ireland, and Chair of Academy of Marketing Research Committee

There are few books on how to do qualitative marketing and management research projects. Professor Hackley is an expert in designing qualitative research projects and analysing qualitative data through interpretive approach. This book provides an invaluable guideline to new and experienced researchers alike.

– Norman Peng, Professor in Marketing, Glasgow School for Business and Society, Glasgow Caledonian University, UK

Professor Hackley presents an excellent guide to using social science-based interpretative methods for researchers and students undertaking qualitative research projects in marketing and management. As he points out, "All research entails interpretation of something," and improving our understanding of social phenomena using qualitative techniques is increasingly important for business students, academic researchers and practitioners.

– Michael Saren, Professor of Marketing, University of Leicester and Visiting Professor, Birmingham University Business School, UK

This book provides a one-stop shop that introduces interpretive methods to marketing and management researchers and research students. Clearly presented, with useful, up-to-date examples that include practical guidance, relevant for a wide range of interpretive research.

– Jonathan Schroeder, William A. Kern Professor, School of Communication, Rochester Institute of Technology, New York, USA

This is an excellent introduction for students who wish to conduct rigorous interpretive research in marketing, consumer research, organization or management studies. The book is well organised, all chapters have clear objectives, and the glossary of key terms at the end of each chapter is a valuable resource. Professor Hackley speaks directly to students and as a result the book is easy to follow and digest. This book is destined to be on reading lists around the world, and it will certainly be on mine.

– Avi Shankar, Professor of Consumer Research, School of Management, University of Bath, UK

Qualitative Research in Marketing and Management

This is a practical and accessible, yet sophisticated introduction to interpretive methods for doing qualitative research projects and dissertations. Bringing together concepts of qualitative research from ethnography, phenomenology, critical discourse analysis, semiotics, literary analysis, postmodernism and poststructuralism this textbook offers an accessible and comprehensive introduction to the subject. Utilising a uniquely pragmatic approach, it bridges the gap between advanced, specialised books on research traditions with more general introductory business research books.

This new edition has been fully updated to include new examples, explorations of the field, and an improved pedagogy with better exposition of key issues and concepts, as well as more schematics and diagrams to aid understanding. The first half of the book considers the practicalities of research and writing a research project, including the craft of academic writing, the critical literature review, the role of the independent research project as part of university courses, suggested projected structures, standards of academic scholarship, and the main techniques for gathering qualitative data. The book's second half deals with abstract concepts and advanced theory by looking at key theoretical traditions that guide the interpretation of qualitative data.

It is perfect for advanced undergraduate and postgraduate students of marketing, management, consumer behaviour and research methods. It will also be useful as a primer for practitioners in qualitative research.

Chris Hackley is Professor of Marketing at Royal Holloway, University of London, UK. He has published more than 200 books, chapters and research journal papers on topics in qualitative research, marketing, advertising and consumer policy.

Qualitative Research in Marketing and Management

Doing Interpretive Research Projects

Second edition

Chris Hackley

Routledge
Taylor & Francis Group

LONDON AND NEW YORK

Second edition published 2020
by Routledge
2 Park Square, Milton Park, Abingdon, Oxon, OX14 4RN

and by Routledge
52 Vanderbilt Avenue, New York, NY 10017

Routledge is an imprint of the Taylor & Francis Group, an informa business

© 2020 Chris Hackley

First edition published by Routledge 2003

British Library Cataloguing-in-Publication Data
A catalogue record for this book is available from the British Library

Library of Congress Cataloging-in-Publication Data
Names: Hackley, Christopher E., author.
Title: Qualitative research in marketing and management : doing interpretive research projects / Chris Hackley.
Other titles: Doing research projects in marketing, management and consumer research.
Description: Second Edition. | New York : Routledge, 2020. | Revised edition of the author's | Includes bibliographical references and index.
Identifiers: LCCN 2019042882 (print) | LCCN 2019042883 (ebook) | ISBN 9781138332195 (hardback) | ISBN 9781138332218 (paperback) | ISBN 9780429446801 (ebook)
Subjects: LCSH: Management—Research. | Marketing research. | Consumers—Research.
Classification: LCC HD30.4 .H28 2020 (print) | LCC HD30.4 (ebook) | DDC 658.0072/1—dc23
LC record available at https://lccn.loc.gov/2019042882
LC ebook record available at https://lccn.loc.gov/2019042883

ISBN: 978-1-138-33219-5 (hbk)
ISBN: 978-1-138-33221-8 (pbk)
ISBN: 978-0-429-44680-1 (ebk)

Typeset in Sabon
by Apex CoVantage, LLC

Visit the eResources: www.routledge.com/9781138332218

This book is dedicated to my wife Amy and my children, Michael, James, Nicholas and little Dulciebella. I'm so proud to say that they all have an inspiring drive to try to make sense of the world by reading, writing, thinking and scholarship.

Topic 1 - Pg 5-10
Topic 2 - Pg 142-160
3 - Pg 26-47.

Contents

Foreword   xi

Introduction   1

PART I
Doing qualitative research projects   5

1 Qualitative research student projects and
   interpretation   7

2 Deciding on the topic and designing the study   33

3 Writing high quality research projects: From
   description to critique   59

4 Gathering and interpreting qualitative data sets   88

5 Sociological paradigms and research philosophy   115

PART 2
Working in theoretical traditions of interpretive
research   137

6 Practical existential phenomenology for student
   researchers   139

7 Ethnography, digital ethnography: Autoethnography:
   practice theory   160

8 Literary theory and qualitative research   183

 9 Critical research: Power, ethnicity, gender   202

10 Discourse analysis   219

    References   232
    Index   258

Foreword

Since the first edition of this book was published almost two decades ago, there have been many more PhDs, books and top journal publications in the marketing, management, organisational and consumer research areas that use interpretive theories to analyse qualitative data sets. This reflects the growth in reach and influence of qualitative and interpretive research in the last 20 years across many disciplines of social research. In spite of the boom in qualitative research, I am convinced that there remains a need for an introduction to interpretive approaches for qualitative research that bridges the gap between the general research methods texts that don't really look in any depth at interpretive theories, and the very advanced texts written for PhD students in specialised interpretive subject areas. This extensively re-written and updated second edition is a practically oriented guide for the first-time student researcher, and for the practitioner or academic who wants a primer on interpretive research. I am gratified that the first edition has helped a lot of students get to grips with theoretically informed qualitative research, and I hope students and their supervisors will feel that this new edition is not only updated, but greatly improved.

Chris Hackley September 2019, Oxfordshire

Introduction

This book draws on interpretive traditions of social science research to illustrate how these can be applied to qualitative research projects. It is aimed primarily at first time researchers in marketing, management, organisation and consumer research. We hope that it will also prove useful as a primer for more experienced researchers in these and other social fields who are not familiar with the wealth of philosophical perspectives, data-gathering techniques and analytical methods of interpretive research. The book offers many practical examples and also suggests possible topics of study for students.

Interpretive research perspectives have become highly influential in many fields of social science research, both as ways of developing rigorous constructs for quantitative research studies and as ends in themselves for researchers seeking 'rich descriptions' of, and qualitative insights into, social phenomena of all kinds. As management, marketing and consumer research studies have grown in popularity, powerful traditions of interpretive research have emerged within these fields. For example, qualitative research has a long history in marketing (Levy, 2006). Today, many qualitative studies informed by anthropology, ethnography, qualitative sociology and critical theory have been subsumed under the Consumer Culture Theory (CCT)[1] label (Arnould and Thompson, 2005) with countless methodological variations amidst a growing empirical scope (Belk, 2006, 2017; Belk et al., 2012; Hackett, 2016). Other more closely defined interpretive research initiatives include the biennial EIASM Interpretive Consumer Research Conference (Cova and Elliott, 2008) and various other conferences and workshops in management and organisation studies. The well-established qualitative approach of Grounded Theory (Glaser and Strauss, 1967) has been extended (e.g. Goulding, 2005) and is a frequently used approach to business and management PhDs, whilst new methods of qualitative research have emerged and grown to embrace the digital era, such as Netnography (Kozinets, 2015).

Qualitative studies have been regularly published in the top academic marketing journals such as the *Journal of Consumer Research*, the *European*

Journal of Marketing, Consumption, Markets and Culture, Marketing Theory and the *Journal of Marketing Management*, and many more are published in other top ranking journals in related fields such as sociology, human relations and organisation studies. There are journals that specialise in qualitative inquiry, such as *Qualitative Market Research: An International Journal*, but qualitative studies are regularly published in general research outlets such as *Journal of Advertising, Journal of Business Research*, the *British Journal of Management*, and the *Journal of Marketing*.

There is now a well-established book series, the *Routledge Interpretive Marketing Research* series,[2] which brings together the work of leading international writers on diverse interpretive traditions in interpretive marketing research. Published studies include those providing ethnographies of management in differing organisations and cultures and in contrasting management functions; studies focusing on consumption as a major site of meaning and social identity in differing cultural and economic settings; studies examining the situated symbolic practices of management in organisations; studies focusing on consumption and the symbolism of marketing techniques and concepts. Many other studies have explored issues in gender, race and equality in the areas of management, organisation and consumption through methods such as ethnography, autoethnography, or discourse analysis. These studies contribute to our understanding of cultural, social and policy issues as well as management issues.

Interpretive approaches have also become increasingly influential in management practice. For example, the fields of brand and marketing consultancy and advertising employ research techniques deriving from ethnography, semiotics and cultural studies. The author has found that the world's leading advertising agencies increasingly employ interpretive techniques drawn from anthropology in their pursuit of penetrating consumer insights that they can use to inform the development of advertising and communications strategy (Hackley, 2002, 2003a). Since the emergence of account planning as a key discipline in advertising (Griffiths and Follows, 2018) qualitative research has become identified with 'creative' advertising research, the research that is done to develop viable and effective creative executions, as opposed to the more quantitative emphasis of advertising research that seeks to measure the effectiveness of advertising campaigns after they have been launched (Hackley and Hackley, 2018a).

The intense interest in interpretive concepts, techniques and philosophies that originated in anthropology and qualitative sociology has led many more student researchers in university business schools, media departments, social studies and communication faculties to adopt interpretive perspectives for their own undergraduate or postgraduate research studies. However, student researchers who wish to find out more about interpretive social research find a vast library of texts that deal with a huge number of methodological variations, many of which are written for readerships already well versed in research practice and philosophy. Relatively few texts are available for first-time student researchers in management, communication, cultural and consumption fields who are interested in learning more about interpretive perspectives for qualitative research.

This book brings together major themes of interpretive research within a practical guide to researching and writing a research project. It is inter-disciplinary in spirit in that it acknowledges the common ground and over-lapping areas in the various management and business and related sub-fields and allied fields of social studies. The first part of the book reflects this inherent cross-disciplinarity as it takes a generic approach to focus largely on practical advice for the pragmatic first-time student researcher or inter-ested practitioner. The later chapters offer informed introductions to a selec-tion of important interpretive research traditions and suggest practical hints on how to apply these to produce a successful research project.

Qualitative Research in Marketing and Management has a distinctive approach that combines practical hints and insights with interpretive theo-retical developments. This approach emphasises everyday, practical manage-ment and social or market problems and issues; creative, inductive research designs and the use of qualitative research data sets.

Notes

1 http://cctweb.org/about
2 The Routledge Interpretive Market Research book series. https://www.routledge.com/Routledge-Interpretive-Marketing-Research/book-series/SE0484

Part I

Doing qualitative research projects

Qualitative research student projects and interpretation

Chapter outline

This chapter explains the scope, perspective and structure of the book. It goes on to list just a small selection of the countless research projects for which interpretive methods could be appropriate in the area of marketing and management. The chapter gently introduces some of the key concepts, assumptions and values of the interpretive research standpoint, before finishing with some comments on the student research project, its educational rationale and its assessment.

Chapter objectives

After reading this chapter the student will be able to

- Appreciate the interpretive research standpoint
- Begin to understand the actual and potential scope of qualitative research projects
- Understand some fundamental terms and concepts of interpretive research
- Understand how the independent research project helps to develop the student's intellect, knowledge and employable skills as part of their Higher Education

The approach of this book

This book is written primarily as a practical, but theoretically robust guide for students doing a research project for the first time. The book's primary audience is the student researcher, from bachelor level to postgraduate, who is new to interpretive research and wants to conduct an independent research project to satisfy the requirements of their bachelor or master's degree in management, marketing, organisational or consumer research. However, it will also be useful for those with some experience of social research in business and management fields who want to learn more about interpretive theories and methods, either for academic purposes, or for practice in industry. The book is written so that it can be usefully read from beginning to end, but it can also be 'dipped' into for tips on particular topics. Throughout the text there are examples and illustrations drawn from completed student research projects. The author and colleagues have supervised and conducted many successful research projects at first degree, master's degree and PhD level, as well as engaging in consultancy projects. Some of these projects are referred to in this book in order to show new student researchers what kind of interpretive work using qualitative data sets is possible and how it can be accomplished.

The book emphasises *qualitative* data-gathering methods and theoretical perspectives that draw on the interpretive social research traditions. This implies a creative and cross-disciplinary, yet theoretically well-founded approach to social research in marketing, management and related areas. It is hoped that student researchers can use the book and the many sources that are cited within it to make their independent research project a more satisfying, rewarding and, perhaps, less stressful experience.

The book is organised into two parts: Part 1 deals with the key practical issues of conducting qualitative student research projects, while Part 2 addresses the main theoretical traditions that are used to interpret and frame qualitative research projects. Chapter 1 introduces fundamental issues and explores the educational rationale for the independent student research project as part of the requirement for a bachelor's or master's degree. Chapter 2 looks at choosing the topic and designing the study, while Chapter 3 examines the issues in writing a research study and suggests a structure for the finished research project or dissertation. Chapter 4 introduces some of the typical approaches to gathering qualitative data sets and outlines some initial issues of data interpretation. Chapter 5 completes Part 1 of the book by introducing key issues in the philosophy of qualitative social research that will be important if the student researcher's analysis is to achieve the required academic standards.

Chapter 6 begins the focus on theoretical traditions for framing and analysing qualitative data sets with an outline of existential phenomenology, perhaps the most influential theoretical approach (or, rather, two theoretical approaches combined) for interpretive research studies based on qualitative data sets. Chapter 7 introduces another highly influential theoretical tradition in qualitative research, ethnography, including a number of other approaches that are used alongside, or as variations of, ethnography. Chapter 8 examines literary traditions of interpretive theory for qualitative research, while Chapter 9 looks at critical approaches including critical theory. Finally, Chapter 10 rounds off the book with another important theoretical approach to qualitative research data analysis – discourse analysis.

The independent student research project

The independent student research project (also described as a 'thesis' or 'dissertation', depending on different countries' traditions) is an entirely new experience for many students on taught bachelor's or master's degrees, and a radical departure from taught courses. It demands new skills and deeper levels of understanding compared to examined courses. University departments do provide research workshops and dedicated personal academic supervisors, but the research project must, in the end, be completed by the student as an independent researcher.

The typical research project requires students to design a study to gather data in order to answer a set of questions or problems that the students have identified. The student will position the study as a contribution to a given research area, write up a review of relevant academic research literature, then gather *primary data*, that is, original *empirical* data, to analyse. Increasingly, some departments are moving away from the empirical research dissertation model to adapt dissertations in two main ways (see Figure 1.1). One version is a practice-based project focused on a specified problem, which requires a practical solution, with less theoretical context. With this type of project there is a less demanding requirement for a thorough literature review and theoretical analysis. It would normally entail a case study (or comparative case studies), sometimes informed by a primary data method such as *participant observation*, to investigate the problem at hand and suggest practical solutions. On the other hand, some other departments are prescribing dissertations based on literature reviews only, without any need for primary empirical data gathering or data analysis. Figure 1.1 does simplify the different types of independent project/dissertation offered in that some now provide quite explicit frameworks for students to follow, so that student researchers do not need to decide on every stage in the project process themselves. This book focuses mainly on the traditional empirical project so that every aspect of the process is covered, and student researchers conducting more guided projects with less empirical data gathering or more structured literature reviews can benefit from the sections that are most relevant to them.

This book will be of help to students doing all variations on the independent research project/dissertation. The kinds of research approach described in the book are used in professional marketing, advertising and consumer research, in various forms, and hence lend themselves well to project-based work that does not have to have an extended theoretical development. For students doing literature review-based projects, the book will help introduce them to a range of interpretive research published papers, while it will also serve as a primer in understanding the conceptual vocabulary used in such work.

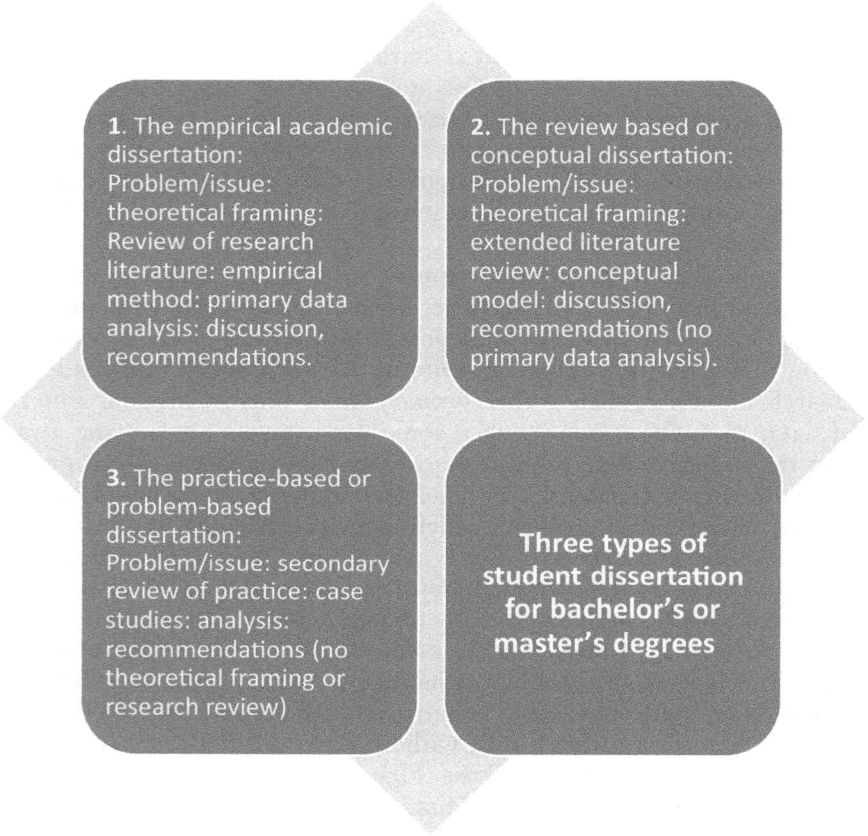

1. The empirical academic dissertation: Problem/issue: theoretical framing: Review of research literature: empirical method: primary data analysis: discussion, recommendations.

2. The review based or conceptual dissertation: Problem/issue: theoretical framing: extended literature review: conceptual model: discussion, recommendations (no primary data analysis).

3. The practice-based or problem-based dissertation: Problem/issue: secondary review of practice: case studies: analysis: recommendations (no theoretical framing or research review)

Three types of student dissertation for bachelor's or master's degrees

Figure 1.1 Three types of student dissertation/project

The fact that the independent project is independent implies several things that demand a degree of maturity. Academic supervisors have different views on contact. Some insist on regular meetings throughout the research process. Others want only an initial meeting to establish the topic and research design. Then, once the student researcher has conducted the work and written up a full draft, they will agree to read it and offer comments and advice prior to final submission. It is important for the student researcher to meet with the supervising academic to get a feel for his or her personal style in order to judge the degree of contact required. Of course, this will also depend to some extent on the needs of the student researcher, the formal processes in the university or department, and the nature of the project undertaken.

Even with the guidance of an excellent supervisor, an independent research project still represents a far greater challenge than taught courses, as we note above. Students on research degrees of PhD and MPhil can find that writing their first-year progress report brings them into contact with issues of research philosophy, data-gathering methods and data analysis that they have not encountered in detail in their studies of taught courses. The relative lack of research theory in the vocationally orientated curriculum of most business and management degrees means that the student then has a very wide gulf to cross to write a successful research dissertation. For many students the very idea of 'research' seems removed from their everyday experience of vocationally oriented teaching. This sense of research as a special activity distinct and separate from conventional studies can seem particularly strong in business and management courses. Indeed, some popular business and management textbooks claim that they are practical guides that can do without any theory. The truth is, they are simply unaware of theory and blind to the theories that underpin every claim they make. Even for relatively non-complex practical problems, a little knowledge of social research theory goes a long way to help to design coherent research interventions that can generate insight and understanding into the problem and sometimes to suggest possible practical solutions.

Interpretive research and qualitative data sets

This book makes the assumption qualitative data sets cannot speak for themselves. They require interpretation. The book aims to show student researchers how to conduct theory-driven qualitative research studies that will meet the criteria of scholarship and rigour required by good universities. With this in mind, we locate qualitative research primarily in the interpretive research *paradigm* as conceived by Burrell and Morgan (1979) although we do point out that many qualitative research studies overlap with other paradigms. A paradigm in social research is a set of values and assumptions about how social research should be done in response to certain types of research problem or question. The book introduces more about research paradigms later in this chapter, and then develops greater detail in Chapter 5.

Although there has been much development since Burrell and Morgan's (1979) work, the interpretive paradigm remains a relevant broad label reflecting the main philosophical standpoints that underpin the qualitative research methods that are discussed in the book. The key assumption of the interpretive paradigm is that the social world is created by individuals and the main priority for researchers is to investigate the ongoing processes of how individual actions constitute the social world. Saying that the social world is created by individuals differentiates interpretivism from paradigms that assume that the social world is created by unseen drivers emanating either from human biology and psychology, or from economic and social structures. Hence, one criticism of interpretivism is that it invests too much *agency* and autonomy in individual actions and behaviour. One could say that our actions as social beings are agentive, that is, we are the authors of our destinies, or they are not agentive, that is, we are subject to greater forces that dictate our behaviour and even our thoughts. However, one could counter the criticism that interpretive approaches overstate human agency by suggesting that alternative paradigms, such as structural/functional approaches, sometimes fail to capture the sense of volition or agency that characterises subjective human experience.

We can, though, set the more abstract debates aside for the present: the student project will not resolve the central sociological question of whether we are agents of our own destiny in life or whether our destinies are set by the social structures and institutions around us. We might even suggest that the key to understanding our experience of being human is to pick apart the spaces where we seem to exercise agency within, or in spite of, the powerful constraints of class, economic status, gender, race and other aspects of social structure (Askegaard and Linnet, 2011).

Traditionally, in management and organisation studies, the interpretive paradigm has been less popular than the functionalist paradigm. Nonetheless, it has retained an important place in research and, as noted earlier, many more studies working broadly in this paradigm are published today in marketing, management and consumer research than was the case when Burrell and Morgan (1979) published their work. Many barriers against qualitative research have been broken down in the last two decades and qualitative PhDs and master's dissertations are now common in university business schools, as are academic careers based on the publication of qualitative studies.[1] The key to the increased acceptance of qualitative work is a greater understanding that the theory-driven approach to qualitative research demands the highest academic standards and can generate powerful and resonant findings.

Almost from the beginning of the book there will be technical terms and concepts that may be new to the reader. The book tries to introduce these specialist terms gently and places many of them in glossaries at the end of each chapter. Part of the key aim of the book is to demystify interpretive research, and it is hoped that readers will at times enjoy learning that some of the esoteric terminology of interpretive research can in fact be useful for enlightenment, as well, at times, as for strategic obfuscation.

One of the most exciting things about qualitative/interpretive research is that it can be used to investigate and make sense of everyday, practical activities. Far from being abstract and difficult, such studies can help to connect the participants of research with research in ways that are highly accessible. The book advocates ways of researching that can be directly relevant to practical issues, using theoretically informed analyses of (often small sample) qualitative data sets. Interpretive studies have used qualitative data sets to investigate topics as diverse as the sub-cultural social practices of biker gangs or other consumer groups such as swap meet fans, dance clubbers or drinkers, advertising workers, and even religious adherents, the elderly, or white water rafters (Schouten and McAlexander, 1995; Belk et al., 1988; Goulding et al., 2013; Hackley et al., 2015; Svensson, 2007; McAlexander et al., 2014; Schau et al., 2009; Tumbat and Belk, 2011). As the book progresses we will encounter many more examples of interpretive research studies that took everyday situations, and tried to understand them in everyday language, but using theoretically informed qualitative data.

Some introductory research methods texts emphasise the construction of questionnaires, and the administration and statistical analysis of large-scale surveys. This text, in contrast, emphasises the research value of naturally occurring qualitative data such as conversations, interviews and observations, or similar forms of qualitative data that are elicited through interviews, participant observation, focus groups or other semi-structured data gathering approaches. The samples in qualitative/interpretive studies can be relatively small, there is no need for hypotheses, and the goal is to develop 'rich descriptions' (Geertz, 1973) of the social worlds investigated, not to develop positivistic assertions about the world that can be generalised across time, culture and history. Interpretive research seeks, well, to arrive at theoretically informed and well-supported interpretations of what is really happening in social situations.

The book cannot make the research project a simple task, but it does attempt to provide a number of clear signposts for students who want to do an interesting, creative and perhaps cross-disciplinary research project that reflects their own interests and abilities.

Finding a viable research topic

More will be said about how to choose a topic in Chapter 2. However, it is worth pointing out now that new student researchers typically think in terms of big categories when they first think about what to research. They often suggest studying 'branding', 'car retailing' or 'advertising', or they suggest that they will look at, say, factors affecting brand choice in mobile phone markets, or factors affecting consumer engagement in online fashion markets. It is essential that a research project topic choice is viable, that is, it needs to be something that can reasonably be accomplished. It doesn't have to change the world, and it doesn't have to generate new knowledge, unless it is a PhD level study. It just has to be do-able.

Later, many students learn that setting out a research project is both more complex and simpler than they realised. It is more complex in the sense that the way the research questions, issue or problem are phrased is crucial for the research design. Putting a research topic in a particular form of words carries implications about the data-gathering techniques and analytical stance of the research. On the other hand, research projects are also far simpler than students often think – there is no requirement and no expectation that the project will generate a solution to a gritty management problem, or that it will generate a brand new insight that could change an industry. A good student research project does not try to invent a grand theory but states a coherent question that can be investigated in a reasonably systematic and thorough way, given the time and resources available to the student researcher. The research project that is part of a taught higher degree simply has to demonstrate that the student has acquired certain academic, intellectual and practical skills. If the project is interesting and creative, or perhaps even generates findings that could be useful to someone, then so much the better.

Incidentally, if you're wondering what was wrong with the above project ideas, well, branding or advertising are very large fields. Exactly which area would the project focus on? Marketing and management have been university subjects with published research for about 100 years – that's a lot of literature. The viable project needs to frame its scope in a less vague way. However, even the topic suggestions 'factors affecting brand choice in mobile phone markets', or 'factors affecting consumer engagement in online fashion markets' will not quite work. For example, how many factors influenced the almost 8 billion humans in the world to purchase the more than 9 billion mobile phones[2] that exist in the world today? Clearly, a student project conducted during the course of two or three months cannot hope to engage coherently with such a huge question. What is more, a research question that begins 'what factors' really set up the student to fail, since there will inevitably be factors that the student cannot consider. Luckily, interpretive research studies are flexible enough to explore 'how' questions rather than trying to specify the unspecifiable with 'what' questions. So, if this student is interested in the mobile phone market, they could set out to explore how a given sample of mobile phone consumers choose between, say, three alternative mobile phone brands, by setting up focus groups and interviews with members of the relevant group.

The critical point when deciding on a research study is to frame the study in such a way that it is possible to succeed. There are some other examples in Box 1.1. These examples are general topic areas that could be framed into viable studies, if the student researcher settles on a specific market sector, a specified region and a specific consumer market segment to study. The list is an ad hoc selection of topics, there are many more possible and it is not to be taken as a selection of 'good' or 'advisable' topics – how good studies that adapt these topics might be all depends on the execution. Of course, an infinite number of different and possibly better topics exist so students should absolutely explore their own interests and chosen fields.

Box 1.1   Some general topic areas that can be researched using the approaches in this book

- Managerial or critical examinations of consumption practices and issues with regard to particular product or service categories (e.g. new technology products), industry sectors (e.g. banking, leisure, manufacturing) or market segments (e.g. the 'cognitively' young older consumer, the 'generation X' younger consumer)
- International marketing studies with a particular industry/product focus (e.g. the design and management of international market entry strategies)
- Cross-cultural comparisons of consumer or advertising activities and practices
- Managerial or critical investigation of management activities and processes in specific organisations or settings
- Case study comparisons of business success factors in comparable industry sectors
- Explorations of management techniques in particular settings
- Critical examinations of the social role, organisational implications and human consequences of marketing and management activities and practices
- Localised case study research based on live in-company projects
- Studies of small business growth and development
- Studies of environmental management issues
- Qualitative psychological studies of consumer choice behaviour in particular consumption settings
- Studies that focus on a specific managerial aspect of marketing in a specified product/market such as pricing, promotion, distribution effectiveness
- New product development and innovation processes in a given organisation or industry
- The management of, and consumption in, creative industries and the arts
- Creative processes in management practice
- Studies of relationships and control issues in the management of sourcing and supply
- Studies that focus on the human dimension of management such as reward systems, performance appraisal methods, motivation, job choice and satisfaction
- Gender-based studies focusing on a particular context of consumption or management

- Studies of management perceptions of the operational efficiency of specific management systems and processes
- Studies of tourism management in particular national and international settings
- Strategic planning models and practices in higher-level organisational management
- Effectiveness and/or efficiency in organisational marketing management assessed through inter-company or intra-industry comparisons
- Approaches to the management of key accounts or other aspects of 'relationship' management in service sectors
- Intra-organisational studies of communication and information systems framed, for example, as 'internal marketing' studies
- Managerial marketing segmentation practices in specified product industries
- Experiential studies of managing and being managed in organisational settings
- Experiential studies of consumption and its role in identity – construction and social positioning in specified social settings with regard to particular categories

Interpretation and the research process

All research entails interpretation of something (O'Shaughnessy, 2009). All *empirical research* entails looking for patterns in samples of data, and that entails interpretation of the findings, and of the implications of the findings. Calling a research paradigm 'interpretive', then, is a little nebulous, to be sure. However, there are implications in the term that are important. The implication is that *qualitative* data sets need to be interpreted, whilst hypothesis testing or experimental research findings based on *quantitative* studies, that is, studies that rely on statistical analysis of numerical data sets, do not, at least in the same way. If a *hypothesis*, an assertion about the world is being tested quantitatively, then the findings either support the hypothesis, or they do not. Of course, there is an interpretive process going on here, but aspects of the interpretation are closed off and bracketed from discussion in quantitative research in ways they are not in qualitative research. If, say, a relationship between variables is being tested, then the relationship will be statistically significant, or not. Of course, the matter is not so simple since all manner of interpretive judgements have to be made to reach that point, and the implications of null findings have to be interpreted just as do the implications of significant findings. Nonetheless, the point is clear enough – some research designs yield findings that can be reduced to measurable and clear outcomes, whilst others require a good deal of interpretation whatever the findings may be.

Exploratory studies, access and 'messy' data sets

Interpretive studies based on qualitative data sets tend to be *exploratory* in nature in the sense that they are exploring a particular phenomenon without presupposing what they will find. Such exploratory studies require an interpretive process in order to develop a deep and nuanced understanding of the phenomenon that is being explored. Just because qualitative data are used does not necessarily mean that the research is interpretive, since qualitative data sets are sometimes used in much the same way as quantitative ones, to confirm a hypothesis or proposition that might, in principle, be generalisable, without there being a theoretical basis that is informing the way those data sets are understood. The term interpretive research then, in this book, refers to research designs that use qualitative data sets and develop a theoretically driven interpretation of those data sets.

Interpretive research, then, tends to emphasise an approach that uses sources of data that are relatively unstructured, such as conversations, unstructured or semi structured *depth interviews*, written (textual) accounts of events or experiences, internet chat or posts, photographs and video, and observation (including participant observation). There are several advantages to this perspective. These unstructured data sets are sometimes called 'messy' data as they are not, well, neat, like survey results that will be fed into an SPSS analysis. Analysing messy qualitative data entails a more thoroughgoing interpretive process since the researcher has to decide how to make sense of it in a very fundamental way. Of course, there are qualitative research conventions such as sorting and coding qualitative data sets involved in analysing messy data sets, and the book discusses these in Chapter 4.

One major issue with student research projects can be data access. Quantitative projects have to deal with poor survey response rates or integrity issues with data sets (such as whether the sample is subject to high rates of *non-response error*). Qualitative studies have to deal with the question of how to access the people and places that are relevant. The kind of *data sets* that are emphasised in interpretive research are particularly suitable for student research projects because they can be relatively easy to access (but see below) and *samples* need not be *randomised – convenience sampling* can be fine, provided the sample is *representative* of the whole population of interest, that is, provided the sample has the same characteristics as the whole population of interest.

Of course, access to the relevant research participants can be difficult, especially for students who would ideally like to interview senior practitioners in the fields they are investigating. One of the author's former PhD students, Dr Benaliza Loo, showed great enterprise to get interviews with leading global fashion designers, and this eventually formed the basis of her PhD study (Loo and Hackley, 2013). In another example from one of the author's former PhD students, Dr Dina Bassiouni managed to gain access to children as research participants for her study on the role of video games in children's socialisation and development (Bassiouni and Hackley, 2016). Getting such access is not easy in the UK because of various laws and sensitivities around safeguarding and the ethics of using children as research participants.[3] Incidentally, both the above examples were published from PhD studies but they began as MPhil studies (master's level) and could very well have been adopted, in shortened forms, for master's or even undergraduate projects.

These two examples were exceptional, and other students also sometimes are able to gain access to extremely valuable sources of data. However, all things considered, for most bachelor's or master's students, getting some friends, friends of friends, and/or peer group members to agree to an interview or to take part in a focus group is often enough, and a great deal easier than getting several hundred questionnaire responses (or interviewing world leading experts in their field).

In this book we suggest that interpretive studies are not only useful in the pre-testing phase of large sample hypothesis testing research, but can be used as a self-contained research approach for complete studies. Insight, not *generalisability*, is the goal of interpretive research. It is important to note that not only do many quantitative research studies have qualitative elements; many interpretive studies have a *quantitative* element to data gathering. The categories qualitative and quantitative are not mutually exclusive in research. Most research studies are a mixture of both with an *emphasis* on one or the other.

The interpretive standpoint, then, aims to provide a well-informed, systematically analysed, theoretically coherent and credible interpretation of relatively unstructured or 'messy' qualitative data sets. The researcher undertaking an interpretive study will not claim that the interpretation favoured by the researcher is necessarily the only one possible. The researcher will not claim that their study has 'proved' any relationship or hypothesis. Proof is a matter for mathematicians or high court judges. What interpretive research studies can do is to make a claim about the researcher's interpretation that is credible, justified empirically and grounded in careful, systematic scholarship, evidence and reasoning.

The educational rationale for the research project

A research project conducted as part of the requirements of a taught university degree is part of the student's broader education. The work will not be judged on whether or not it generates new knowledge (only the PhD degree is required to do this) or whether it provides a new and viable solution to a problem of policy. Rather, the work will be judged on the extent to which it demonstrates a synthesis of the students' learning over the course of their taught studies. The finished project should demonstrate the ability to conceive of, to articulate and to systematically investigate a coherent issue or question. It should demonstrate a high order of scholarship through a review of relevant published work, which shows that the student can conduct a literature review, and can read, understand, synthesise and critique a selection of published work in order to set the dissertation topic within a trajectory of earlier research. Students who will gravitate into employment will need to demonstrate that they have skills research and scholarship that inform their reasoning and decision making. These skills include research design, problem formulation, data gathering, analysis and interpretation.

More pragmatically, management students often use the research project as a 'way in' to an area of work. They can make industry contacts and acquire specialised knowledge of a key area that will be of benefit to potential employers. In addition, the research dissertation is thought to improve student employability (Sinkovics et al., 2015) through the skills and critical independent thought it develops. There are many topic areas that students can use for the dissertation that might increase their knowledge of that area with a view to future employment. In recent years, the author has supervised student marketing and management projects into communications technology, mobile phone telephony pricing strategies, Internet music distribution, agile systems, digital transformation, international market entry strategies, interactive advertising planning and many other vocationally motivated projects.

Many students, then, choose a topic area that they feel might help them deepen their knowledge of an area they would like to specialise in later on. Sometimes, if they are lucky, they solicit interviews or other help from practitioners and develop useful contacts. So, although vocational aims are not the main purpose of student independent projects and dissertations as part of a university course, they can often be of considerable help to students in furthering their vocational ambitions and interests by developing their employability (Sinkovics et al., 2015).

Interpretive research and the 'hermeneutic circle'

The interpretive research perspective rests on a set of assumptions about the nature of human understanding. While this book offers practical advice on how to conduct research projects throughout the range of marketing and management and other related topic areas, it is important to understand that interpretive research is based on a view of the world. This stance is informed by the *hermeneutic* tradition of social research.

Hermeneutics, the study of interpretation, derives from Biblical exegesis. For Holbrook and O'Shaughnessy (1988, p. 400) the idea of the *hermeneutic circle* is helpful in explaining the interpretive process (see also Thompson et al., 1994).

> In the Hermeneutic Circle, an interpreter's tentative grasp of the whole text guides an initial reading of its parts. The detailed reading, in turn, leads towards a revision of the original overview. This dialogue between reader and text then proceeds through subsequent iterations of a circular process that . . . tends towards its own correction.

Social research is often concerned with the analysis of texts in the sense that research data are crafted into a textual representation (Hackley, 2003c) of what is being researched. For example, a questionnaire survey generates results that can be represented on paper in words, statistics and perhaps bar or pie charts. The written-down results are a representation of what took place (a questionnaire survey), which is itself a representation of the phenomenon that was the subject of the survey. It is the task of a researcher to interpret the results of the survey, write the results down in a text and then to interpret the results.

Similarly, a *depth interview* can be transcribed into a text of a dialogic exchange between researcher and interviewee. The text that results is a representation of what took place (the depth interview). The subject matter of the interview, the phenomenon of interest about which the interviewer was being interviewed, is also represented in the text, through the words of the interviewee. Social research is a hermeneutic task in the sense that the reader of the text (the written representation of the interview) is engaged in a cycle of re-interpretation and substantiation. The researcher engages with the text to draw meaning from it. The meanings that the researcher reads in the text are then communicated in the research report and substantiated with direct quotes from the interview text. Typically, in qualitative research, the researcher would engage in a process of sorting and coding (Chowdhury, 2015) of the data as they read and re-read the textual transcripts of interviews or any other data sets they have. The researcher would sort data extracts according to particular themes, applying a code or a title to instances of a theme they find in the data set. Eventually, after many re-readings and further sorting, the data set will be collated into a series of extracts that fall under a number of overarching themes. These themes will structure the findings and discussion in the project.

There are many other forms of qualitative data other than interviews, such as photographs, video, captured internet chat and social media posts and so on. But, in a broad sense, a social text refers to anything that can be described and rendered into words. The process of hermeneutic interpretation would apply whether the researcher is analysing conversations, interviews, news clippings, pieces of elicited writing or indeed any kind of data sets that can be described. The process is often one of repeated engagement with the text and refinement of the researcher's understanding. For example, as part of his PhD, the author undertook a number of interviews with advertising professionals, recording and transcribing these interviews into printed texts. These texts were read, re-read and re-read multiple times before the research findings began to take shape, as the reader's interpretive understanding of the texts developed further with each re-reading (Hackley, 2000).

Interpretive strategies and the 'two cultures' of art and science

English author C.P. Snow spoke of art and science being two very different and opposing cultures of human understanding.[4] This division is (still) reproduced in management fields such as marketing (Brown, 1996). Holbrook and O'Shaughnessy (1988) put it this way: they argued that different forms of understanding are employed in the physical sciences on the one hand, and the humanities and social sciences on the other. Humans are seekers after meaning and we live 'embedded within a shared system of signs based on public language and other symbolic objects' (p. 400). They suggest that there is a need for an interpretive social science that does not assume that the physical and the social world are entirely analogous.

In other words, they agree that researchers should not necessarily bring the same assumptions to research in the physical and social sciences. They suggest that researchers can acknowledge that the material being researched in each case has different characteristics. The way we might understand and describe the activity of a tree and its cells reflects a different kind of reality to the way we might understand how an idea or an emotion percolates through a particular set of social practices for a given group. The assumption is that the behaviour of managers and consumers is self-determined and self-aware in a way that the behaviour of cells is not.

The division between these two cultures remains quite pronounced in social studies and management. Since the Ford and Carnegie reports on US Business School research in the 1960s there has been a strong emphasis in American University Business School research on natural science models of business and management research (Brown, 1995; Hackley, 2009a, b). Time has broken down some of the barriers to qualitative research that this political intervention created. Management and social studies are huge academic fields and there is unquestionably considerable plurality in research methods across many sub-fields today. Nonetheless, the division is keenly felt by many university academics and opinions are strongly held. There are still those departments where there is a clear hierarchy of research methods in which adherence to a quantitative, natural science model of research is at the top, and qualitative research is regarded as second best. There are also departments where there is greater incidence of qualitative studies. There is a general acceptance of mixed methods studies, although the natural science model holds that qualitative investigation should normally be a route to construct development and a precursor to measurement and/or hypothesis testing, hence the hierarchical relation of quantitative versus qualitative studies in some university departments.

There is clearly room for, and indeed a necessity for, both approaches, but it must be said that in some departments quantitative surveys seem to be the default research approach that is taught to students, whilst the case for qualitative research as a stand-alone method has to be made. Perhaps this book and the many others on the same subject will help to make this case stronger.

Situated knowledge, hermeneutics and objectivity

In much quantitative research, the stated goal is to achieve an *objective* point of view and to eliminate *bias*. Indeed, the most pressing criticism of qualitative research from quantitative researchers is that it is not objective. Interpretive researchers counter with the argument that objectivity is a chimera – no researcher can stand apart from the social world they are investigating. If researchers want to be sure that trees fall in an empty forest, they have to be there to observe that phenomenon and their presence has ineluctably changed the environment in which it happens. Of course, the entire point of research is to arrive at agreements about the state of the world that are more robust, more secure than personal, subjective opinion. In this sense, both qualitative and quantitative research has the same aim – to generate findings that are robust, transparent and well-supported by evidence. This is not about objectivity or the elimination of bias, as if that were possible – it is about good research design and strong scholarship and research practice. A softer meaning of objectivity would be not that the researcher can be eliminated from their effect on the phenomenon being studied but that the researcher is trying to achieve a detached evaluation of the phenomenon without their judgement being swayed by their emotional feeling of what they would like or expect the findings to be. All researchers from all paradigms could probably agree that that softer meaning objectivity is a virtue in any kind of research study – the goal of science after all is to achieve knowledge and understanding that is better than heresay, intuition or wishful thinking.

Thompson et al. (1994) discuss the ways in which the idea of the hermeneutic circle is used in consumer research. Holbrook and O'Shaughnessy (1988) invoked the hermeneutic circle to discuss what they see as the culturally situated character of scientific knowledge (p. 433). In other words, they use the hermeneutic circle to articulate their view that there is not a science or method that can stand outside history beyond interpretation. The hermeneutic circle is often invoked in consumer research in the context of qualitative data interpretation (Thompson et al., 1994, p. 433, citing Hirschman, 1990; Thompson et al., 1989, 1990). Thompson et al. (1994) suggest that the hermeneutic circle is "a general model of the process by which understandings are formed" (p. 433). They see it (p. 433, citing Benhabib, 1992, as support) as a model that offers insights into the nature of human understanding:

> Personal understandings are always situated within a network of culturally shared knowledge, beliefs, ideals and taken-for-granted assumptions about the nature of social life.

Human understanding, then, is necessarily mediated by social context. It cannot be objective in any pure or absolute sense. We make sense of our everyday experience by deploying strategies of interpretation. These strategies can take many forms but are drawn from the cultural and social context of which we are part. Hermeneutic research seeks to elicit insights into the 'unspoken' background of socially shared meanings by which a person interprets his/her experiences (Thompson et al., 1994, p. 432). Hermeneutics, then, is the field of study that broadly informs the interpretive research perspective. It acknowledges that research is a sense making process, in which we try to make sense of the social world, and it acknowledges that this is a process that is conducted by human beings operating within social and cultural contexts.

Askegaard and Linnet (2011), discussing one paradigm of interpretive research, Consumer Culture Theory (CCT) suggest that there can be an accommodation between the traditional emphasis of interpretive theory on the ways in which individual agents make the social world (Burrell and Morgan, 1979) and the influences of social and institutional structures of which individuals may not even be aware, what they call the context of context. They propose an *epistemology*, that is, a philosophy of knowledge, for CCT research, that embraces the individual's agency and the force of social structures that both frame and impede that sense of agency:

> We . . . suggest an epistemology for CCT that explicitly connects the structuring of macro-social explanatory frameworks with the phenomenology of lived experiences, thereby inscribing the micro-social context accounted for by the consumer in a larger sociohistorical context based on the researcher's theoretical insights.
>
> (p. 381)

Askegaard and Linnet (2011) situate CCT research in a hybrid paradigm that ostensibly overlaps two of Burrell and Morgan's (1979) paradigms:

the interpretive and the *humanistic*. We suggest that this can be appropriate for interpretive research in general – there is no requirement that interpretive studies ignore the effects of sociohistorical structures on individual experience, and equally there is no need to eliminate the human sense of agency from structural studies. Interpretive studies, after all, seek to achieve a rounded account of social action in its situated context.

For the first time student researcher, all this means is that they can say what they see. If the research participants raise issues that are complex, perhaps contradictory, then report the contradictions and complexities. If social phenomena appear to entail a mixture of individual autonomy (or what is experienced as such) and structural social influences, then these complexities can be part of the findings and discussion. One of the advantages of interpretive research is that the social situation under study does not have to be distorted to fit the research method. It can be reported fully, with a literary sensitivity to the lived experience of participants.

Exploratory research designs

Earlier, we touched upon the matter of qualitative and interpretive studies being used to assist in construct development as precursors for quantitative studies. At the risk of seeming defensive, a little more should be said here about quantification in social research. Many introductory research methods texts demonstrate relatively simple statistical tests that can be usefully used in small-scale research projects, such as T-tests, Chi-squared tests, cross tabulations, Wilcoxon and other tests of statistical significance. There is value in this approach, particularly since basic statistical and numerical understanding is indispensable for students aspiring to a managerial career. However, there is also a strong case for developing intellectually rigorous research designs that do not employ statistical tests because they can form a key part of the student's education in research philosophy and critical thinking.

There are many possible reasons why a research project may not require a substantial quantitative element (see Box 1.2). It was noted above that qualitative research is often conducted in the early stages of research projects to generate constructs and hypotheses that can eventually be measured in a quantitative study. However, not all qualitative research implies the possibility or the desirability of measurement. Interpretive traditions offer means of making sense of qualitative data as an end in itself. At undergraduate and master's level students may well wish to investigate a chosen area, question, problem or issue in order to develop insights and deepen understanding of the phenomena in question. As their knowledge develops they may wish to formulate a more specific research objective but this may not require measurement, since the student pursuing an interpretive project may not wish to generate generalisable facts about the world. If a student wishes to investigate a topic that has not specifically been the subject of previous

Box 1.2   Reasons for not moving to a quantitative phase in a research project

Pragmatic reasons

- Lack of statistical competence
- Lack of time/resources for sampling rigour
- Low survey response rates, non-response error
- To develop research skills based on qualitative data-gathering techniques and non-random sampling approaches
- To advance personal knowledge of a chosen area of marketing management
- To engage with personal experience and interests and to connect with practical management issues and practices
- To develop knowledge and skills relevant to a chosen career area
- To investigate under-researched and cross-disciplinary topics

Theoretical reasons

- Exploratory research design
- Theory-driven research objectives
- Generalisation of findings is not appropriate
- The interpretive stance of the researcher

studies, then an exploratory research design based mainly on qualitative data may be the most appropriate.

Many topics that fire students' interest have arisen from their own observations and experience of marketing and management or consumption. These interests may not fall neatly into existing theoretical categories or frameworks, hence an 'exploratory' research design is often appropriate. This does not mean that the exploratory research design would by implication be ground breaking or wholly original. It might simply be that the researcher wishes to investigate, say, the social dynamics of decision making in a local company. The empirical data set and context would indeed probably be original, in the broad sense that this problem or issue will probably not have been investigated in exactly this way using this method and this context, but the general issue might well have been explored many other times before in different contexts with different data sets. Exploratory studies, simply, do not presuppose their findings. For example, where a confirmatory study might seek to test a hypothesis, that is, it tests a statement of putative fact about the world, such as 'eating more carrots improves the social skills of adolescents', an exploratory study might set out to explore the social skills of adolescents in particular demographics and locations.

Some students find it difficult to reconcile such an exploratory perspective with the need to have a relevant literature review as part of their work. But, even if the topic is one that has not specifically been researched before, there will inevitably be existing research that is broadly relevant to the topic in hand. From a pragmatic point of view, an exploratory study is a useful device for the first time student researcher whose knowledge and understanding of the topic area will evolve as the project progresses. Doing an exploratory project leaves some latitude for changes, for example to the working title, to the data sample selection or to the literature review, as findings begin to emerge and the research perspective changes.

Interpretive projects and 'cross-disciplinarity'

'Cross-disciplinarity' occurs where researchers combine features from different research traditions in their research designs. In other words, they work 'across' disciplines. Many students who come into postgraduate marketing, management and consumer studies from social science and humanities backgrounds, have useful knowledge they can draw upon to give their research a sense of coherence with their previous education. They may have a theoretically informed idea of their own particular 'take' on a marketing/management topic. Students of literature, for example, have a range of interpretive strategies that they can bring to their understanding of texts in marketing.

In the author's experience of teaching master's courses in marketing over the course of some 25 years, often to international students from many countries outside the UK, the discipline of the student's bachelor's degree really does not matter when it comes to being successful on a marketing master's course. Indeed, some of the least likely backgrounds can be very apt. For example, students with bachelor's degrees in the arts, communication, literature, music and languages often take very well to the 'messy' and open-ended nature of marketing subjects. Of course, many students come to marketing from a background in science or engineering, and their numeracy skills are increasingly in demand as a basic grasp of marketing metrics, at least, become essential to understand marketing in the digital era. Marketing, though, will always be an art, as well as a science (Brown, 1996) and the 'soft' skills of imagination and creativity, insight synthesis and sensitivity to cultural trends, will be needed alongside 'hard' skills of coding and quantitative data analysis. Cross-disciplinarity, that is, looking at one discipline through the intellectual perspective of another discipline, can be highly productive in generating new ways of looking at issues.

Box 1.3   Reasons for conducting an exploratory research project to satisfy taught degree criteria

- To develop research skills based on qualitative data-gathering techniques and non-random sampling approaches
- To advance personal knowledge of a chosen area of marketing management
- To engage with personal experience and interests and to connect with practical management issues and practices
- To develop knowledge and skills relevant to a chosen career area
- To investigate under-researched and cross-disciplinary topics

---

Cross disciplinarity works both ways and literature searches for marketing topics can find useful sources in many research journals outside the marketing (and management, and organization or consumer research) journals. Within social sciences such as psychology, cultural studies, youth and childhood studies, economic psychology, food studies, the sociology and anthropology of consumption, and also in some humanities areas such as social and economic history, the importance of marketed consumption is increasingly acknowledged in research and teaching. Sociologist Colin Campbell is quoted as saying 'You are what you buy'[5] and, from a sociological point of view, much can be learned about society, power and relationships by studying consumption practices. From a managerial point of view, many social scientists work in consumer psychology to learn what motivates and excites consumers so that advertising agencies and manufacturers can respond accordingly. Within organisations, organisational and occupational psychologists are interested in how managers manage their organisation's activities, especially its contact with consumers. In all of these cases it is clear that management and marketing topics and issues are accessible to a wide range of research perspectives and disciplines. While business education tends to be driven by practical management problems, it is also part of the broader intellectual tradition of the social and cultural sciences. The approaches taken in research projects (see Box 1.3) should rightly reflect the breadth and variety of approaches in social research methods.

The skills gained through the independent research project

The independent research project conducted as part of a taught academic course is a demanding, essential and, at best, exciting and liberating part of a student's higher education. It is a means of teaching, and of learning, and it is thought to offer huge benefits to students in the skills developed that enhance their critical thinking, their intellectual maturity, their knowledge of a subject area, and, hence, their employability (Sinkovics et al., 2015). The skills needed to research and write a successful academic research project are both practical and intellectual. While the assessment of the research report itself is largely based on academic and intellectual standards, these standards imply many practical skills. The practical skills involved in conducting and writing a research report include gathering and organising data, planning time and scheduling work, selecting appropriate information, negotiating and other interpersonal skills. An intellectually persuasive research report will imply high attainment in many or all of these practical skills.

For example, there are many social and communication skills required in doing research (see Box 1.4). The supervisory relationship must be maintained by keeping in contact, observing deadlines, following advice and maintaining goodwill. The student must be able to communicate his or her research ideas clearly, and he or she must also be able to listen to the supervisor's advice and act on it. The student's own life must be managed to sustain personal motivation and to plan for the required time and resources that the research project will demand. If practicing managers or other academics are asked to give time for interviews then this access must be negotiated by the student. Busy practitioners are more likely to grant interviews to student researchers who are well-organised, who can write a grammatically correct and well-structured email or letter, who can attend meetings on time, and who can strike the right tone in communications. If interviews, group discussions or other qualitative data-gathering approaches are to be conducted then these require social, communication and interpersonal skills too. The need for the student researcher to demonstrate complex sets of skills such as these explains why the independent research project is so important in the overall assessment of taught bachelor's and master's degrees. Not only does the independent research project assess the student's ability to synthesise information and demonstrate higher order academic skills, it is also a measure of the students' personal and intellectual maturity. The independent research project is not just an outcome: it is a process.

The skills listed above are interdependent: one is often implied in another. For example, reviewing or changing existing beliefs in the light of new knowledge is an intellectual quality. It is also a feature of emotional maturity that one is able to do this. Adept negotiation skills and self-motivation are also qualities which reflect emotional maturity, as well as demonstrating management skills. Although there is considerable blurring between skills it is useful to set out a number of them in this way because it can show students that the research project is not just a barrier to their degree success, it is a vehicle for personal development. It does not matter if the research

Box 1.4   Examples of some of the skills required to successfully complete research projects

Intellectual skills

- Critical reading, understanding, evaluating ideas
- Integrating new learning with existing knowledge
- Skills of logical inference: drawing on evidence and reasoning to construct persuasive arguments
- Selecting and summarising relevant points from appropriate information sources
- Drawing logical connections between differing research studies

Communication skills

- Communicating research ideas clearly, verbally and in writing
- Writing the research report in a succinct and lucid academic style
- Listening to and acting on advice from supervisors or others
- Skills of editing and sub-editing prose to create a clear and persuasive report structure

Interpersonal skills

- Negotiating access for research interviews or other data gathering
- Managing the supervisor, negotiating goals, gaining agreement on topics
- Handling qualitative data-gathering sessions with sensitivity and professional competence

Practical/emotional skills

- Time management: sustaining motivation to meet deadlines
- Breaking down activities into sub-goals for scheduling and prioritising
- Reflecting and learning from experience: modifying views in the light of new knowledge
- Interviewing and other primary research skills such as empathy with the research participant

has not produced a striking or novel business solution or a new theoretical advance. Carrying out and producing the research project report is itself an achievement that demonstrates advanced intellectual, personal and managerial skills.

Chapter 2 will examine initial issues of deciding on the research topic and designing the study.

Glossary

Agency   individual, autonomously generated action and thought. The old sociological dilemma is between agency and structure, referring to the extent to which the social world is generated through individual action, or imposed by social structures and institutions such as class, race and economic status.

Confirmatory research design   A research design that seeks to confirm or refute a hypothesis.

Convenience sampling   A sample selection that is convenient, say, using a friendship circle or work colleagues as research participants.

Data set   The research material gathered by the researcher.

Depth interview   A long interview that explores an aspect of the world of the interviewee's experience.

Empirical   Using data that can be observed or otherwise verified by sense experience. In classical philosophy the counterpoint to an empirically-based argument would be an argument drawing on pure reason, without empirical evidence.

Epistemology   A theory of knowledge, especially referring to the distinction between mere belief, heresay or opinion, and verifiable knowledge.

Ethnographic data   Ethnography entails the scientific description of cultures through first hand observation.

Exploratory   An exploratory research design seeks insight and understanding into a novel or unfamiliar topic area or question, it does not presuppose its findings or seek to confirm generalisable facts.

Generalizability   The aim of producing a research finding that can be universally true, that is, it can be generalised across all populations.

Hermeneutics   The study of the theory of interpretation.

Humanistic   An approach to research that places lived human experience at its centre.

Hypothesis   A hypothesis is a statement of fact about the world that can be tested by observation. Hypothesis testing research usually applies statistical tests to quantitative data sets.

Interpretive research 'Interpretive' refers to a broad and diverse category of research traditions that assumes that the social world is created by individuals and employs the theoretically driven analysis of qualitative data sets.

Literature review An extended critical discussion of previously published academic work that is relevant to the research topics under investigation. The literature review sets the context for the research project and identifies issues, research gaps and analytical concepts that may be used in the project.

Non-response error Many quantitative studies seek random samples in order to be able to generalise their research findings. Non-response error refers to the fact that most social studies based on random samples are not in fact random because some contacted participants did not respond.

Objective A judgement or empirical observation that is not influenced by human emotion or predisposition (*bias*).

Paradigm A set of values and methods for research underpinned by a worldview.

Participant observation A data generating method that entails the researcher taking part in a social process as both participant and observer. Common in *ethnographic studies*, the researcher would normally record observations in making field notes, and perhaps also by conducting interviews.

Plagiarism Use of another author's written words without proper acknowledgement.

Primary data Primary data are original empirical data sources that have not been previously sampled for the same purpose. This contrasts with *secondary data* sources that are already in existence, having previously been compiled for some purpose e.g. government demographic data.

Qualitative 'Qualitative' data sets are made up of material such as transcripts or audio-recordings of interviews, field notes of researcher observations, photographs, video, projective test exercises, written reflections or accounts of events, observation and any other form of research data that cannot easily be rendered into numerical form.

Quantitative 'Quantitative' data sets are any form of data rendered into numerical form, usually for statistical analysis.

Randomised A random or randomised sample refers to a data set, each element of which had an equal chance of being selected and in which no human judgement was involved. Random samples are often generated using random number generators. A sample that is ad hoc, that is, there are no explicit criteria applied to select the sample, is not random because it entails a degree of human judgement in the ad hoc selection.

Representative A sample that is not random but which shares key characteristics with the whole population of interest.

Sample   Researchers cannot collect all the primary material that could possibly be relevant to their study. They must be content with a partial sample, selected according to certain criteria.

Notes

1 It is only right to note that in the business and management area, there are probably far more academic research careers founded on quantitative research than there are founded on qualitative research.
2 www.bankmycell.com/blog/how-many-phones-are-in-the-world
3 The study was conducted with the children's welfare uppermost in mind and Dr Bassiouni obtained permission from all the children and their parents and carers, and also gained approval from the university research ethics committee.
4 www.telegraph.co.uk/technology/5273453/Fifty-years-on-CP-Snows-Two-Cultures-are-united-in-desperation.html
5 www.theguardian.com/education/2002/dec/19/highereducation.uk2

Chapter 2

Deciding on the topic and designing the study

Chapter outline

This chapter focuses on the choice of research topic because this important decision must be considered in the light of its implications for research project method, scope and structure. The choice of topic, and most importantly the way it is phrased, has major implications for the success of the project. This chapter aims to help student researchers to think through their research project ideas and to judge whether a particular research problem, question or issue can make a viable project.

Chapter objectives

After reading this chapter students will be able to

- understand the importance of the choice of research topic
- understand the importance of how the research topic is crafted and expressed
- appreciate the need to think about the research design that is implied in the research question

Initial considerations: topic and design

As Box 1.1 in the previous chapter suggests, the choice of possible topics for a research project in marketing, management, consumer research and related fields of social research is very wide indeed. There are many social phenomena that can be researched from one or all of these perspectives. The scope of such studies may be broader than many student researchers realise. Marketing, for example, is a functional area of organisational management but it can also be conceived as a pervasive presence in citizens' lives in developed and developing economies. Successful marketing may be indispensable to organisations, but the institutions, values and activities of marketing have a reach and influence far beyond the organisations it serves. In many indus-trialised and post-industrial economies marketing activity is often seen as a source of social problems, as well as a means of generating wealth (Hackley, 2009a; Maclaran et al., 2007). In less developed countries the lack of a marketing infrastructure is considered a painful absence and a major barrier to the creation of wealth and the reduction of poverty. Marketing is a man-agement field: practically every organisation engages with markets at some level, in some way, even if the terms of engagement may often be far from the familiar world of consumer goods transactions. People are employed to 'manage' this engagement and to manage all other organisational activi-ties and relationships. Marketing management is not just about big organi-sations, executive managers and consumer goods markets. It is, crucially, about consumers and consumption in every context, since all marketing activity is premised on assumptions about the nature, needs and social prac-tices of consumers. Therefore, student researcher should realise that it is not compulsory to conceive of a management research project as, simply, an attempt to help business sell more stuff or help them to do so more effi-ciently. Marketing is a ubiquitous influence in social and cultural life and any aspect of this influence is a legitimate research topic, where it concerns the marketing of alcohol to young people and the potential harms this may bring (Szmigin et al., 2011), the ideological influence of fashion magazines on gender (Minowa et al., 2019), the subtle and exploitative interplay of advertising and entertainment (Hackley, 2019) or the ethical issues of decep-tion in brand product placement (Hackley et al., 2008).

Box 2.1 offers a list of things to consider in deciding on a research pro-ject topic. These are pragmatic considerations of course – if the student

---

Box 2.1   Checklist for choosing a project topic

- Is the topic interesting to you?
- Does the research problem make sense to people when you explain it to them? Is it clearly and succinctly expressed?
- Does your supervisor feel that it is an appropriate topic? Does it fall within the required subject domain? Is it sufficiently important/ interesting?
- Can you say, clearly, how you would investigate it? In other words, is it do-able?
- Is enough relevant published research-based literature available to support a substantial critical literature review?
- Does the topic depend on access to confidential or sensitive information?

is passionate about a particular topic or question, then that weighs the decision heavily in favour and the other issues are secondary. However, they are all important to the successful completion of the project. The answer to each of the questions does depend on many considerations. In particular, the 'do-ability' of the project is a question that the student researcher will be far better equipped to answer after having read this book. Do-ability is the key pragmatic issue with a project. Student researchers can probably quite easily think of topic areas they find interesting, but whether or not the project is viable, that is, whether it can be done given the time and other constraints facing the student, is a question that requires some understanding of research methods and the research process to answer.

To be sure, the range of possible topic areas for a research project in this area is so great it can be daunting. The world of consumption is a vast arena of symbolic human practice that is rich in research possibilities from many perspectives. The analogy of consumption is a powerful one: we can be said to 'consume' not only perishable items such as food, drink and fuel, but also clothes, motor cars, theme parks, service encounters, even the sheets we sleep on are 'consumption' items in this sense. Any aspect of consumer experience is valid material for researchers in marketing since it all contributes towards a greater understanding of the end of marketing activity: consumption. It has been suggested that consumption has become the primary symbolic human activity in developed economies. This may take the consumption metaphor too far for some tastes, but it can hardly be doubted that marketing actively seeks to transfer meaningful values and norms from their origins in non-consumption social life to the products and practices of marketing. Hence, as consumers, we are encouraged to realise our aspirations, wishes and fantasies of fulfilment through our consumption of marketed brands, products, services and lifestyles (Elliott and Wattanasuwan, 1998; Larsen and Patterson, 2018; Bardhi and Eckhardt, 2017). The student's preferred research topic might evolve from a particular industry issue or problem, or it might entail a more personal issue perhaps deriving from experiences as an employee, a consumer or a researcher. We all experience marketing activity as consumers and form ideas of how this activity might be managed. For example, we queue in shops and banks (service delivery quality), we buy products that we like (customer loyalty and relationship marketing) and products we dislike or products that were delivered poorly (relationship recovery, marketing operations). We take part in social rituals of consumption when we go out to restaurants, to see a show in a theatre or cinema, or to watch a football match. We read newspapers, eat advertised chocolate snacks, drive branded cars and wear branded goods. As consumers our practices of consumption might generate ideas for research projects. Our experiences of being 'managed' either as consumers or as employees might also generate ideas.

Whilst the research area of consumption has a vast scope, 'Management', too, is a broad and amorphous category encompassing all manner of directing, coping, co-ordinating, strategising, organising, resourcing, allocating, investigating and making judgements, from the executive pomp of major global corporations to the humble local store, small business or charity. Management goes on with vast resources and armies of subordinates, and it also goes on with no resources and no subordinates in small business. The management experience is vast and varied and its engagement with markets and consumers offers a fertile source of research topics, including the critical study of dysfunctional management practices (Knights and Willmott, 2017; Spicer et al., 2009).

The project topic may evolve from an interest in *functional* managerial issues, for example the student might be interested in examining how service quality might be improved in a particular industry context, say banking or restaurants. It may be that the student simply has an interest in an area and wants to learn how things happen, for example how advertising strategy is developed in an advertising agency. There may be a particular question that interests the student, such as how tourism destinations are influenced by the service quality of travel agents and their staff, or how tourism operator brands influence the internet purchase of 'packaged' holidays. The limit of the topics that can be explored in a qualitative management research project is the student's imagination.

Relevance

Much has been said and written about relevance in management studies. This chapter so far has tried to show how relevance can be conceived in a far broader way than simply in terms of a short-term solution to a management problem, such as how to make advertisements/distribution, chains/pricing strategies/service standards better and more managerially effective. This book assumes a scope of management and organisation studies that includes the social and cultural dimensions of this vast subject area. It also assumes that the focus point for many organisations is the consumer – anything that concerns the consumer should also concern the organisation that serves consumers. Consumer health and well-being, rights, ethical concerns, environmental concerns and happiness should all rightfully fall within the scope of organisations and, especially, within the scope of management education. The author has had many students worried about the adequate 'relevance' of a research project topic that interests them. They absorb the very narrow view of managerial relevance that obtains in many basic management textbooks and courses and think that research should follow the same path. Part of the aim of this book is to show that the student research project can be far more interesting, more creative and broader in scope than naïve managerial textbooks and courses suggest.

There are many traps to avoid when deciding on a project title and topic. For example, it is very important not to choose a topic merely because it seems interesting. It must also be one that can be researched easily in the available time and with the available resources. 'The impact of US Government economic policy on the level of marketing activity' might sound impressive but how would you go about studying such a broad question? Perhaps narrowing it down to a particular industry sector (motor manufacturing) and a specific aspect of government policy (say, monetary policy) might help but this remains a huge question for a 10–20,000 word research project that has to be completed within one or two semesters. Even if one case study of one organisation was conducted, attributing marketing activity in the firm to US Government policy would not be easy. There could be other causes, such as shifts in consumer demand, competitor activity or internal marketing initiatives that might equally influence the level of marketing activity. And what would constitute a good measure of marketing activity? Many research projects that initially sound good to the first-time researcher come apart at the seams under more careful examination. It is essential that the research title and topic are picked apart, criticised and thought through at the very beginning. The cost of not thinking carefully enough about the title at the beginning could be a research project that runs aground when it is too late to start again.

The exploratory project trajectory

We will return to the topic of exploratory research projects that we introduced in Chapter 1 because it is germane to the matter of how a research topic is framed and crafted in words. To reiterate, at undergraduate or master's level, research projects, especially qualitative projects, do not normally need to have a hypothesis. A hypothesis driven study would normally fall into the category of confirmatory research. Exploratory studies rather than hypothesis testing confirmation studies are often more suited to the student researcher. For example, the research question deriving from a *functional* or managerial interest can usefully be cast as a broad exploration. Say the research question is looking at the influence of travel agency staff on consumer choice of tourism destinations. An exploratory research design builds fewer assumptions into the research question and makes it less likely that the inexperienced student researcher will find the project speeding down a 'dead end'. In other words, if a research question implies that there is a relationship between two variables (in this case, travel agency staff attitudes and consumer destination choice) then the research may discover late in the study that the relationship does not hold. Tourism destinations may not be influenced by travel agency staff at all. The staff may be influential in the choice of tour operator or airline, but the destination choice may be more influenced by other factors. Too specific a research question, for example, one that postulates a direct causal relationship between variables, may be searching for a causal relationship that isn't there, setting the student and the project up for eventual failure. The great advantage of exploratory research designs is that you are investigating a topic, and not looking for a relationship that may not be there. A functionally driven research question (i.e. one to do with managerial efficiency or effectiveness) might presuppose a link or causal relationship, say, between sales promotional activity and sales, or between celebrity endorsement and brand equity. It might proceed from essentialist categories such as 'quality' or 'strategy' or 'brand equity' that are not necessarily useful in describing or explaining organisational action in practice. An exploratory research design leaves the possible findings open and gives the student researcher the flexibility to adapt the research to new knowledge.

As Figures 2.1 and 2.2 imply, the exploratory project (beginning with a 'working' title that can be adjusted as the work progresses) takes a different trajectory to the confirmatory project. Typically, the confirmatory project will assume or propose that a fact or relationship exists in the world, and sets out to test that with a *hypothetico-deductive* study. If the anticipated relationship turns out not to be statistically significant, or the response rate to the survey/experiment falls short of expectations, the project could grind to a halt half way down the pyramid. Of course, student projects and indeed published research studies do report null findings, that is, they report non-statistically significant findings. However, this is demotivating for the student and (usually) far less interesting to do, the student having a strong sense of trying to make a silk purse out of a sow's ear (to use an old English idiom) as they labour through the final stages of writing up their work.

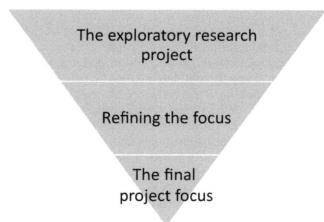

Figure 2.1 The development trajectory of the exploratory research project

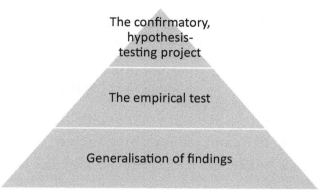

Figure 2.2 The development trajectory of the confirmatory research project

Of course, if a confirmatory study is well designed and based in a rigorous review of previous studies, then the chances of null findings could be reduced. The easiest way to do this would be to try to conduct a *replication study*, that is, to replicate a previously established finding with a new survey or experiment. The problem with replication studies is that A) findings in social research are notoriously difficult to replicate and B) it is not particularly a creative or interesting thing to do.

Being realistic about the scope of the project

There may also be an assumption implied in the research question that the student with little or no experience of a particular industry can solve problems that practical people encounter every day. 'Managerial' research projects are particularly prone to this weakness. Seeking to find a solution to problems in marketing or management processes may be a laudable aim for a student research project, but is it realistic? If experienced people have been tackling a particular problem every day of their working lives, how likely is it that a student project can find the best way for direct entry into the Chinese motor car market for a Western car manufacturer or solve an industrial relations issue in the coal mining industry? Functional research projects may well provide new insights into problems or new ways of conceiving of the problem, but it is important for the intellectual quality and practical credibility of such projects that they are framed modestly as explorations seeking insights and understanding, rather than making grand and hollow claims about finding sweeping solutions to major industrial problems.

If the research project topic is too ambitious or unrealistic in its aims the research is going to get sidetracked into arguments that are needed simply to defend the basic assumptions. This is a sure way to stifle research creativity. It also takes the fun out of research if you can't change your mind and explore something unexpected but interesting that emerged from the investigation. Furthermore, it is a poor research ethos that forces researchers to ignore issues that arise because they don't fit into the *a priori* categories that were built into the research question. For all these reasons, first-time student researchers often find that broad, exploratory research questions or issues are the safest and most appropriate.

The 'working' title and student motivation

A 'working' title is statement of a research question, issue or area that is phrased broadly so that it can be made more specific at a later stage. It is useful in exploratory research that research questions have some flexibility. If a person starts out by, say, researching branding effectiveness in a particular product market and then, mid-way through the project, decides that communication is central to the issue, it would be an intellectually flawed exercise if they could not adapt their research to take in a change of emphasis from branding to brand communication. Research projects should not have to perform logical somersaults to defend the coherence of the question. This would be a little like setting out on a world back-packing trip with a bad map, then insisting that the map is right – therefore this mud patch on the left must be Copacabana Beach.

Research questions should initially be couched in exploratory terms even if the original interest from which they evolve is one of a *functional* managerial, *normative* nature. The term 'managerial' used in research tends to refer to research that seeks to solve a management problem, while the term 'functional' refers to one of the typical organisational management functions, such as marketing, accounting, or Human Resources (HR). The term 'normative' is sometimes used to refer to managerialist texts that purport to offer such solutions; they offer frameworks for *doing* management tasks successfully. 'How can this work better?' is a natural question to ask for people attracted to marketing studies through a managerialist vein of thinking. In most cases an intellectually honest investigation will reveal the assumptions built into the question and hence lead into an exploration of the preconditions for the problem. In other words, the question 'how can we sell more stuff' would, if it is being investigated thoroughly, not simply focus on advertising, sales force management and distribution but also on pricing, product development ('are we trying to sell the right stuff?'), HR ('are our staff any good at selling?') and, of course, customers.

In any case, in marketing and other management fields, people working in that field feel that they already know how things could work better. They feel that the hard part is trying to implement the necessary changes, because there are always barriers to organisational functions, both internal barriers such as inefficient internal systems, poor reward systems, poor sales support and so on, or external barriers such as stiff competition, difficult macroeconomic conditions or trends and fashions in consumer tastes. Self-evidently, in most cases, since implementation of managerial practices and solutions is difficult, the problem itself is not as simple as it may appear to the naïve researcher. A project entitled 'Resolving customer dissatisfaction in service encounters in the motor car hire industry' is quite likely to generate some useful insights into customer experiences in that context, but it cannot do as it claims and 'solve' the problem, because it is a complex and continuing issue of management. What is more, finding out what a problem is is quite different to solving it. Research questions should be realistic about the limitations of research and suitably modest about their ambition. A working title that is phrased with some strategic vagueness can be useful because it can be adjusted as the researcher learns more about the complexity of the issue they are investigating.

There is also the question of student motivation. The project needs to be motivating for the student, and learning half way through it that the hoped-for aims will not be achieved, the promised interviews will not be forthcoming, or the anticipated relationship between variables is not there, are deeply de-motivating experiences. The exploratory format, and a 'working' title that can be tweaked, allows students the flexibility to investigate a topic of their interest in ways that are satisfying to them and can, if necessary, change emphasis half way through as the student learns more about the topic area. The choice of topic must be motivating for the student otherwise the research experience will be a chore, and commitment and performance levels will drop.

The student–supervisor relationship

The question of motivation is connected to the supervisor. Some supervisors are highly motivated, and motivating for the student, when supervising a committed student who is studying something that is of interest to them. Other supervisors might be supervising 30 undergraduate and/or postgraduate dissertations[1] and need to parcel out their time carefully for the sake of their health and sanity. The supervisor can help the research student to clarify issues and assumptions involved in the topic idea. Wherever possible research dissertations should not be a mere chore for the supervisor because where they are the student will quickly sense this and a key element of the motivational framework for doing the dissertation is flawed. This may be out of the hands of both student and supervisor if the faculty administration dictates the issue. Nonetheless, maintaining motivation is an issue of key importance to the success of the project and establishing a good relationship with the supervisor can be a big part of this. As a generalisation, supervisors tend to be more motivated and more responsive if they feel that the student is also committed and fully engaged with the process.

The student researcher's success depends a lot on their supervisor. It is always wise, and simple good manners, for students to attend meetings when requested, reply promptly to emails, listen to the advice offered, and meet deadlines when asked to do so. It is very unwise to fail to contact the supervisor for months on end, then to demand advice and guidance by tomorrow. In the great majority of cases supervisors sincerely want their research students to do well and many will go an extra mile or two to help. However, students must be aware that it is a two-way street. 'Independent' research project means exactly that. Students must work independently but under the guidance of the supervisor. Too much contact, or too little, can have a negative effect. In almost every case a little consideration and good-will on both sides solves any problems.

Many university departments set out procedures for making contact with supervisors. Some allow a good deal of flexibility. Some supervisors prefer regular meetings and updates. Others expect their students to go away and work independently once a careful initial discussion has set out just what their topic is to be and how they should go about researching it. Supervisors of this inclination would usually want to review only one draft before sub-mission. Both supervisors and students have differing needs and preferred ways of working: the main rule is that friendly and courteous consideration on both sides can make the process more satisfying for both parties.

Supervisors have a wide range of knowledge and expertise but their most important attribute for the student researchers is their experience of judg-ing, evaluating and designing research projects. In many cases it is not nec-essary that a supervisor be a specialist in a given sub-area of marketing or management for he or she to be able to give useful advice and to judge the success of a research project at undergraduate or master's level. Academics are often required to read and judge a wide range of papers in their work as reviewers for academic journals, research funding bodies and PhD propos-als and theses. Student researchers should be aware that experienced aca-demics have read, and in many cases written, a great many research papers and have developed strong research skills that enable them to help students research a wide range of topics.

The need to choose a topic and stick to it

Having a working title for an exploratory project does not mean that the stu-dent researcher can change their topic. What they can do is change aspects of it, such as tweaking the method, the sample, or the research questions. Doing the research project entails acquiring knowledge that is new to the student researcher. This new knowledge then, obviously, changes and informs the way the problem or issue is conceived. However, there must be a clear and well-defined although broad topic area and a general perspective that cannot be changed. It is unsettling for students and worrying for the supervisor if students change their minds about the topic they want to research halfway through the process. Research projects that are part of taught degrees are often conducted in a tight time-scale and with limited resources. Supervisors are often responsible for large numbers of students. Therefore, a radical change of topic mid-way through the process can present special difficulties. Indeed, some universities forbid students to change the topic after the proposal has been approved. It is, again, therefore, wiser to phrase the project title in such a way that its exploratory nature is evident and in a way that does not presuppose findings. Before writing the proposal students should take time and trouble to explore different topics, different research designs and different problem formulations. This is why academics always try to encourage students to begin thinking about their research project long before it is time to submit (advice that is, unfortunately, often not heeded). Then, when the student has decided on a topic proposal in discussion with their supervisor, they need to stick to the topic area, even they can sometimes tweak the theoretical approach, method and/or the empirical scope or sample.

For example, a student might decide to investigate comparative advertising strategies for motor cars in the UK and China. As they progress in gathering data they might decide to focus on a particular brand or class of car. They might also refine their project to focus on a specific market segment. They could even change the emphasis of analysis from a broad concern with 'advertising strategy' to some aspect of creative execution, such as the portrayal of speed in motor car ads, or the representation of masculinity that is produced through the visual imagery of the ads. They might be let down by brand managers in the car industry who had previously agreed to grant an interview but who now do not have time. In this case they might seek alternative interviewees, perhaps from the advertising agencies themselves. All this can change the emphasis of the research question and the consequent analysis and discussion. The important thing is that, however the emphasis of the project may change, the broad topic, scope and aims do not. That is why a broad, exploratory working title for the project proposal is often, pragmatically, the best starting point.

The project proposal

The research project process often begins with a research proposal that represents the initial ideas on how the project will unfold. Many universities require students to produce a research proposal that has to be approved before they can commence the project. As mentioned above, in the initial stages of the project a 'working' title that can be slightly adjusted may be sufficient. For example, a project entitled 'The relationship between advertising and sales in the laptop segment of the UK computer retailing sector' would be rather too broad. This would be a somewhat over-ambitious project that reveals a naïve understanding of the complexity of the issues involved. Such a project would need to be radically modified at a later stage, when the student researcher realised that they could not satisfactorily establish the stated relationship. However, if the same project proposal is worded in more general terms as, say, 'An exploration of advertising strategy in the laptop segment of the UK computer retailing sector', then there is scope for the precise aims of the project to be re-appraised later in light of the information that is gathered and the understanding that is developed. An over-ambitious, sweeping project proposal can risk setting the student up for failure. A more modest, carefully qualified proposal is usually wiser. Proposals must be interesting to the student (and if possible to the supervisor) and they must have a point or a question that will structure and drive the research. However, this can be phrased broadly in the initial stages because the project may then reach its full potential in an evolutionary way.

Writing the proposal

Different universities ask for slightly different things in their project proposal. They all, however, have the same general purpose. Proposals are designed to get the students to think carefully about their research project and to begin to think through and plan how they are going to complete it on time and to an acceptable standard. Many institutions try to get students to think about their proposal quite early in the year even though the project often does not have to be submitted until the very end of their course. Academic staff often find that a high proportion of students leave serious project work until rather late in the year, leading to a panic when submission time is near. The project is itself a major learning experience for most first-time student researchers and it is unreasonable to expect that they can anticipate the whole process in detail in advance. However, if students take the proposal seriously it can save a lot of stress later. The things that are normally required in the research project proposal are listed in Box 2.1.

It should be unnecessary to state that the essential elements of a proposal are that it is a carefully proof-edited text that is written clearly and uses a

---

Box 2.2   Research project proposal checklist

1   Topic area and working title
2   Major research questions/issues/problems to be investigated
3   Areas of literature (topics, academic journals, article titles) relevant to the review
4   Methods of data gathering (for empirical projects)
5   Research activities/time-line for research

reasonably accurate *referencing* style (Harvard style is specified by many universities). Some project proposals will require some elaboration on each point. For example, some universities will ask students to write a 2000 word proposal. This means that they can devote, say, some 300 words to a working title and an explanation of the topic area and a list of three or four main research questions, 1000 words to an outline literature review, 500 words to the methods and 200 words on a time line of the research process. Leaving enough words for a list of the references used would also be a good idea, so that the marker and the potential supervisor can see that the student knows how to use citations properly and how to list them at the end of the work.

The importance of reading the academic literature

One of the best ways to prepare a proposal is by reading the academic research on the topic the student is thinking about researching. As a rule of thumb, the more reading the student does, the better your project is likely to be. This will mean taking the trouble to use the databases of academic literature that are usually available in most university libraries such as 'Proquest', 'Emerald', 'ABI-inform', 'EBSCO' and ATHENS. University library staff are the experts in 'literature searching' and they are usually only too happy to advise students doing research projects, if advice is needed. Of course, being able to source research papers on a given topic is a fundamental scholarly skill and many universities will expect their undergraduate students to be fully able to do this by their final year.

Reading the academic literature has several benefits. First, students begin to understand the academic style of writing, including the use of conventions such as *Harvard citation style*. Second, acquiring a good understanding of the published research in relevant areas is a major part of the project process. For a bachelor's or master's dissertation or project the university will not expect the student to have a grasp of the entire field they are investigating, but it is a key requirement of the work that the study is contextualised by a good review of some of the main areas of work relevant to the research question. Reading research papers in a field increases the student's depth and breadth of understanding about a field of research and might even give the student ideas about a possible research topic or method.

The author studied for a taught MSc in marketing some (actually, rather a lot of) years ago. He was particularly interested in marketing and corporate communications, both to external and internal audiences. The independent research project he produced for his final (3rd) year assessment grew out of some reading on 'mission statements'. A group of researchers had collected many examples of published mission statements and had then analysed their content using a simple content analytic framework. The author extended this work by collecting more mission statements from a particular industry sector (higher education) from the organisations' published reports, websites and other communications. He adapted the previously used frameworks by adding a few categories, although what he did was essentially to replicate an earlier study, slightly modified, with a new data set. The study served for the author's MSc in marketing research dissertation (at the University of Salford, UK) and was published (Hackley, 1998)[2] with some theoretical development that had not been present in the original project.

Dealing with a scarcity of published research

Access to primary data is not the only potential difficulty in research design. Both empirical and conceptual projects must have a substantial literature review as their basis. If the chosen topic is novel or new there may not be very much published literature that deals with that precise topic. Even if the student researcher finds some useful sources, some fields, such as digital marketing, are changing so quickly that the books and articles that are in print quickly fall out of date. This makes it difficult to ground the project in an adequate literature review. One solution to this problem is to investigate a new or novel topic as a subcategory of an old one. For example, a student who wishes to do a project on interactive media would, at the time of writing, find relatively little authoritative published academic research that could be the basis of the project literature review. Instead, the novel topic could be presented as a subcategory of a well-established one, for example by calling the project 'The role of interactive media on media strategy decisions in advertising'. There is plenty of available academic literature, books and practitioner articles on media strategy in advertising. By locating a new topic within a well-established one the student can be sure to find plenty of existing published work on which to base a thorough literature review.

Originality of research

Many research projects are essentially adaptations, extensions or replications of previous projects. Student researchers are sometimes worried about the originality of their work if they adapt or extend a previously published research study. Adapting previously published research studies should not be confused with plagiarism. It is not only entirely legitimate: it is an extremely useful way of carrying out a first research project without 're-inventing the wheel'. Student research projects must be original in the sense that they must be the student's own work. They do not have to be original in the sense of being an entirely new, never-before-thought-of idea. Indeed, no research falls into this category. Every individual researcher researching in good faith from their own particular perspective will produce original work in the sense that it is their own 'take' on a given topic and the sample, the results, the findings, and the discussions and interpretation of findings, are all likely to be somewhat different to the original study. Indeed, as noted earlier, it is notoriously difficult to replicate studies in social research.

Students should not worry about the originality of their topic (provided they are doing different studies from the other students in their class of course!) because there will invariably be some things that are different if it has been conducted in good faith as a new piece of work produced entirely and wholly by the student.

Most academic published research is linked with or extends previous published work in various ways. *Conceptual* papers, that is, published research that does not draw on primary data sets, review previously published research to draw attention to theoretical anomalies or gaps and to suggest new lines of discussion or investigation. Empirical research papers that do use primary data sets often reproduce previously used research designs and use them on new sets of data to test the findings. Such papers also often explore old data with new theory, or they explore old research problems with a new angle or concept. 'Originality' in academic research consists in the particular arguments, style and combination of ideas employed. To repeat, originality in student research projects does *not* mean never-before imagined ideas or findings. Reading published research and drawing ideas, examples and ways of working from it is absolutely the best way for student researchers to form their own ideas about the kinds of research possible and the appropriate academic style of research writing.

'Deductive' and 'inductive' research designs

The *research design* refers to the overall design of the research method and its rationale for an empirical project. This would include details on research question(s) and/or problems, sampling, data gathering techniques and data analysis. We will note a few broad issues on research design at this stage.

The terms 'deductive' and 'inductive' are often used in research theory. *Inductive* means reasoning from the general to the particular. For example, if something seems true in many varied circumstances, it may also be true in specific circumstances. If, for example, you find from your lived experience that brown-eyed people tend to be generous, and green-eyed people less so, then you might form a rudimentary theory that brown-eyed people are generous. This is an example of inductive reasoning, although of course the sample size is so small that the results cannot be extended beyond your personal experience.

Deductive means reasoning from the particular to the general. Say, for example, you wanted to test if your personal, informal theory that brown-eyed people are generous is true of the whole population of brown-eyed people in the UK, you could form a hypothesis – 'Brown eyed people are generous', then design an experiment or survey to test the hypothesis empirically on a large random sample. This would be a deductive research design.

In social research exploratory studies would normally be designed on an inductive model, that is, the study would explore a phenomenon to see if any patterns or themes emerge. Strictly, inductive research looks at many cases in order to induce general patterns or relationships. However, major research studies can go through both inductive and deductive phases. If, say, a hundred sales people are interviewed about their motivation, a researcher might be able to induce a general proposition about sales person motivation that seems to be true for a large number of the interviewees. The researcher might feel that this proposition has not been considered in the previous research and theory on sales force motivation. Perhaps a large number of interviewees mention that having a boss with good communication skills is very important for their motivation. The researcher could then use a deductive research design to 'test' this proposition on an even larger number of cases, perhaps by means of a questionnaire. The finding would then provide material for reflection and modification of a theory of sales person motivation. If the study is trying to find a cause-effect relationship between the sales manager communication skills and sales force motivation, then this is sometimes called an abductive form of reasoning.

A qualitative, exploratory project then would normally use inductive or abductive reasoning because the researcher would be looking at a complex situation and trying to induce conclusions from the observed patterns in the data. For example, the previously mentioned study of children and video games (Bassiouni and Hackley, 2016) sought to explore the role of video games (played on any platform or device) in children's lives. Interviewing children about their video game usage enabled the researcher to draw some tentative conclusions about this role, even though only a dozen or so children were interviewed. The findings were tentative but nonetheless, powerful, but perhaps only characteristic of this sample of children and their particular circumstances. The reasoning used was broadly inductive in the sense that the reasoning moved from the general (the interview data) to the particular (conclusions drawn about the role of video games in children's lives induced from the interview data). The Grounded Theory style of qualitative research (Glaser and Strauss, 1967) is regarded as inductive in reasoning style.

Of course, induction and deduction both have a role in thinking and reasoning. Arguing and analysing necessarily draw on both inductive and deductive thinking in the process of reasoning about a particular problem or issue. For example, if I go out of the house three days in a row and get wet because it is raining, I might take an umbrella on the fourth day. I have induced a hypothesis: 'If I leave the house without an umbrella I might get wet'. Therefore I carry an umbrella to prevent getting wet when I leave the house. However, if I decide to test this hypothesis deductively when I go on summer holiday to southern Italy, I will find that my hypothesis does not hold true in that situation. I could carry my umbrella around in Rome for weeks in the summer and never get wet, unless I fell into one of the fountains. In our daily life we use deductive and inductive thinking to understand the world and to make predictions. If we relied exclusively on one or the other thinking style we would not manage very well at all. Many large-scale research designs, as in the illustration above, move from inductive to deductive and back again as theories are refined and developed. It is therefore rather a simplification to say that a research design is either inductive or deductive. Research is always both, to an extent.

Research philosophy

We will address the topic of research philosophies in greater detail in Chapter 5. For now, we will discuss some initial considerations. Interpretive research tends to be based on a social constructionist ontology. An ontology is a set of basic assumptions about the nature of life and the world. Social constructionism is the belief that the social world is self-constituting in a way that, say, trees or mountains are not. Trees and mountains operate to fixed laws of biology and geology that hold true for all trees and mountains on earth. They do not make up their own ways of being. The social world, according to the social constructionist ontology, is rather different – it does make up its own ways of being and does not always operate to universal laws.

We have already mentioned positivism, a term which refers to the belief that empirical research ought only to study things that can be observed and measured. An ontological assumption that can go alongside positivism is realism, the belief that the social world can be studied as if it operates according to universal laws, just like the natural world of trees and mountains. Positivism and realism are terms that are often used interchangeably in management research books, although they are not really the same thing.

For our purposes in this book, we can say that, normally, hypothetico-deductive research studies tend to be based on a realist-positivist ontology, whilst interpretive research studies tend to be based on a social constructionist ontology. That is, hypothesis testing studies tend to be based on the realist world view, they assume that whatever they discover might turn out to be a universally true fact or relationship between variables. Interpretive studies on the other hand, based on a social constructionist worldview, would not make the claim that their findings have discovered a universally true fact or relationship. Rather, they would offer an interpretation of what they have found that might be more widely true of similar groups but which also might connect with a human sense of truth, much as a novel might do the same by highlighting a truth that may hold for many people in certain situations.

Some university departments would expect students to understand which ontological assumptions they are making in their research design. Others would not. However, it is useful for all student researchers to understand the basic distinction between the realist ontology and the social constructionist ontology because of the implications for research design and also for the kinds of claim that can be made from the findings. Each style of research design tends to follow rather different conventions. One way of really getting to grips with the differences is to read a number of published studies that fall into each camp.

Hypothetico-deductive research studies based on a realist ontology tend to work best where there is already robust theory that can make strong predictions. Some interpretive researchers have argued that there are few examples of this kind of theory in the management and marketing area. Others would disagree. Inductive, interpretive studies tend to work best where the researcher is conducting an exploratory study to learn in greater detail about the dynamic that is operating in a given social situation.

'Empirical' and 'conceptual' research projects

The chapter will now discuss another important distinction, briefly mentioned earlier, in the kinds of project that can be undertaken as part of taught degrees. Some research projects at taught degree level in management and marketing are based mainly on existing sources of information such as academic papers, published economic data and/or internal company records. Such projects are often termed 'conceptual' projects to distinguish them from projects that make use of original information that is gathered first hand by the research student. Projects that generate original data are often called 'empirical' projects. The section below will elaborate on the issues and problems of each kind of project. It will then return to important issues of what topic to research given the special demands of these two categories of research.

Empirical projects

Marketing, management and consumer research projects in higher education can be either predominantly empirical, conceptual, or they can include elements of each. *Empirical* knowledge derives from experience and empirical research projects utilise first-hand experience of primary data sets from, for example, interviews, survey data or observation. The primary data sets are placed in the context of available literature (in the literature review) and are then analysed for insights or patterns. An empirical project report will represent the student's own systematic investigation into the topic. It will include a critical review of relevant research literature, perhaps including important practitioner literature (trade press, industry reports) and published market studies too. The general findings from the review are then evaluated in the light of the student's first-hand experience of the particular topic area, that is, their interpretation of the empirical data that have been gathered.

The amount of primary data in the empirical project can vary greatly. In research projects that are part of taught courses, data sampling may be based on very small samples for practical reasons. Qualitative data-gathering techniques use sampling approaches that are not required to provide a basis for statistically significant generalisation. Data can be based on *convenience samples* and need not be *randomised*. For example, a student investigating the use of fashion blogs in fashion purchasing might enlist their friendship group to form three *focus groups* of six people each. Primary data sets can be used to enhance a primarily conceptual project or it can be used as the major basis of argument for a project. One MSc student project the author has supervised used three focus groups, another used four *depth interviews*. The amount of primary data that might be useful depends on the research question or questions. It is important for student researchers to remember that even if small samples are representative of larger groups, that is, if they share the major characteristics of the larger groups, findings are still limited to the immediate research context and should be expressed cautiously in view of this. It is an important principle of inductive research that even if a particular fact or relationship between variables is true in millions of cases, we cannot know for sure if it will be true in the next case we examine.

Many projects combine elements of both conceptual and empirical approaches. One way of combining the two approaches is to focus on the literature review while carrying out a limited number of short 'pilot' interviews to get important practitioner or consumer perspectives on the topic. These perspectives can then be acknowledged and used in the discussion. Many projects in marketing and management that investigate a live problem do so by reviewing relevant literature on research and practice and then comparing the major findings with first-hand interviews with practitioners. In this way an empirical component can be added to a mainly conceptual research project. Conducting interviews with practising managers also has the added benefit of sharpening students' research interviewing skills and filling out their knowledge of the area. It can also be a useful exercise in getting contacts in an industry that might offer employment prospects after graduation.

'Conceptual' projects

Conceptual projects with no first-hand data are also often acceptable at undergraduate and sometimes at master's level, depending on the rules at the particular department in question. Conceptual projects are not based on primary data but use mainly existing published sources of information. Conceptual projects consist of an extended critical review of available research literature around a particular set of research issues, questions or problems. Students who survey academic literature will see that many published research papers in marketing, management and consumer research are like this. They report no empirical findings and have no data as such, but they explore issues or problems related to research. Many are simply a critical review of previously published literature that explores the state of knowledge in a particular area. Such a review would normally try to spot gaps or neglected areas or issues on previous research in order to make suggestions about how future research might contribute to greater understanding. Other conceptual papers are more intellectually complex in that they develop sophisticated themes or conceptual models, or they discuss research philosophy and methods and the scope of research in that field. Some conceptual papers offer historical analyses of particular traditions of research to show how it has developed and what influences have shaped that development.

The 'conceptual model'

Conceptual projects can induce a *conceptual model* from the literature review. A *model* in management and marketing research is a *representation* of an event or process that illustrates something important about that event or process. A critical path model of, say making buttered toast could be represented in a conceptual model. Similarly, a management process such as, well, the process of research design could also be represented in a conceptual model. Placing some related ideas in a conceptual model can be quite a powerful textual device for making particular points or summarising particular relationships. Models in basic management and marketing text books are often, simply, related concepts placed in boxes with arrows showing the supposed direction of causation or the flow of decision-making. In advertising research, for example, there are hierarchy-of-effects models of advertising effects; in marketing there are models of sales cycles and new product diffusion; in management there are models of employee motivation and decision-making. The model in the conceptual student project will be drawn from a synthesis of findings from the literature and will suggest possible implications of this synthesis for management practice or for future research.

For example, one of the author's MBA students once wrote a project on advertising ethics by first reviewing literature on the topic. She then developed a taxonomy or list of ethical problems that can arise with particular advertisements. These included mis-description, overt use of negative social stereotypes, sexually provocative imagery and so on. The researcher found that, while countries tend to have their own regulatory systems for advertising, individual advertisements often seem to succeed in by-passing these criteria with subtle use of symbolic texts and imagery. She then induced a conceptual model of criteria for evaluating the ethical status of particular advertisements. This conceptual model included the major criteria that could be used to judge an individual advertisement's ethical status. The research report applied the conceptual model by giving several examples of advertisements and judging their ethical status by applying the content criteria in the conceptual model. In this example the study was not purely conceptual, it did have some empirical data, but it used this to induce a conceptual model.

Another of the author's students was interested in the ways advertisers seem to target the insecurities of young women. The project was framed as a study in 'social fear'. The concept of social fear was intended to express the appeal of advertising that targets young women to sell products that exploit their fear of being unattractive or being rejected by the peer group. Products such as treatments for fresh breath, products to get rid of body hair and to prevent spots came into this category. She conducted an extensive literature review that addressed issues such as theories of advertising effects and ethical issues in advertising. She then collected a selection of print advertisements and creatively induced from them a typology of social fear in advertising. The typology of social fear was the conceptual model in the research project.

Other conceptual projects do not develop a conceptual model as such but, rather, develop abstract ideas and themes. One project explored the claims that research in marketing often makes to being a kind of science. The student wrote a reflexive, first-person research project expressing his bewilderment at the conflicting views in marketing. He discussed the various ideas he had been exposed to on his taught MSc in the light of his own career aspirations in marketing. A reflexive and relatively unstructured research project only reads as a credible piece of work if it is well written and well informed. This project was based on many articles published in marketing research journals that discuss research theory in marketing. It evaluated articles that claim marketing to be a science, and articles that pour scorn on that presumption. It reflected on the implications this lack of academic consensus has on the education of aspiring marketing professionals. It did so in a lively and scholarly written style. Conceptual, literature-based projects that draw on many published articles and challenge conventional wisdom and practice in the field are a pleasure to read from an academic's point of view, at least if he or she is sympathetic to the critical view expressed. To make such a project credible the student must demonstrate that they have read and thought about a large number of high-level academic papers and, moreover, understood them. Another MSc student wrote a conceptual project that entailed a critical appraisal of the literature on the sub-field of political marketing. Again, to make this piece of work credible as a research project she had to show that she was familiar with much of the current and recent literature and ideas in that field. The writing style had to be mature and elegant and the themes developed had to demonstrate a good working understanding of research in the field.

It is wise for any student researcher considering a conceptual project to discuss it carefully with the supervisor. Projects that criticise conventional wisdom and practice need careful handling. Critical projects fit best with critically inclined supervisors. Some supervisors prefer student researchers to limit the scope of their research to exploring smaller-scale questions rather than critiquing fundamental aspects of the field as a whole. The conceptual, literature-based project is no less demanding than the empirical project – in its way, it can be more demanding.

'What', 'why' and 'how' questions

We have already emphasised the importance of the choice of words in expressing the project proposal and title. Of particular importance is the kind of question that is implied in a research proposal. Different kinds of question imply different methods and analytical approaches. Students new to research are often unaware of the implications different kinds of question have for their whole project.

'What' questions

For example, many topics entail 'what' questions. A common way of crafting a research question in marketing is to ask 'What is the connection or link between x and y?' Very often this will be cast in terms of the possible impact of a marketing variable in a particular managerial intervention.

This could be a question of causation such as 'What is the impact of celebrity endorsement on sales of a brand of sports shoes in the UK?' or 'What is the effect of a 10% price reduction on consumers' perceptions of the quality of brand X?' Such questions, while legitimate research topics, carry assumptions that dictate the character of the research to be conducted. First, such questions assume that the categories contained in them ('celebrity endorsement', 'brand') are unquestionably appropriate to the circumstances. Defining the terms in no way avoids this problem because the categories, however defined, set the terms of researcher engagement with the topic. As a result there will inevitably be an element of logical circularity to a project in which an essential category is taken for granted.

To put this in another way, the first question assumes that 'celebrity endorsement' has an impact on sports shoe sales. In social research in marketing, management and anything else, you can always find what you think you are looking for. If you assume that 'celebrity endorsement' is what drives sales in the sports shoe market then that is what you will 'find'. But there could be other ways of conceiving of this relation. Perhaps the brand exposure is the important thing and the celebrity component is incidental. Perhaps celebrity endorsement is the wrong phrase to use: members of the public know very well that celebrities often 'endorse' products that they don't use. Perhaps the celebrity association with the brand is the important thing and not the endorsement as such. Clearly such questions of conceptual clarity and causal relations in marketing can and should be discussed in the research project report. However, in marketing research in particular, it is all too often the case that they are not. Marketing research projects do need to offer a balanced justification of their assumptions in order to satisfy broader intellectual criteria.

It is useful to be aware, also, that in many cases the academic assessing or second marking of the research report may not be inclined to accept that certain concepts and relations can be taken for granted. In the above case it would be wise for the student to pose a broader research question exploring the nature of demand for sports shoes in the UK (or other) market so that should any causal relation become evident during the course of the research, it can be reported in an appropriate context. Alternatively, the research proposal could explore the *role* and *nature* of celebrity endorsement promotion in a national sports shoe market. That way, posed as an exploratory study, the research findings are not presupposed in the research question.

It is an important part of the ethical and the intellectual integrity of management research that conventional or given categories, phrases and relations are questioned and their use critically examined in local contexts. Marketing research does have a record of perpetuating essentialist concepts in self-confirming research exercises. For example, research that investigates the role of the 'marketing mix' in particular product markets legitimises the 'marketing mix' as an important and decisive category of management activity. One may argue that the 'marketing mix' is just that: important and decisive. But research that accepts given categories and the relations implicit with their use is likely to lack a spirit of creativity and critique. A research project is an opportunity to explore creatively an issue or area and thereby intellectually develop and enrich the researcher's perspective. There are plenty of published studies that have investigated how marketing professionals actually do marketing, which conclude that they don't use text book categories such as 'marketing mix'. As an intellectual exercise, a research dissertation should be an exercise in challenging assumptions and picking apart native categories. An inexperienced researcher should not feel bound to decide what they are going to find before they start looking. So the topic chosen can be framed initially as a working title exploring, investigating or examining an issue, problem or relationship. If the topic is cast in this way the issue is left open. The topic may change emphasis or direction depending on what the researcher finds. Initial categories (such as 'celebrity endorsement' or 'marketing mix') should be established by critical inquiry and not simply asserted by definition.

'Why' and 'how' questions

'Why' questions, as well as 'what' questions, can be inappropriately phrased in a way that implicitly supplies the answer. For example, the research question 'Why does marketing orientation offer sustained competitive advantage for commercial organizations?' is clearly a question that has answered itself. Incidentally, this is a question that, even phrased in an exploratory style, is probably beyond the scope of a student project unless they can get access to senior executives of several organisations. 'How' questions also need to be used with caution. The question 'How do car sales people maximize their effectiveness in sales interviews?' assumes that direct selling is an important sales channel for cars. Many car buyers, though, will arrive at the franchise already knowing which car they want to buy. The salesperson's job is not to sell but to 'upsell', that is, to sell add-ons such as gap insurance and extended warranties. It would be more useful to the student who is interested in this area to explore either, a) car sales conversations in a given market context, or b) sales interview styles in any context. In general, it is a useful practice for first-time student researchers to pose open questions so that they are not caught out later by the presuppositions implied in particular kinds of question.

We tend to phrase social research questions in terms of 'what', 'why' and 'how' when we first embark on an independent study project. Students new to research cannot be expected to know that they set traps for themselves in phrasing questions in this way since they presuppose particular ways of knowing and understanding. It is far from unusual for a student to do a conscientious research project investigating such a question only to be told at the end that they were not awarded a better mark because their research question was too narrow or was otherwise inappropriate to the subject. 'What', 'why' and 'how' imply that there is a 'what', a 'why' or a 'how'. In social research there may be highly complex relations between an event and its consequences or antecedents. At undergraduate or master's level, an open investigation into a topic tends to be a wiser exercise for the student. It is also a more creative exercise to conduct an open investigation that is not stunted by the need to defend the assumptions implied in the question.

Chapter 2 has discussed the design of the research study, beginning with how the title of the project is phrased, which is of key importance to the successful completion of the project because of the implications it has for the research design, method and findings. The chapter has also touched on issues of research design and research philosophy. Considerable thought must be given to the way the topic title and research proposal is drafted. Getting this right and thinking it through can save a great deal of stress later in the process. The next chapter discusses the outcome of the research project process, the project report, also called the dissertation or thesis. It is particularly important for student researchers to understand that a written document, a text, is the goal of their efforts. If student researchers appreciate the likely structure, tone and style of this text at the beginning of the process it can make research design and planning much easier.

Glossary

Conceptual project A project that does not make great use of primary data but, rather, develops a conceptual analysis from a synthesis of published research and existing available data.

Deductive Normally refers to reasoning that proceeds from the particular to the general. In research, refers to hypothesis testing or hypothetic-deductive studies.

Depth Interview A long interview with one person, lasting anything from half an hour or more, that probes a topic in considerable detail allowing the participant to reflect deeply on the questions.

Focus Group A group formed to discuss a particular topic area under the guidance of a convenor.

Functional In this chapter 'functional' refers to research projects that seek to address a functional area of business such as accounting, operations, marketing, service or manufacturing from a managerial problem-solving point of view. 'Functional' has a different meaning in sociology and cultural anthropology, often described in terms of a biological metaphor that emphasises the systemic interdependence of parts (known as functionalism).

Harvard referencing The style of referencing used in this book. It entails citing references in the text with author and year. The full reference is placed in the references section in alphabetical order at the end of the document.

Hypothetico-deductive A style of research that derives a hypothesis from a body of theory, tests it empirically and uses the findings to inform or modify the theory.

Inductive Reasoning that moves from the general to the particular. In research, usually identified with qualitative, exploratory studies.

Normative Much managerial writing and teaching is normative in the sense that it purports to tell the student or reader what they ought to do in a given management situation. There are implied judgements in the normative managerial tradition of thinking and writing, which may not be made clear or explicit.

Positivism   In social research the term usually refers to a set of assumptions about reality and knowledge that have some similarity to the precepts of a branch of philosophy of knowledge called 'logical positivism' (Ayer, 1936). In management research 'positivist' often refers to research that assumes that the social world can be treated as materially real in the same way as the physical world, and can be observed and measured. Indeed, for logical positivists, if a phenomenon cannot be observed and measured, then it belongs in the realm of metaphysics.

Realist ontology   A world view that holds that the social world can be researched in the same way as the physical world.

Replication study   A research study that attempts to reproduce the finding of a previous study by using the same research design. It is notoriously difficult to replicate findings in social and psychological research.

Research design   The overall design of the research method and its rationale for an empirical project, including details on the research question(s) and/or problems, sampling, data gathering techniques and data analysis.

Social constructionist ontology   A world view that holds that the social world is self-constituting in a profound way that distinguishes it from the natural world, therefore it requires different (interpretive) research methods.

Notes

1   Thirty is unusual but not unknown. Some universities insist that supervisors are handling no more than six student projects at a time.

2   A copy of the paper is available here www.researchgate.net/publication/235273251_ Mission_statements_as_corporate_communications_the_consequences_of_ social_constructionism and it is cited in a subsequent study by Desmidt (2015) www.researchgate.net/publication/279167305_The_Relevance_of_Mission_ Statements_Analysing_the_antecedents_of_perceived_message_quality_and_its_ relationship_to_employee_mission_engagement

Chapter 3

Writing high quality research projects

From description to critique

Chapter outline

This chapter focuses on the structure, tone and style of the written document that must be produced for a research project. The aim in dealing with this issue early in the book is to give student researchers a rounded view of the whole text that they must eventually produce, so that they can see how the parts fit into the whole. Having this view will help with the student's confidence, research planning and time management. The chapter looks at key issues of research writing such as academic tone, style and critical thinking.

Chapter objectives

After reading this chapter students will be able to

- see both the parts and the whole of the research project structure
- plan the research knowing what kind of text must be produced
- understand the central role of writing in the production of research
- grasp some of the stylistic issues of academic writing such as 'tone', 'critique', 'reflexivity' and argumentation.

'Writing up' and the research process

'Writing up' is often considered to be the final stage in the research project and is usually treated as an afterthought in the student's research methods education. In fact, research writing is a highly specialised genre that demands skill in the art and rhetoric of writing research texts. Writing and rhetorical skills are central to the success of professional researchers, in marketing studies areas (Brownlie, 1997, 2001; Brown, 2005; Hackley, 2009a) and equally in other areas of management and social studies. For example, McCloskey (1983) pointed out the centrality of skill in persuasive rhetoric in successful economic theories, as others have done with regard to marketing texts (Brown et al., 2018; Hackley, 2003b) and ethnography (Jarzabkowski et al., 2014). The research project is not a work of literature – and yet, it is, in the sense that it is a piece of writing (with other forms of representation included, such as numerical, pictorial, graphical, diagrammatical) that is designed to take the reader on a journey that will, ultimately, be persuasive. In this chapter we will consider the student research project as a written text that must be written with appropriate stylistic conventions and rhetorical devices.

It is strongly advised that student researchers think carefully about the written document that they must produce right from the beginning of the project process. By doing this, student researchers form an idea of the whole picture of a research project before they embark on it. In contrast, many first-time student researchers begin the project without appreciating the nature of the desired end-result. They attempt each stage without knowing why it is important and how it fits into the whole. This can result in poor planning and loss of direction. Academics are very familiar with student research projects that are flawed because they are poorly structured. Indeed, 'poor structure' is one of the clichés of academic criticism, because it is an easy one to make of a lot of student written work. If students have a holistic idea of what kind of text they must produce then the process can be much less stressful and more successful. Later in the chapter we will present some suggested structures for interpretive research projects.

The common idea of 'writing up' research implies that the research process is separate from the writing process, and also that 'writing up' somehow requires less attention than the research. Neither is correct. Research is constructed through writing. Research cannot be communicated unless a narrative is constructed to tell the research story. Therefore, it makes perfect sense to consider the narrative conventions of research as part of research design. This does not imply that there is one right way to write research projects. People plan and write their research in different ways. The process of writing, and the style in which the researcher writes, can differ widely. Different research genres tend to have different styles. For example, a piece of quantitative research would generally be written to different conventions than an interpretive study.

Some student researchers gather data and literature over time and then write up a draft of the whole project in one go. Others prefer to do their literature search first and write up the project chapter by chapter. If the project is hypothetico-deductive in style, the literature review will be the basis for the hypothesis so it will need to be written in full early in the process. If, on the other hand, the research is inductive in style (see previous chapter for discussion on deductive–inductive research designs) there will be an initial literature review followed by a phase of data collection, followed by another more closely focused literature review (as in grounded theory studies, Glaser and Strauss, 1967). The research report will, however, be written up in the same sequence as for the deductive research project, with the literature review early in the sequence of chapters. This is because research writing does not always have to accurately represent the process of research. Indeed, it would be impossible to do this. A research study that takes several months and entails false starts and blind alleys would not make easy reading if it were described in every detail. The sequence of actual research activities depends to a large extent on personal preference (and on the preferred style of the supervisor) and upon the nature of the project. The report itself need not necessarily reflect this sequence of activities. It is more important for a research report to satisfy some of the accepted narrative conventions of research in that field. In other words, it must look like a research report (or thesis, or dissertation) in order for readers to accept that it is one.

Students conducting a research project have to construct their research question, to read widely around that topic, to choose a suitable method of inquiry, and to reflect on their own assumptions as they attempt to make sense of their question and of the answers. Many university and business school faculties have their own conventions for style, tone and structure of such projects, typeface and references style, contents and chapter headings. Many academic supervisors have individual preferences in such matters. It is wise for students to make sure they understand exactly what conventions they are expected to observe in their research project. However, there are principles of good practice that apply to every research project. Research reports need to have certain things, like literature reviews, research objectives, findings, references and so on. The various sections have to be presented in an appropriate sequence. The report also has to be written in an appropriate style or 'tone'. The next section will develop some themes on this most important aspect of research writing.

The academic writing 'tone'

The 'tone' of a piece of writing refers to what it conveys through, for example, its grammatical conventions, sentence structure and vocabulary. Tone can be generally formal, informal, conversational, authoritative, amusing, serious, technical and so on. It is difficult to define tone since it is a matter of interpretation. The best way to address the issue for research writing is to say that the tone must seem to the reader to be appropriate for a research text. The written text produced by the student researcher needs to strike a suitably academic tone of writing, although as we discuss below there are different ways of conceiving this. Some academics criticise student work if they feel that it is too 'conversational', 'anecdotal' or 'journalistic'. Of course, all these styles can be virtues in the right context, but for many academics there is an academic tone of writing that is distinct from the tone you use when writing or talking to a friend ('conversational'), when relating an anecdote, or when a journalist writes a feature article. Precisely what that difference is, is difficult to define and no-one in academia (including this author) can tell you exactly what it is. What we can do is to mention some of the stylistic conventions that typically characterise academic writing.

One aspect of academic writing, in social science in particular, is the use of academic jargon. Another is the use of long sentences. Academic writing styles can sometimes seem obscure and pretentious to readers more familiar with newspapers or popular novels. Indeed, some academics argue that academic writing is generally bad writing, partly because it is so often obscure and strewn with the technical jargon of social science. Sentences are often long and often carry multiple subclauses as academic writers build in contingencies and conditionals to everything they want to say. Sometimes, reading academic work, it seems as though the author has spent a whole page very elaborately *not* saying something, lest they open their paper up to counterarguments. It is important to recognise that, while some writers are obscure because their thoughts are not clear, much academic writing uses technical terms and stylistic conventions because they have become part of the accepted way of writing in that field, and academic work is principally written for the approval not of casual readers but of other academics. A lot of the jargon is shorthand for academics to refer to issues and arguments that they feel must be stated before they move on to the next stage in the argument. It is an important part of the student researcher's task to begin to understand the purpose of this style and to write in a way that is somewhat like it, hopefully without giving in to the worst excesses of convoluted and arcane academic writing.

The 'third person'

Some of the stylistic conventions of research writing are fairly easy to grasp. For example, most research papers are written in the 'third person', as when the authors refer to themselves as 'the authors' instead of simply saying 'I'. This convention can rhetorically produce a sense of detachment or objectivity. It makes the research writing sound more depersonalised, which is intended to make it seem more authoritative or credible (and less 'conversational'). It is often a good idea for student researchers to adopt this convention although it is not always required. Some interpretive traditions of research writing, such as autoethnography (Hackley, 2016) adopt the first person grammar and use 'I' when referring to the author. Different academics have different preferences. If in doubt it is a good idea to write in the third person because that is the traditional approach in academic writing.

Writing in the third person, while a somewhat artificial and stilted prose style, can help to encourage a disciplined approach to writing up the work as a piece of systematic research rather than as a personal story. Some published researchers have, though, written very personalised accounts of their research. Holbrook (1995) has even devised an interpretive method of research he calls 'Subjective Personal Introspection' that has been used in various published interpretive consumer research studies (e.g. Shankar, 2000). Brown (e.g. 1995) has produced some of the most vivid, and funniest, pieces of writing in academic marketing using an exclusively personalised style. Marketing authors have used poetry and lyricism to shed new insights on marketing as a Romantic endeavour (e.g. Brown et al., 1998, and in consumer research, Sherry and Schouten, 2002). Brown (2005), Brownlie (1997, 2001) and others have challenged the stodgy conventions of academic writing to call for livelier, more personal, *better* academic writing. It is probably fair to say, though, that you have to be a very experienced and creative scholar, and a confident writer, to produce a credible research report in as subjective a style as these authors. For most student researchers, writing in the third person is the safer option.

Making 'claims' and supporting 'arguments'

Another important aspect of writing tone concerns the way 'arguments' or points of view are constructed and assertions made. The entire research report is an argument, in the rhetorical sense that the text is written to be persuasive of the author's point of view. The research project process can be seen as a test to see whether the student can develop or explore points of view of some complexity drawing on a variety of sources. In the research report he or she must show that they can sustain this for 8,000, 10,000, 12,000 or 20,000 words, depending on the requirements of their department. The report will attest to the student researcher's standard of scholarship. For academics, a high standard of scholarship is difficult to define, but they know it when they see it. It consists in plausible, clearly expressed, thorough and well-supported intellectual work. Most important of all, the work has to amount to an *argument*, that is, it must be persuasive. Academics argue in very stylised ways, which to the non-academic observer don't look like arguing at all. But don't be deceived – there are subtle codes of academic argument that don't involve typing in capitals or using multiple exclamation marks.

Academics use terms such as academic 'rigour' (Gioia et al., 2013) or we might refer to arguments and discussions that are 'robust'. What we mean when we use these terms is that the writing is persuasive and credible, to an academic.

Credible research writing depends on not making incredible 'claims'. Academics refer to making claims when a piece of academic writing makes an assertion of fact or draws a conclusion about a topic. Such assertions are claims and they should be supported by careful reasoning or evidence from previous research or case examples. Academics are looking for a good quality argument when we read student work, and that means supporting and/ or qualifying any assertions or claims carefully. The acquisition of more knowledge usually makes people less extravagant (or assertive) in their claims about their research findings, therefore more modestly styled prose suggests to the reader that the author has more knowledge. In other words, a mark of good academic writing is not overselling the author's opinion (although the popular genre of academic marketing text books, it must be admitted, break this cardinal rule of scholarly tone by making an art of overselling) (Brown, 1995; Hackley, 2003b).

The stance of the true researcher is that one knows enough to know how little one really knows. In fact, William Goldman's famous axiom from the movie business applies very much in business and management research: Nobody knows anything (Goldman, 1983). Knowledge progresses in very small stages, if it can be said to progress at all. Academics working in a particular field know a lot, but this knowledge shows them how much more there is to know. This does not mean that one has to write only about topics that can be reduced to tiny subtopics. Neither does it mean that research writing should be excessively cautious in making assertions of any kind. There is plenty of scope for creative exploration in ideas, as long as the writer is frank about what is speculation and what is a more substantive claim. Assertions, claims or suggestions should be carefully and logically supported with reasoning or evidence.

Any assertion made in a research report (such as 'Management researchers still understand relatively little about motivation in the workplace') needs to be supported very carefully with references to published authorities, to other sources or by careful reasoning. Inadequately supported assertions are probably the most common reason for losing marks in a research project report. The examiner will not normally judge the student researcher's writing on whether or not what they write about is true. Much of social science is speculative and can only be judged on its coherence or its logical connection to other bodies of theory or evidence. The examiner is, however, looking for quality of argument and discussion. Whatever the point being argued, the examiner wants to see persuasive and well-rounded argument. Authors should show that they are aware that their point of view is not the only one that may be right. Authors of research reports should show that they are aware of a number of possible points of view. A mark of good argumentation is to give suitable acknowledgement to opposing arguments, even if this is simply as a rhetorical device to dismiss them more persuasively. There is a lot of published research literature on employee motivation so the above assertion would, at least, need to be placed in a context of a careful review of a good range of that literature in order for the examiner to accept that the writer has sufficiently supported the claim. For picking up useful information and for absorbing the writing style of academic research, there is no substitute for reading published academic papers.

So, before embarking on the research report, remember to read as many academic research papers as possible to grasp the academic style and to become familiar with a range of research in the field of interest. Second, remember that academics who have devoted their entire career to researching a specific topic often feel that, while they know a lot, they still know much less than they'd like to. Consequently, the last thing they want to read is a piece of student research from a writer who thinks they've cracked the whole problem in a semester. Popular business and management texts tend to use grammatical conventions which imply that they offer solutions: 'Managing quality better in financial services'; 'Relationship marketing, the new paradigm for business success'; 'Emotional intelligence: the key to effective management'. These are not, to my knowledge, the titles of real books, though they could be; I've made them up. They employ grammatical styles that are very (too) common in this field. Students should be aware that a research project should not make too much use of the popular, consulting style of writing that is seen in many teaching texts. Write in a style that shows caution towards assertions, supports points with careful reasoning and evidence from literature and research, and shows awareness that there may be alternative points of view that have not occurred to you, the researcher.

Plagiarism: how to avoid the charge

Most university research project guides have a section on *plagiarism*, warning of dire consequences for the student if the work submitted is found to have plagiarised any other work. Many of these guides are now quite detailed and contain a lot of useful information, plus essential procedural information on how accusations of plagiarism will be dealt with in each university department, so they should be read carefully by student researchers. The growth in online businesses selling pre-written essays and dissertations has created a sense that this is now a 'problem', so universities are increasingly sensitive to the issue. The independent research project must be entirely the student's own work. It is vitally important that the criterion of 'independence' is satisfied. However, it is also true that few ideas are truly original and research projects do contain elements that are substantially a review of previously published ideas. This is why there is often confusion over what, exactly, constitutes plagiarism. How can it be copying if the ideas are already out there in the public domain? And even more confusing, why do students get disciplined for plagiarism when they had no intention of passing off other's work as their own?

Plagiarised work is research or other writing that is reproduced in a project report to appear that it is the author's own words when in fact it has been copied from another source. Many students, especially those working in a second language and trying to understand a new educational culture, find it difficult to distinguish plagiarism from legitimate paraphrasing and quotation. The *literature review* component of the research project report describes, summarises and evaluates the published work of writers in a field. For some international students, especially those who were educated in traditions that regard rote learning and reproduction of academic work as absolutely fine, it can seem odd, and even presumptuous, to re-word the written work of published academics. However, the research project is not merely an extended paraphrase of the work of established researchers. It is the student researcher's discussion and views on this previously published work. The distinction between copying or plagiarising and legitimate quoting and paraphrasing is difficult to grasp for some students, but it is essential that they do so.

Literature reviewing demonstrates important academic skills. If a student researcher can summarise a particular piece of research or theory succinctly it demonstrates that he or she has read and understood the work. This kind of engagement with the published research of established researchers is an important part of the Western university tradition. The biggest downside to deliberate and flagrant plagiarism is that the student will have missed out on a key part of their higher education. They will have failed to develop the higher order academic, scholarly and personal (and interpersonal) skills that the independent project is designed to develop.

Using direct quotes in research projects

All written or graphic material that is reproduced unchanged from a source should be accompanied by the author and page citation (e.g. Smith, 2003, p. 4); written material that is a direct quote of the work should be placed within full quotation marks, again with page number. Footnotes may be used where appropriate, depending on the convention of the student's university. A paraphrase of a short section of work should also normally have the original author cited, even if it is not a direct quote. *It is very important to note that changing just a few words of the quote is not enough to render it into the student's own words.* This confusion is probably the single most common source of plagiarism charges – the student thinks that they do not need to represent the work as a direct quote because they have changed a couple of prepositions.

Using direct quotes can be a powerful technique of exposition, and good research projects often make liberal use of them. However, there are three things students should remember about using them. The first is that they should not normally be too long (check out published papers for guidance). Second, they should not be left to speak for themselves. A direct quote should be preceded, and followed, by extensive discussion that explains what point the quote is being used to make and how it connects to the overall reasoning in the section. Finally, and third, a good dissertation does not have too many direct quotes – to do so suggests that the researcher was struggling to write their own narrative.

School students of literature are often asked by the teacher to describe, criticise or discuss a particular piece of poetry or prose. Many direct quotes are useful for this purpose but there can be no mistake that the discussion must make use of the student's own original ideas and words. The student's considered views on the piece of work are being sought and their ability to demonstrate their understanding by articulating those views will be assessed by the teacher. Similarly, the independent research project requires students to engage with published research studies in an active and critical way so that the original author's words are reinterpreted by the student researcher. This is what strictures against plagiarism are designed to encourage. Plagiarism is a serious charge and, where proven, can prevent graduation, so student researchers should make every effort to ensure that they cannot be accused of it by carefully citing every source that they have used and making sure that direct quotes are cited correctly.

The use of references

The use of references in the text can seem a cumbersome device that impairs read-ability but it is essential to academic writing. If a general assertion is made (say, 'research in marketing has neglected the role of internal communications in organisational marketing effectiveness') there needs to be a citation of one or more published works that support this assertion. If a student researcher makes any assertion that they want accepted as a statement of fact, there does need to be this support from credible published research, even if the assertion seems rather conventional and uncontroversial. The published work should, preferably, come from refereed academic journals of good standing, but it is also relevant to cite websites and trade press articles when the text is discussing business conditions or case examples. As a general rule, the more references the better, provided they are relevant to the point being supported. Citing other work signals that you understand how your research is thematically linked with previous research. It is a mark of good scholarship to master a fluid style of referencing so that citations are woven elegantly into the text.

All works cited by author and date (Smith, 1995) in the text of the research report should be listed in full in alphabetical order by author at the end of the report (See Box 3.4). The term 'bibliography' is sometimes used to indicate all work read as part of the research even if it is not cited in the research report. However, viewed negatively, a bibliography can be seen as a list of books that the student didn't quite get around to reading, as it is sometimes used to list works that were not cited in a text. This is why the term 'references' is better for academic work. All works listed in the references list at the end of the project text must have been cited in the main body.

Box 3.1   Harvard style referencing

In-text citation
(Author, year) or Author (year)
e.g. Smith (2019) or (Smith, 2019)

Reference List by First Letter of Family Name Alphabetical Order
Books
Author, (Year) Title. Place Published: Publisher.
e.g. Smith, P.J. (2019) Interpretive Research Methods: London: Routledge.
Articles
Author, (Year) 'Article title'. Journal Title, volume (number): pages.
e.g. Smith, P.J. (2019) 'The role of interpretive research in improving outcomes from therapeutic psychological interventions", Psychological Research International, 40 (2): 342–363.

Standards of scholarship

The independent research project conducted in a higher education context is a test of a student's scholarship. Scholarship consists in assimilating different sources of information into a new piece of written work. The standards required are high. Not only do research project reports have to be clearly structured with a well-defined problem or issue, logically ordered and written in appropriate and grammatically correct English, they also have to satisfy standards of good scholarship. 'Good' scholarship is not easy to define. It has many dimensions.

Some universities use tables of marketing criteria to try to itemise the different levels and different elements of good scholarship. In Box 3.2 we can see one such example. This is fairly typical of many such 'rubrics' as they can be called. This extract from a UK university rubric for master's dissertations in business and management is not intended as a template, it is just one example of how such a rubric can be constructed.

To this example of a general marking rubric for dissertations, we can add an example of a generic rubric for undergraduate written work in Figure 3.1. Neither of these examples, it should be said, are particularly good – rubrics in general tend to be exercises in synonym generation for stating the obvious, or, at the other extreme, some go to such lengths to display the full range of Bloom's taxonomy that it hardly seems worthwhile to do the work, such is the precision with which its features have been described. Academics often find it very difficult to describe what excellent, adequate and poor work looks like, but they do know it when they see

Box 3.2 An adapted example of a master's dissertation marking rubric

Overall Mark

85–100: An exceptionally high level of understanding and outstanding research potential.

70–84: Very high competence and excellent research potential.

60–69: Evidence of some creativity and independence of thought.

50–59: Sound understanding of the literature, but lack of accuracy or originality.

0–49: Insufficient or no understanding of the topic, poor quality of work.

Marks allocated under particular categories of achievement

Knowledge of subject (25)

21–25: Deep understanding and near-comprehensive knowledge.

18–20: Deep understanding.

15–17: Very good understanding.

12–14: Sound knowledge of relevant information.

10–11: Basic understanding of the main issues.

0–9: Little or no understanding of the main issues.

Organisation of material (25)

21–25: Of excellent quality.

18–20: Arguments clearly constructed; material very well organised.

15–17: Well organised; aims met with no significant errors or omissions.

12–14: Coherent and competent organisation.

10–11: Lack of clarity in written presentation or aims only partially met.

6–9: Major flaws in arguments; aims of project not met.

0–5: Arguments are missing/deficient. Disorganised or fragmentary.

Originality, interpretation and analysis (20)

17–20: Significant originality in the interpretation and/or analysis; project aims challenging.

14–16: Some originality; evidence of excellent analytical and problem-solving skills.

12–13: Good attempt to interpret and analyse existing literature.

10–11: Minor flaws in interpretation/analysis of existing literature.

5–9: Poor interpretation/analysis or project aims too simple.

0–4: Little or no interpretation or analysis; project aims trivial.

Evidence of reading (10)

8–10: Independent reading especially of research papers.

6–7: Good use of reading.

4–5: Some evidence of reading.
0–3: Little or no evidence of reading.

Referencing (10)
9–10: Excellent, comprehensive, few minor errors
7–8: Good referencing
5–6: Poor referencing.
3–4: Poor or little referencing.
0–2: No referencing.

Style, spelling, punctuation and grammar (10)
9–10: Clear and fluent, few minor errors of spelling, punctuation or grammar.
7–8: Very minor errors of spelling, punctuation or grammar.
4–6: Some errors of spelling, punctuation or grammar.
0–3: Many errors of spelling, punctuation or grammar.

it. Of course, it is the detail that differentiates good from poor academic work, and this book attempts to articulate some of the detail that cannot fit into a rubric when it discusses academic writing tone, style, referencing and possible dissertation structures.

Both Box 3.2 and Figure 3.1 do, in spite of their limitations, highlight the ways that academics struggle to be more fair and transparent to students by trying to systematise the way they assess levels of student work.

For academics, scholarship is a complex craft that is very difficult to itemise in list form and it is evident in published articles in well-established academic journals. In an important sense, scholarship is an aspect of rhetoric because the best 'scholarship' consists in the highest quality of argument. 'Argument' in this sense does not carry its everyday meaning of acrimonious or antagonistic disputes. In academic work 'argument' is a general term that refers to all kinds of scholarship conducted in written form. All written academic work is an 'argument' in the very broad sense that it is written to persuade.

A typology of the characteristics of scholarship in Jankowicz (1991) includes careful use of evidence to support arguments, care and accuracy in the identification of information sources, and thoroughness in the coverage of the subject matter. 'Thoroughness' implies that arguments and points of discussion are well balanced. This in turn implies that alternative points of view are acknowledged and evaluated. A further characteristic is integrity in the use of data and the formation of arguments and points of discussion. The reader must believe that the work has intellectual integrity. In other words, the reader must feel that the work and arguments presented

	High pass	Good pass	Pass	Fail
Content	Critical, deep, comprehensive understanding, creative interpretation	Deep understanding, some originality	Basic understanding, limited originality or insight	Limited understanding, lacks focus
Structure	Logically coherent, clear, fully meeting the brief	Logically structured	Logically unclear in places, could be better organised	Lacks logical coherence and clarity
Reading	Excellent synthesis of secondary work, reading beyond the set texts	Very good coverage of relevant sources	Basic coverage of key work, some omissions	Little evidence of relevant reading and/or understanding
Referencing	Accurate, precise, comprehensive coverage of relevant work	Accurate, thorough coverage	Some errors in Harvard referencing, gaps in coverage of relevant work	Inaccurate and/or absent referencing
Writing	Fluent, fluid and penetrating academic style, excellent use of supporting citations	Clear, grammatically correct, relevant, solid academic style	Clear, largely grammatically correct with some errors	Uneven and unclear writing, incoherent at times

Figure 3.1 An adapted generic rubric for written academic work

represent a sincere attempt on the part of the writer to investigate and report a topic whatever the findings may be.

The project report structure

Each kind of project (empirical or conceptual/review) has similar require-ments that it must follow in order to satisfy the intellectual standards of university degrees. The chapter headings in Boxes 3.1 and 3.2 are offered as flexible guides to the broad content of an independent research project.

Whether a research project is mainly empirical or mainly conceptual the student researcher still needs to demonstrate an informed point of view in a carefully developed and structured piece of written work. It is not enough to simply summarise a series of articles or book chapters and pass this off as a conceptual project. In both styles of project there must be a problem/issue formulation, a set of criteria for selecting relevant literature and a way of evaluating or discussing the theories and findings in that literature. The findings of the empirical project, or the conceptual model/findings of the conceptual project, will form the basis for the analysis/discussion, so in both there must be a clear point of view that can be developed logically.

Box 3.3   An outline empirical project chapter structure

Project Title – must be clear and carefully phrased
Abstract: 100–150 words summarising the project aims and main findings
Contents page
Chapter 1: Including the introduction; overview of research issue/problem; research objectives; major theoretical assumptions; outline of the project as a whole
Chapter 2: Critical literature review; locating the issue/problem within relevant published research; identifying key concepts and issues
Chapter 3: Method: offering an explanation and justification of the particular approach chosen; referring to published authorities to back up the chosen approach; explaining why the chosen approach was most appropriate in the circumstances
Chapter 4: Empirical research report; reporting findings from primary research
Chapter 5: Synthesis of literature review with empirical findings; discussion of major issues
Chapter 6: Concluding comments and recommendations
References: Harvard method, full reference for every authority cited in the dissertation
Appendices: May include additional graphs or data that would have interrupted the flow of the text, such as interview transcripts

---

The particular structure chosen for the project can vary but every project will contain, in whatever form, the elements of these suggested structures. That is, the project must contain a clear research problem, issue or question that the supervisor has agreed is appropriate. It must contain a careful, substantial and critical review and evaluation of relevant research papers and other published sources. Finally, it must contain a careful interpretation of the data to summarise the major findings and to discuss the needs of future research and/or the implications for current and future practice. The following sections will discuss in more detail the particular problems and issues arising at each stage in these suggested project structures.

The project structure

Abstract and chapter one

The abstract and chapter one can sometimes be written last of all. That is because with exploratory research one does not know how the story will

---

**Box 3.4   An outline conceptual project
chapter structure**

Project Title: Must be clear and carefully phrased

Abstract: 100–150 words summarising the project aims and main
findings

Contents page

Chapter 1: Introduction: overview of research issue/problem; project
objectives (e.g. to review current developments in a particular field);
outline of the project

Chapter 2: Extended critical literature review; locating the issue/
problem within relevant published research, identifying key concepts
and issues

Chapter 3: Conceptual model; inducing the major features or findings
from the literature, or developing main arguments regarding future
research or practice

Chapter 4: Applying the conceptual model to a set of case examples

Chapter 5: Synthesis and discussion

Chapter 6: Concluding comments and implications

References: Harvard method, full reference for every authority cited
in the dissertation

Appendices: May include additional graphs or data that would have
interrupted the flow of the text

---

turn out until the end. Hence the abstract and chapter one, and indeed the
title, could change before the final write-up. This is to some extent a matter
of personal preference. As noted earlier, some researchers prefer to gather
data, think about the issues, make notes and reflections, draft some sections
and collect relevant research articles until the last moment then write a first
draft of the project report in one go. Others prefer to start at the beginning
and write a chapter at a time in sequence. The abstract will summarise the
whole project in about 150–200 words. Chapter one will explain in more
detail what the project is about, what its main aims and subject matter are. It
will also set the background context and explain why the topic is of interest.
Chapter one can outline the whole narrative arc of the project, to give the
reader a clear steer about how the story of the research project will unfold.

The chapter can begin with a problem statement about what issues the
research will seek to address. It can then set out some background to set
the report issues within a broader context of a particular industry, a particular tradition of literature or a specific problem. It will need to set out
three or four major research objectives. Finally, the chapter can outline the
whole project report, indicating what each chapter deals with, how the

---

Box 3.5   Chapter one – suggested content

Abstract: 150–200 words that describe topic, problem, method – logical standpoint and main findings.

Introduction: statement of the research problem or issue, and the reasons why it is important and/or interesting

Background: setting the context with regard to particular industry or research issues

Main research objectives

Major method(s) or philosophical/conceptual standpoint

Brief outline of the chapter themes that follow

---

research was conducted and briefly summarising the major findings and/or conclusions. This gives the reader a good idea of what to expect and, more importantly, shows that the report is the result of a carefully structured, well thought-through and systematic piece of scholarly research (see Box 3.5).

Research aims and objectives

It is important to remember that repeating the aims, objectives and themes of the research in the abstract, in chapter one and in the final chapter, is not only appropriate but necessary. It is necessary by convention and also as a rhetorical device to remind the reader that what is being written is structured according to a consistent set of questions or themes. The objectives would usually be set out in chapter one, returned to at several stages during the report, and finally restated in the concluding comments. In this way the writer clearly signals to the reader that the research was well conceived and systematic. In general, it is a good idea in research writing to make it easy for the reader to see why particular points and sections are relevant to the main theme. A degree of necessary repetition can help in this aim. In addition, 'signposting' is very useful. At regular intervals in the narrative, remind the reader why this particular point being discussed is germane to the research problems/issues.

Research aims and objectives are very important, though it should be remembered that they need not be complex. It is not necessary to produce an original contribution to knowledge in a taught master's or undergraduate degree course. For this level of research project objectives can be quite simple and straightforward. They are important because they indicate that the researcher had a focus for the research and that this focus is the basis for the narrative structure of the report. A report must tell a story of a piece of research. A story must have a plot that develops through a beginning, a middle and an end. A research report that drifts along without a point of focus will give the reader the impression that the researcher never quite thought through what it was they wanted to find out. The research objectives also provide an internal measure of the success of the research. If the final chapter can say to what extent the objectives were achieved, this is a good sign and clear and coherent (and also realistic) objectives are a great help.

As mentioned in the previous chapter, the research report is not a temporally linear representation of the research process. That is to say, the report is not the same thing as a research diary and does not necessarily describe the precise order of events. In exploratory research, the objectives may be crafted in final form at the end of the research process because they, like the broad research question, will be modified during the research. Some research objectives, such as 'To critically review the existing state of theory from a selection of leading journals' need not change during the process. This is a broad and straightforward objective for a conceptual project. Other, more specific objectives might well evolve and change in emphasis, although they will have been present in some form from the beginning.

For example, a research project might set out 'To find success factors in entrepreneurial marketing'. The researcher might find that this objective was too broad. Research interviews with marketing entrepreneurs might well generate interesting findings regarding the origins of the entrepreneurial mentality but these insights may be personal, rooted in the entrepreneur's particular biography and experience. The phrase 'success factors' implies that 'factors' are the same for every entrepreneur in every entrepreneurial situation. Furthermore, entrepreneurial activity is conducted in many different industries and takes differing forms. To be entrepreneurial within a health service implies different behaviours, outcomes and priorities to being entrepreneurial in, say, a television production company or a small retail business. Hence the broad objective could be refined to accommodate the specific research context and priorities.

Many research objectives are very simple. For example, the student researcher might wish to use words such as investigate, explore, evaluate or examine a particular area or problem in an exploratory study. They might wish to craft more precise objectives if they wish to investigate relationships between events or variables, but these, too, can be phrased carefully, as in, say, 'To explore the relationship between executive pay and company financial results'. Objectives that are carefully crafted can pave the way for a good project because they signal that the student researcher understands the complexity of the issue or problem that is under investigation.

Reflexivity in research writing

Interpretive research reporting traditions often adopt a *reflexive* stance. *Reflexivity* in research means, broadly, being aware of being aware, although it must be admitted that different writers in management research tend to use the term in slightly different ways (Johnson and Duberley, 2003).

In research writing, reflexivity generally implies open and transparent acknowledgement of all the circumstances of the research context, including the ways in which the researcher's personal perspective influenced their interpretation of the research findings.

Interpretive research traditions give a voice to the researcher. That is, reflexivity is more accepted and expected than it is in realist/positivist research. However, both paradigms of research require a basic reflexivity in the sense that the researcher needs to demonstrate that they are aware of weaknesses and limitations in their study. For example, it is important for the researcher to show that there is awareness of limitations of method, of sample, and of ways in which the findings may have been influenced by the assumptions, beliefs and research style of the researcher.

In a reflexive research project it is quite appropriate for the researcher to comment on how the research project evolved. There is no need to pretend that it all went without a hitch. Indeed, the examiner will normally want to see that the student researcher has developed his or her research skills and subject understanding through reflecting critically on how the project was conceived and carried out. If things went a bit wrong in some ways, it is ok to say so, and this is an opportunity to demonstrate a deeper understanding through the way that the student researcher responded to setbacks.

'Critical' thinking and the literature review

Whatever research topic is decided upon, it is essential to locate it in an appropriate body of literature. The research project should evolve out of a careful consideration of previous research in similar related areas. Some research projects (conceptual projects) consist mainly of an extended review of literature. Other, managerially oriented projects, may be based around a particular industry problem. For an academic research project, though, trying to solve a managerial problem is not enough. The problem, and the means of solving it, must be set within a context of previous and recent research. This entails reviewing a cross-section of published academic journal articles relevant to the research topic. The literature review must be 'critical', that is, it must employ critique, in order to satisfy a major criterion of higher academic accomplishment. For academics, 'critical' analysis means strong, good or persuasive analysis, but the types of critical thinking and writing in research and scholarly work can differ.

The word 'critical' is often used colloquially in managerial writing as a synonym for 'important' (as in, for example, 'marketing is a critical business function'). But this is not the sense in which research academics use the word. Academics feel that 'critical' thinking or critique is inherent to intellectually 'rigorous' thinking. The ability to think critically is demonstrated by the student researcher showing that they can understand research perspectives well enough to be able to evaluate the strengths, weaknesses and key assumptions of each perspective. Doing so suggests that differing theories and perspectives have not simply been accepted at face value by the researcher. Rather, the critical or rigorous researcher has compared and evaluated each theory or perspective in terms of their apparent qualities and shortcomings. Work that does this well demonstrates a deeper level of understanding and a more penetrating quality of intellect than work that takes a passive position towards theories and merely accepts them uncritically. In other words, the literature review that merely repeats the views of several authors on a topic is not 'critical'. Research writing that is 'critical' demonstrates a deeper level of intellectual engagement than this.

However, to add to the student's confusion, writing and thinking critically does not mean simply being critical. That is, saying that a particular theory isn't very good, doesn't cut it. It would be necessary to say exactly why the theory isn't very good, and it would also be necessary to state what assumptions the writer is making to make the judgement about what constitutes a 'good' or poor theory in the context being discussed. Of course, it would be simplistic to say that a theory is either just 'good' or not so good. Theories are like cars – some are fine for popping into town, but you wouldn't want to drive across the country or tow a trailer in them. The point is, a theory needs to be evaluated against exactly what it purports to explain. There are many ways of understanding what theory means and what counts as theory (Merton, 2017). For the current purpose, we are not concerned with the philosophy of science but with a basic appreciation of critical thinking and how it might appear in research projects.

Figure 3.2 is a schematic that shows one possible way of categorising critical thinking for research to help students to incorporate it into their work.

Level 1: uncritical thinking

Uncritical thinking is exemplified by referencing a theoretical or conceptual model (an example in marketing could be E. Jerome McCarthy's Marketing Mix and the Four Ps of Price, Product, Physical Distribution and Promotion) in application to a marketing management issue without any caveats or qualifications to critically examine how useful or relevant such models are in providing a management solution in a given situation. The marketing mix, that is, the Four Ps are still mainstays of introductory marketing courses, but of course they are not theories in a sociological sense because they have no evidence base and no capacity for prediction. Arguably, they might have some explanatory value. Then again, they have been coruscatingly critiqued for their logical circularity and apparent irrelevance in many cases of marketing success (Brownlie and Saren, 1992; Brown, 1995; Hackley, 2009a). Of course, students on taught courses who are presented with these models in class are entitled to take them in good faith. But when the same students are writing a research dissertation, they will be reasonably

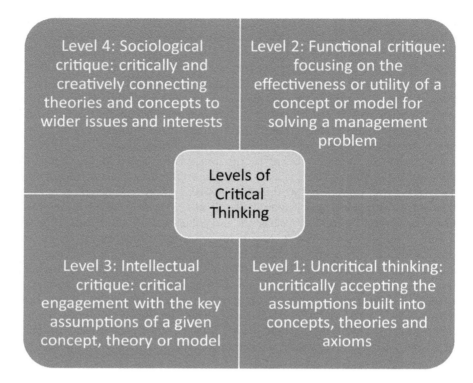

Figure 3.2 Levels of critical thinking for research projects

expected to have thought a little more deeply about these useful classroom models and to have read at least some of the volumes of criticism they have attracted. For example, they might have grasped that the mix rests on assumption such as the following:

a   that the marketing mix cake-baking analogy is indeed analogous to practical marketing management
b   that the framework is internally coherent so that logical inferences can be made from it
c   that it generates insights that have practical utility to marketing professionals
d   that it has universal applicability to any marketing context
e   that the mix elements are decisive in market success
f   that marketing managers have strategic control over all mix elements

The marketing mix framework might be defended against these criticisms, but research projects that fail to acknowledge fundamental criticisms of the constructs and conceptual frameworks used are usually confined to the uncritical level of analysis.

Level 2: functional critique

Thinking at this level entails analysing the usefulness of the theory in terms of how it might deepen insight into a particular issue. It therefore goes beyond the uncritical thinking described in level 1 above. There are two particularly pertinent questions:

a   Does the conceptual model/theoretical knowledge add to or go beyond experiential, 'common-sense' understanding?
b   Does the theoretical model fit well with the situation under investigation?

If the answer to either of these questions is negative, a third question is begged: what other theoretical framework would be useful? The onus is on students to explore a range of theoretical work with application to the particular problem. So, to extend the example, if the student researcher were to apply the marketing mix framework to a particular marketing management problem or issue, they would need to begin with an extensive evaluation of the mix in their critical literature review. The review would have to address criticisms of the practical usefulness and managerial relevance of the framework, discussing weaknesses, strengths and the implicit (and explicit) assumptions that are built into it. The review would seek to move towards a frank appraisal of the mix framework as a basis for managerial problem solving. It would also acknowledge that other frameworks may offer different but equally useful insights.

Level 3: intellectual critique

Brownlie and Saren's (1992) critique of the Four Ps addressed the logical coherence and lack of empirical grounding in the Four Ps. In fact, there is no evidence that these four elements are key to marketing success. Many organisational marketing managers would complain that they do not, in any case, have control over pricing strategy (that'll be the finance director) product policy (R&D) or even promotion, since the advertising is often created by an agency outside the marketing manager's remit and under the control of the marketing or communications director. This does not mean that the mix has no descriptive value: self-evidently, marketing strategies usually have a price strategy, a distribution and supply chain, a product design, and a promotional campaign, amongst many other things. The point is that this list in itself is merely a list – the explanation for marketing success or failure in any given case is inevitably more complex, nuanced and, often, cross-functional.

This brings us to level 3 of critique, the critical engagement with the assumptions of the model, theory or concept in question. Again taking the example of the marketing 'mix', the review might question the social scientific basis for the model. What grounds are there for this framework? What evidence is there that it is a practically useful or intellectually viable way of categorising certain managerial marketing activities? This level of thinking is an advance on level 2 because it not only focuses on managerial problem solving, but also begins to evaluate concepts and frameworks in social scientific terms. The marketing mix is, arguably, a framework that evolved from a business consulting perspective and was popularised in marketing management text books. Does this make it an appropriate basis for intellectually rigorous work in an academic context?

Level 3 thinking begins to engage with the difficult philosophical question of how it is possible to 'know' anything at all. This should not be too daunting to advanced students: after all, many primary schools find it useful to teach philosophy to very young children. The aim is not to resolve philosophical questions but to acknowledge them in order to improve the student researcher's quality of thinking. 'How do you know that it is your own hand on the end of your arm?' is a classic philosophy degree exam question that forces the student to engage with the problem that we rely for our empirical knowledge on our senses, but we rely on our reason to judge whether or not we can trust what our senses seem to be telling us. The relevance of this to critical thinking in research is that scepticism towards knowledge is the mark of the mature thinker. Note that scepticism is very different to the kind of ill-informed cynicism that drives people to reject science and believe in bizarre conspiracy theories. Scepticism is the habit of not trusting our own judgements about the world until we have carefully engaged with and evaluated the various arguments and evidence behind all the differing points of view.

Many marketing academics argue that marketing has a body of theory that is *normative*, that is, it is designed to assist practical action. This, they suggest, gives it a special character that cannot be evaluated in traditional social scientific terms. Others (Hackley, 1998b) argue that this may be all right for consulting projects but that academic marketing and management research cannot claim to be a special kind of knowledge set apart from the rest of social science. Marketing and management are practical business disciplines, but academic study of them demands academic standards be applied. Words on a page or in a class case discussion can never be direct conduits to management practice, whatever some marketing texts may claim (Hackley, 2003b).

Level 4: sociological critique

The phrase 'sociological critique' is used here to emphasise a particular mentality in social research. This mentality questions the 'ordinary' and the 'obvious' in social life on the grounds that what is ordinary or obvious seems so by virtue of a profoundly complex process. This very fundamental level of critique asks what alternative ways the situation under investigation could be represented and questions the assumptions that underpin presumptions of knowledge. It asks this on the grounds that every way of describing something suppresses other alternatives and carries certain assumptions and interests (see the section on critical discourse analysis in Chapter 8: see also Fairclough, 2010).

This level of thinking and writing may cut across into other disciplines in its breadth of perspective and conceptual scope. Many marketing and consumer research projects engage with their subject matter in this way and ask how the consumption of goods in specific social contexts helps consumers to construct a sense of meaning and identity, hence, for example, a discussion about consumption practices in a given context might connect with psychological theories of identity. Managerial projects can ask how managers make sense of what they do by using metaphors and stories to articulate their experience of organisational work (Ardley, 2009). Managerial work and consumption need not be seen as ontologically 'fixed' or 'given' realities but can, rather, be understood as dynamic processes in which people impose meaning on to their activities through the language and social practices they employ. So, for example, a managerial project would not only ask how effective the marketing mix is in a particular problem – solving context. Rather, it would ask what managers accomplish by using the language of popular managerial marketing (if indeed they do) to articulate, rationalise or justify their actions (Ardley and Quinn, 2014; Svensson, 2007).

Theories and models

We have already mentioned the idea of the conceptual 'model' as a representation of a process or event. Many academic textbooks (in marketing, especially) refer to 'theories' and 'models' (for a critical review see Baker and Saren (2010)). These terms are often used interchangeably in marketing texts, although the scope of a theory tends to be broader than the scope of a model. A model tends to be a representation of a particular process, such as a model of the life cycle of a new product (Levitt, 1965) or a model of consume behaviour (Engel et al., 1990). Models try to show what elements are important in a process. They also try to show the relationship between elements. Students conducting a conceptual research project might try to put together a basic model to illustrate a process or the relationship between elements in a process.

Theories are attempts to explain or understand a group of phenomena. On occasion, a theory can be reduced to a representation, that is, they can be modelled. In disciplines such as biology, physics or chemistry, a theory would both explain a phenomena and make predictions on the basis of that explanation.

Theories in management and social research tend to lack the ability to predict, they more often purport to explain phenomena, with some broad predictive capability implied in the explanation.[1] Of course, some theories predict without being able to fully explain why the predictions are accurate, such as theories of economic behaviour from the behavioural economics perspective.[2] Other, similar theories, induced from 'big' data such as Google Trends or other sources of empirical observation, sometimes also predict without being able to explain why the predictions are accurate (Davidowitz, 2017).

Writers in the business field sometimes refer to 'theory' as counterpoint to organisational 'practice'. This rhetorical use of theory is often used pejoratively, as when books promoting consulting solutions claim that they are 'practical' rather than theoretical, meaning that theory implies ideas that are impractical, not relevant, or self-indulgent. Another use of the idea of theory refers to speculative, as opposed to factual, discussion and thinking. 'All very well in theory' is a common complaint levelled by organisational managers at business school texts and teaching. 'In theory' it is easy to find solutions to business problems. In practice most solutions have been tried before and failed for some reason. Student researchers need to disentangle the rhetorical uses of the word 'theory' (like the use of the word 'critical') as a device of persuasion from its more substantive use as a form of carefully grounded explanation. Theories can be very practical indeed, and there is no world of practical action that is immune to the reach of theory – theories help us to explain what people regard as common sense or self-evident ways of thinking about and acting in the world.

Research 'method' and empirical projects

'Method' is important in social scientific research (and business and management research draws on many social science research traditions for its foundations) because it distinguishes research from opinion, hearsay or intuition. The presence of a method in a research project implies that what has been investigated has been done so systematically, carefully and from a theoretically informed intellectual basis. The 'method' is central to the narrative structure of the research story. It gives the research project shape and structure. It signifies that the project has engaged with *epistemological* issues (that is, issues of what kind of knowledge can be generated) to offer insight into a particular area. In this way the 'method' section shows the examiners that the project has, at least, reached levels 2 or 3 of critical thinking in its intellectual standards.

If a research project has a 'method' it implies that the research was not merely ad hoc or made up on-the-hoof but was thought about carefully, planned and executed systematically, that it proceeded according to rules, and that it satisfied some of the criteria of social scientific knowledge. If a research project at master's or undergraduate level demonstrates the ability to apply a given methodological perspective and to show some awareness of its limitations and weaknesses, a major outcome of the research process will have been satisfied. There must be a carefully referenced explanation and justification of the particular approach chosen. The author must explain why the chosen approach was most appropriate in the circumstances, and perhaps also discuss why other methods were not chosen.

The 'method' section will explain which data-gathering approach was taken and why. It will then explain how the data were analysed. The competent use of a method, any method, is most important in student research projects that use empirical data. Social research is an enterprise that attempts to produce and/or communicate ideas, truths and insights that are not normally publicly known through everyday 'common sense' understanding. The use of some kind of methodological and/or theoretical perspective is what makes social research a distinctive way of trying to discover, generate, communicate or test new knowledge. Methods are never perfect or infallible. But in a sense, they are all social researchers have.

Triangulation in interpretive research

Triangulation is a common term in qualitative research. It is a nautical metaphor that refers to verification of research findings by reference to more than one source. If a researcher looks at something in more than one way, say by getting two assistants to agree on the interpretation of some data sets, then that is a form of triangulation. Using a method of triangulation can mean that findings are more persuasive to readers. However, the concept of triangulation is not always helpful in interpretive research.

The use of triangulation can imply that there is only one version of social truth and, furthermore, that it is available to the researcher, rather like the view that obtains in realist/positivist research. Interpretive research often proceeds on a *relativist* basis in the sense that it acknowledges the legitimacy of differing perspectives on social phenomena. Triangulation can be useful, and some qualitative research studies employ the nearest thing to triangulation, called inter-subjective verification, through which two or more people are asked to look at an interpretive process in the hope that they will agree. But, ultimately, interpretation is just that, an interpretation. The interpretive researcher does not claim that their interpretation is the only or the best interpretation possible. They simply argue for their interpretation of the data set using the best quality of argument and most solid standards of scholarship they can in order to make their interpretive process as transparent as possible. If a reader wishes to dispute their interpretation then at least they see the grounds for so doing.

The findings, discussion and conclusion

After the section on research method, the empirical project will report the major findings. 'Findings' are the results, key themes and/or insights that the researcher feels emerged from the primary data analysis. They may consist of themes, patterns, consistencies or other types of insight that seem, to the researcher's informed eye, to be evident in the data. In qualitative research reporting the findings will be supported by many direct quotes and examples from the data reproduced in the body of the research dissertation findings section. Transparency is important in qualitative and interpretive research: the reader must be able to see why the author made the interpretation of data that they made. If there are many direct quotes and the interview or other material is reproduced in the appendices then the reader can make his or her own judgement on the quality of the interpretation. They can see how the researcher arrived at the interpretation they reached.

Discussion

After the findings are reported they must be discussed. The 'discussion' or 'analysis' section evaluates primary data findings in the light of the concepts and issues from the earlier literature review. The discussion synthesises previous research findings in the field with the new findings generated by the project. It addresses questions such as these: Does the primary research yield findings that are consistent with the literature on that topic? Does it appear that there are shortcomings, gaps or limitations in the literature, and, if so, what new research should be undertaken? Or, were there flaws in the project that resulted in a disconnection with previous research findings?

The discussion or analysis chapter is, in several ways, the most important of your report, since it is your chance to pull together the various strands of your research and to say what you really think, based on all the evidence you have gathered. It should demonstrate the student researcher's understanding of the method(s) used and the kind of knowledge or insight that has resulted. It should critically evaluate findings and analyse them for logical consistency and coherence with literature-based theories. It should demonstrate that the researcher has the intellectual ability to integrate primary findings with theoretical knowledge and draw logically coherent conclusions. It is here, in the discussion, that the student researcher can achieve the Level 3 thinking by drawing a trajectory between previous research, the present study and its findings, and possible new horizons for this area of research. Of course, this would be the case in the most well-executed projects, whilst most would probably be more than content with a more modest achievement.

The research report will have a short section of 'concluding comments' re-iterating the research story. What did you do, why was it important, and what did you find? Again, there is some repetition involved here as the story of the research project is briefly rehearsed once again. To what extent did the research concur with previous research? To what extent were the research objectives fulfilled? What were the weaker points of the research and what did you feel worked well?

You can conclude by (modestly) suggesting what implications your work might have for future practice and/or future research. The appendix and detailed (Harvard method) references sections complete your research report.

In Chapter 4 we will develop the theme of empirical research by discussing several popular and effective methods of collecting qualitative data sets.

Glossary

'Datum' and 'data' The research material that the researcher gathers and analyses is the data. Strictly speaking 'datum' is the singular and 'data' the plural, although the word data is often used as a collective noun for a single group of material when 'data set' would be grammatically accurate.

Empirical Deriving from experience. In management research an empirical research project will include data gathered by the researcher. A *conceptual* research project will not, relying instead on existing published sources.

Epistemology The philosophical study of knowledge. It addresses such questions as, how can we know what we know? What kind of knowledge counts as knowledge? And, what is knowledge?

Method Every research project employs a systematic or theoretically informed method of investigation. In social science, 'method' usually refers to the technique of gathering data and also to the assumptions underpinning the interpretation of data. Very often in social science method and interpretive framework are implied in each other. Note that 'methodology' is the study of methods.

Normative A 'norm' is a rule that does, or should, govern a pattern of behaviour: normative work in management and business writing and research seeks to develop norms or rules for doing management and business.

Primary data Original data, obtained first-hand by the researcher.

Reflexivity The experience of being aware of being aware, in other words, the ability to reflect on one's own experience. It is important in a research context because researcher reflexivity gives interpretive research reporting a special character of personal engagement, frankness, self-criticality and self-awareness. In particular, it allows the researcher to be aware of and acknowledge the influence they have on the research process.

Secondary data Existing material that has already been produced for another reason.

Triangulation   This is a nautical metaphor that refers to checking a position from an alternative standpoint. For example, if a researcher feels that a particular finding emerges from data he or she can check that finding by seeking another colleague's opinion (also called intersubjective verification of findings).

Notes

1 If this sounds a little like an academic way of admitting that theories in management and social studies are not very good, the reader is forgiven for reading it in that way.
2 www.behavioraleconomics.com/resources/introduction-behavioral-economics/

Chapter 4

Gathering and interpreting qualitative data sets

Chapter outline

This chapter offers practical advice on a selection of qualitative data-gathering techniques and it introduces some basic principles of qualitative data analysis such as content analysis, thematic analysis and coding. The selection of data gathering approaches discussed can be used with a variety of theoretical approaches, or with no explicit theoretical approach. The chapter makes the point that certain theoretical assumptions are implied in particular qualitative methods, and begins to introduce some of the themes of research theory that will preoccupy much of the rest of the book.

Chapter objectives

After reading this chapter students will be able to:

* gather qualitative data sets using well-established techniques
* understand some of the theoretical implications that are associated with particular data-gathering techniques
* appreciate some of the major difficulties of gathering primary empirical data sets
* understand the influence of the researcher in qualitative data gathering and interpretation

Introduction: interpretation, theory and 'theory'

Gathering qualitative data sets is easy. There are people out there, all you have to do in order to understand what they're doing is to watch them, talk to them, ask them questions and listen to them. Everybody does this all the time. Of course, for academic work, or indeed for practical projects, there has to be some sort of formality and systematicity to the ways in which people are watched, questioned, and listened to. There also has to be some kind of formality to the ways in which their responses are interpreted and made into 'findings' or 'insights'. After all, this book is about social science, with albeit a different way of conceiving science to the way it is conceived in natural science. So, to draw a naïve equivalence between everyday categories and social science paradigms, watching people can be called observation, ethnography or practice theory: asking people questions and listening to their answers happens when researchers conduct in depth interviews, focus groups or ask participants to complete diaries, written reflections or even photomontages, and interpreting these kinds of data might be framed as existential phenomenology, discourse analysis or thematic analysis. We will look more closely at the theoretical framing of qualitative research in Chapter 5. Chapter 4 will try to set up some general principles for gathering qualitative data sets that can be theoretically analysed.

Multi-method approaches

Before detailing single approaches, it is worth noting that the data-gathering approaches in this chapter, and also the theoretical stances in subsequent chapters, are not mutually exclusive. They can be used in combinations, as well as for the main method for a research project (for a variety of approaches to qualitative data gathering for interpretive research in marketing and consumer research area see, for example, Belk, 2006, 2017; Carson et al., 2001; Easterby-Smith et al., 1991, 2018; Moisander and Valtonen, 2006; Gummeson, 2000; Schwartz-Shea and Yanow, 2012). Many of the research traditions introduced later in the book are often used in combination with a number of data-gathering approaches (see Figure 4.1 below). *Ethnography*, for example, is noted for its use of depth interviews, field notes, observation (and *participant observation*) and other, informal data sources, as do *practice theory* approaches to empirical research. *Phenomenological/existentialist* research studies use a variety of qualitative data-gathering approaches in combination, particularly the depth interview, as do many studies framed as *discourse analysis*. Indeed, as we shall see in Chapter 5, several different interpretive theoretical perspectives use similar combinations of qualitative data-gathering approaches, but with differently nuanced data analysis.

It is important to remember that data-gathering techniques are not necessarily theoretically neutral: they carry implicit assumptions about the nature of the material being studied and also about the form of analysis that may be appropriate. In addition, the particular ways that specified data-gathering methods and analytical traditions are applied by researchers are subject to many variations. For example, practice theory and discourse analysis are deployed in many somewhat different ways and in different contexts of application (see Chapters 7 and 8). The following is intended to assist student researchers in practical issues of data gathering, but care must be taken to check that the chosen technique is appropriate to the desired theoretical stance.

Pragmatic data gathering

First, lest theoretical framing sounds too daunting for the first-time student researcher, we should state that student researchers often use empirical data-gathering techniques in a relatively informal way, to aid and deepen knowledge and understanding in a project that is only loosely framed as interpretive research. This is ok – a student who wants to pass their course in business and management does not necessarily have to have a thoroughly worked out, ontologically grounded, epistemologically coherent method right at the beginning. That would be nice, but for most undergraduate student researchers, getting some data, any data that are[1] relevant and useful is a challenge. For example, many students carry out a literature review of an area with respect to a particular management problem or issue. Indeed, for many student researchers, it is the practical problem or issue, not theoretical framing, that is driving their interest and giving shape to their project investigations. They may, for example, use ad hoc interviews with practitioners for material that will enrich their general understanding and can be used to develop lines of discussion in the report. Such a relatively informal approach to data gathering can adopt any of several data-gathering techniques, such as interviews (semi-or un-structured, observation, textual analysis of documents or secondary sources, focus/discussion groups). Empirical data gathering can proceed alongside secondary research in this sense as part of a broad process of exploration. The sequence of research activities does not preclude data gathering at any stage in an exploratory project.

For students working in this way the whole research process can appear a little ad hoc. It is fine to, say, use a small-scale questionnaire survey and/

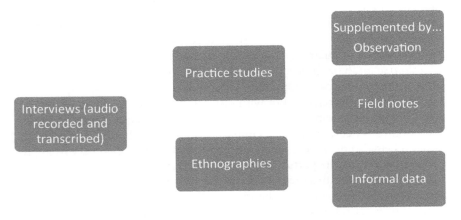

Figure 4.1 An illustration of one data-gathering approach being used by different theoretical perspectives

or some semi-structured or unstructured pilot interviews to deepen general understanding of different issues. On the other hand, a student researcher may wish to conduct a more theoretically driven and empirically systematic and extensive study in, say, an ethnographic style. The student researcher may, indeed, use a mixture of data-gathering techniques including, say, informal interviews, naturalistic observation, some textual analysis of news articles and/or trade press information and perhaps research diaries (of course this would be a lot for a student research project) if they had decided at the outset that they wished to try to accomplish a mini-ethnographic study. The decision of whether to use multi-method data gathering normally depends upon practical constraints of time, availability of and access to data sources, and the research skills of the student, as well as on the aims and theoretical framework of the research project. In student research projects conducted as part of taught courses, ad hoc methods of data gathering used to supplement critical literature reviews can be as useful as more theoretically driven data-gathering approaches. The important thing is how the data are used to enrich the analysis and discussion of a particular set of research questions.

'Interpretive' and 'quantitative' research

We have touched on this distinction earlier but we will return to it briefly because it is the source of a great deal of confusion amongst first time interpretive researchers. Interpretive research typically uses qualitative data sets, giving the rationale for this book. But, qualitative research is not necessarily theoretically interpretive. Qualitative data sets are sometimes used in realist/positivistic research studies. The two terms 'qualitative' and 'interpretive' are often used interchangeably. However, they imply different things. Some research looks at qualitative data to dig out truths that might be tested to see if they can, in principle, be *universalised*, or tested to see if they are universally true. This kind of research is often conducted as a precursor to construct development for a quantitative statistical study, on a realist/positivist ontology. Other qualitative research studies are cast as exploratory or as creative interpretations of the data, and the findings are seen as an end in themselves and not necessarily a precursor to construct development and quantitative measurement. With a non-theoretical qualitative study, the risk for the student researcher is that the academic marking the work sees it as merely descriptive or theoretically naïve, and lacking in analytical rigour.

'Qualitative' and 'quantitative' research categories, though, are not mutually exclusive. A great deal of quantitative research has a qualitative component. As mentioned above, qualitative work (such as interviews or group discussions) can stimulate the researcher to think of 'constructs' that can then ultimately be measured in a quantitative study. To return to an earlier example, a researcher might interview sales people to see what particular factors seem to influence their effectiveness. If many sales people seem to talk about their motivation in terms of the personal qualities of their manager, then the research might generate a scale with which to measure the motivational ability of sales managers. He or she could then conduct a larger study to see if there is any statistical correlation between sales managers' motivational ability as measured by the scale and the sense of motivation felt by their sales force.

Such a study assumes that *nomothetic* (statistically generalised) findings can be useful. This term is often contrasted with *idiographic* research. The researcher seeking nomothetic insights might try to isolate the decisive motivational skill of the sales manager with the intention of making generalised points about all sales managers and their sales forces. The researcher seeking idiographic insights would, in contrast, conduct a depth interview with a few sales managers in order to establish how their approaches to sales management and staff motivation evolve out of their life history and experience.

Sampling for qualitative research

or 'How many interviews is enough?'

Data gathering for interpretive research need not be random, but it should be systematic and/or theoretically informed. The word 'interpretive' implies that data are not used to try to set findings beyond dispute or to generalise findings across time and social context. An interpretation is necessarily one of many possible interpretations. In interpretive research, the researcher seeks to arrive at insights for which he or she will offer as much evidence and reasoning as possible. They do this in order to make their reasoning transparent and to try to make their interpretation persuasive and, if possible, transparent, meeting high standards of scholarly exposition. Given all this, the selection of data for analysis must be purposive rather than randomised. In quantitative research, non-probability sampling is the term used to any non-rando sample, whether that sample is gathered through convenience, snowballing (asking one person to refer their friends), purposive (sample driven by the purpose of the study) and quota sampling (selecting a certain number). What is important is to understand why particular data sets were chosen given the aims of the research. It is also important to qualify findings carefully so that they are grounded within the social context that is being researched.

Sampling issues are often resolved by necessity. In qualitative research, sampling is often based on *purposive* or *convenience* criteria. This means that the sampling decision is driven by pragmatic considerations of convenience or suitability for the particular problem or issue being studied.

First-time researchers might ask ten people for an interview and find that three agree. That, then, has to be the sample. You can't force people to agree to be interviewed, just as you can't make people fill in online questionnaires. Quantitative researchers and qualitative researchers alike invariably find that they are making the best of imperfect samples. If you can show that you have a realistic and well-informed awareness of the limitations, as well as the advantages of your sample, your research can be credible and competent. In some cases, qualitative researchers find that a 'snowballing' effect occurs as they get agreement from some participants who then tell others and more people agree to be interviewed. In this case, the researcher has to decide when they have enough participants to stop.

It is difficult to provide a satisfactory answer to the question 'how much data shall I collect?' The answer is always unsatisfactory because it is always the same: 'it depends'. Unlike in quantitative research, there is no formula. The sample size for qualitative research depends on the objectives, the scale and the resources applied to the research. It depends on the nature of the subject matter, the kind of data sets that are sought, and the quality of the data that are needed. It also depends on pragmatic consideration such as time-scale and costs. In the end, two maxims are worth remembering. For student researchers, any primary data is often better than none at all, and second, few marks are awarded for the amount of data collected. The important thing is how well the student researcher uses the data they have.

The sample should, therefore, be decided on grounds of a) pragmatism, b) representativeness and c) quality of insights generated (see Figure 4.2).

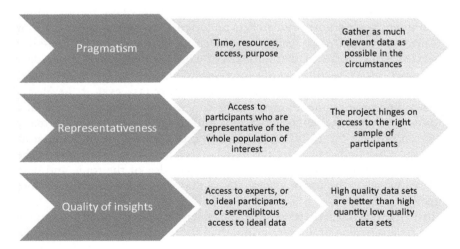

Figure 4.2 Criteria for gathering qualitative data

Interviews – preparatory issues

Access and pilot interviews

Interviews with expert professionals or consumers can be excellent sources of quality data for analysis, or for framing the study through a better understanding of the field of practice. If student researchers can gain access to relevant experts through personal or social networks such as LinkedIn, so much the better. If not, find an address and send an email. Pragmatism dictates that student researchers cannot wait months for organisations to reply to their letters requesting interviews or field access. It is, incidentally, a good idea for students requesting research access to find out the name of a person responsible and direct communications to that person. An initial email or phone call will be enough to determine whether the person has the time or inclination to grant access or interview time. Organisational staff are busy people and some receive many such requests. Student researchers should accept this and thank the people for their time even if the response is negative. It will also be necessary to fit around the person granting the interview, in the sense that, if the student researcher wants a one hour depth interview and the expert offers a 20 minutes chat on the phone, then take what's offered and adjust the research rationale accordingly. Finally, in any communications with practitioners (or indeed with academics) make sure that emails or other communications address the intended recipient appropriately, and are carefully structured and copy edited for spelling and grammar. These things are not quaint old school concerns. They still matter, unless you play tennis with the recipient.

If there are positive responses, the technique of data gathering may dictate the amount of data to be gathered. Depth interviews are very time-consuming. Some student researchers ambitiously set out to conduct 20 or 30 interviews, until they realise how much work is involved. A one-hour interview can generate many thousands of words of dialogue. If the student researcher is to transcribe just one interview to place in the report appendix, as is good practice, this will prove a very lengthy task even if they use a transcribing programme. In general, the data sample should, on pragmatic grounds, be manageable given the time and resource constraints. In many research projects the early interviews in the project will be the longest as the researcher finds out what the major issues are. In later interviews the researcher might have a much better-informed idea of the topic and may well know what the major issues are so that they ask about these more directly.

In qualitative research, as we note above, it is more important for a sample to be representative of a larger group than for it to be random. Randomising a sample is almost an impossible task even for accomplished researchers. Students doing a project as part of a taught degree need to make sure that whoever they access for data, the insights generated will be relevant to the broader issues in their research question. Simply, if you are exploring the exposure of school age young people to alcohol advertising on social media, you will need to access school age young people who engage with social media (and research access, especially to people under the age of 18, requires various permissions to earn the approval of the university research ethics committee that normally has to approve all empirical data collection.)

Assuming access can be gained, a degree of careful thought and preparation is useful. Some researchers conduct *pilot* data-gathering sessions, that is, practice sessions before the main data-gathering phase begins. These can be very useful for refining the questions you want to ask in order to ensure that the main data-gathering interviews are as focused as possible on the key issues of interest. Pilot interviews are also very useful for establishing the parameters of the study, the objectives and the scope. Finally, they are also very useful for practising qualitative research skills of interviewing or convening and moderating focus groups.

Quality of data is often difficult to ascertain before it is gathered. Sometimes, the person being interviewed doesn't say the interesting things that they might have done. Perhaps they're having an off day, perhaps the student researcher didn't ask the right questions in the right way. At other times, unpromising participants can be really fun and interesting and offer insights that change the direction of analysis by throwing an unexpected light on the subject matter. However, expertise in a field should never be ignored – if a request for an interview is read by an expert senior practitioner, then take them up on that. What they say will be useful in the discussion because of their knowledge and experience, and the experience of interviewing and making contact will be valuable even if the person may not fall directly into the original sampling frame.

Conducting the research interview

Conducting research interviews can be useful whatever kind of research design is used. In a project that is problem based rather than theoretical, interviews with practitioners can give a valuable insight into practical issues. This practical insight can then be used in discussion as a counterpoint to the more theoretically informed perspective of the literature review. In such circumstances the technicalities of the interview process are not as important as the quality of the insights generated. In more theoretically informed research projects, the technicalities of the 'depth' interview become more important. There are some general rules of interviewing that are useful to remember (see Box 4.1).

As a general rule, the most relaxed interview participants give researchers the best quality data. Some researchers are able to strike a rapport with their interviewees so that in the interview situation the interviewee becomes

---

Box 4.1   Research interview checklist

- Establish the aims of the interview
- Reassure participant regarding ethics and confidentiality
- Decide on a formal or informal interview setting
- Decide on a structured, semi-structured or unstructured interview agenda
- Decide whether to take notes and/or audio record the interview (only audio record with the participant's permission)
- Decide whether to take a mainly active or passive interview stance
- Formulate some broad, open questions to ask at the beginning of the interview to put the participant at ease and establish rapport

---

candid and expansive. Few of us don't like talking about our life and work, especially if we can do so to a neutral person in a safe and confidential situation. Relaxing interviewees and learning to ask just the right kinds of question at the right time is an art that takes time to develop. Some tips can help the novice interviewer. First, be well prepared. Think through what you want to know beforehand. Prepare a list of questions you can ask if the interviewee 'dries up'. At the beginning, introduce yourself, thank the person for agreeing to the interview and explain just what it is that interests you. Reassure the interviewee that the whole process is entirely non-judgemental and confidential. Explain to them that they can end the interview at any time.

It is a good idea to maintain eye contact in interviews, stay interested and give interviewees the space to speak freely. As noted earlier, employ 'active' listening – plenty of eye contact, nodding and other facial expressions of interest really help the interviewee along. Where digression occurs, it can be used to the interviewer's advantage. The interviewee may be relaxed and expansive and could raise novel or unexpectedly candid issues and insights. If the digression becomes too tiresome the interviewee should never betray boredom or irritation but should gently redirect the topic of conversation. Once, when the author was interviewing one of the Madison Avenue advertising agency professionals mentioned earlier, the interview participant said 'just stop the recording and follow me'. The participant led the interviewer to a quiet room and, with no recording equipment in play, related a very unofficial version of the official version of his working life that he had been relating to the recording device. Without the recording device, he felt more confident in being candid and telling stories that did not necessarily reflect well on the company, or the industry. In such circumstances a research interviewer, much like a journalist, can find a scoop, a real story that will change the tone and direction of the research story.[2]

It is important to remember that being interviewed can be a difficult experience. Many interviewees will feel that there are things they are expected to say, points of view they are expected to hold. For example, practising managers who are being interviewed by students doing an academic research project may imply that their everyday work is more theoretically informed than it actually is. Some will claim that they use marketing textbook models in their work – others concede that they do not (Ardley and Quinn, 2014). This is not dishonest: we all moderate our conversational responses according to social expectations. It is just trying to be helpful. However, a careful research interviewer will try to anticipate and deflect expectations based on conversational conventions in order to improve the integrity of the data that is generated. It is important to note here that in interpretive research the goal of the research interview is not to access some version of the truth that is free from 'bias'. Their role is to interpret the structure and function of what is being said. If the researcher feels that the claims made by the interviewee are not credible, then that means the data set will not be of great quality and the researcher will need to either access better quality data or figure out why the integrity of the interview was poor and discount certain claims. The interview text does not hint at an underlying reality in interpretive research. The interview text is the reality and must be judged as a text. We will look at the matter of data interpretation in greater detail in the second half of the book.

A questionnaire-style interview agenda is rarely necessary in a research interview. This is because the value of the research interview lies, in part, in its potential for spontaneity within the interview interaction. If the interviewer seeks to control what is said by imposing their own prewritten agenda of questions and assumptions then the interviewee's insights, thoughts and reflections might be modified to a considerable extent. The trick of qualitative interviewing is to empower the interviewee while retaining control over the broad agenda. As a researcher, you cannot know this person's job, their life, their problems at work. If you really want to understand their experience as a marketing and management worker in a given context, give them the space to speak.

Structured interviews, though, can be useful in some cases. For example, in the *laddering* technique of qualitative research (Gruber et al., 2008) the interview schedule takes the interviewee through levels of involvement in a consumption decision going from utilitarian benefits of consumption through to the more abstract emotional benefits in a structured progression. The technique, originally developed to assist in generating creative ideas for advertising (Reynolds and Gutman, 1988; Phillips and Reynolds, 2008) is essentially an interpretive method (though arguably not falling within Burrell and Morgan's (1979) interpretive paradigm) for conducting qualitative interviews based on means-ends theory.

Box 4.2 Transcription conventions

= Indicates the absence of a discernable gap between speakers
(.) A pause of less than 1 second
(1), (2) A pause of 1 second, 2 seconds and so on
(. . .) Some transcript has been deliberately omitted
[DB laughs] Material in square brackets is clarifying information
They A word or phrase underlined indicates additional emphasis
[as you can Left square brackets indicates overlapping speech.

Source: (Adapted from Potter and Wetherell, 1987)

Recording the data set

When the interview has come to a close, thank the participant, remind them that everything in the interview will be treated confidentially and that all reporting will be anonymised. It is a very good idea to transcribe the interview into typed text soon after the interview, so that the researcher still remembers the tone, manner and intonations and gestures that gave texture to the interview responses. When transcribing, include the questions and prompts from the interviewer. In qualitative research reporting it can be useful to be able to faithfully reproduce an exchange that consisted of a conversation with several questions and/or interjections.

Audio recorded interviews can be transcribed using software or using a transcription service, but research tends to be better when the researcher or a research assistant who were present at the interview do the transcribing so that every word, pause, intonation and meaning is faithfully reproduced. When transcribing, it can be very useful to use *transcription conventions* (see Box 4.2) to ensure that pauses, stutters, interjections and emphases can also be reproduced in the transcribed text. The use of transcription conventions is more pertinent in the transcription of conversations in, for example, focus group discussions, but they can also be useful for adding nuance and texture to the transcription of depth interviews.

If a research interview takes one hour, it can take far longer than this to transcribe it, so do not underestimate the amount of work involved if the researcher desired to transcribe first hand. The advantage of first-hand transcription is that the researcher has a full record of the discussion that he or she can refer to when arguing a particular point in the research report. The full transcription can be placed in the appendices of the research report so that the reader can see for themselves exactly what was said and make their own judgement on the researcher's interpretation. If full transcription seems too daunting, automated transcription using relevant software or making personal notes from the audio-recording are alternatives. Direct quotes can then be used to support any point of discussion in the report, even if the full transcript will not be available for the reader to peruse. These notes can also be written immediately after the interview if the researcher feels that writing during the interview would distract the interviewee. The notes might include reflections on the manner, voice, intonation, metaphors or any other contextual feature of the interview.

The presence of accurately transcribed data extracts in the main body of the research report, supplemented by transcripts of full interviews in the appendices of the research report or dissertation, demonstrate highly committed research that the author is willing to open up to scrutiny. The presence of full transcripts (or one example with a note stating that 'data sets are available on inquiry') shows that the researcher is fully prepared to share their data and to defend their interpretation against possible alternative interpretations. If, say, ten interviews were conducted it is only necessary to provide complete transcripts of one or two in the appendices.

A further important advantage of transcribing interviews is that interviews are seldom easy to interpret on one or two hearings. In order to understand what the major themes are of a given interview, it can be necessary to hear, reflect on and reread the transcript many times. This is because what is taken for granted in conversation can be the most revealing, but only if it is heard so often that it ceases to be familiar. This may sound odd, but it is an important principle of interpretive research traditions that the everyday, the normal, the taken-for-granted, hides a complex social web of assumptions, codes and obscured, or forgotten, motives. In important respects interpretive research seeks to reveal how the 'normal' is produced. This does not imply that research data generated from interviews are in some way 'biased' or even plain dishonest. The interpretive researcher takes an innocent position towards what they are told: researchers do not try to second guess 'the truth'. What they do is to try to understand where the interviewee is 'coming from' by placing their comments in the broader context of the research topic. Incidentally, having a typist copy type the interview transcript from a recording can be quite problematic. Only the most adept copy typist can capture real time conversation accurately with all its halts, false starts, ahs, ums and digressions. For truly accurate understanding of the interview, the person transcribing simply had to be there.

Focus/discussion groups

The term 'focus group' has a fairly specific meaning in some contexts of marketing research, but in this book we use the term in a general sense to refer to research data that are gathered from a small group of about three to six people, simultaneously and interactively, guided by a research convenor. That is, the group of people is in the same space at the same time and they can communicate with each other as well as with the researcher. The focus of discussion may be broad or narrow: the motive for the research may be exploratory, developmental, strategic or tactical (see Box 4.3).

Box 4.3   Focus/discussion group principles

- Group discussions can be audio-recorded or video-taped and transcribed
- Group convenors (researchers or research assistants) stimulate, guide and record the discussion
- Group convenors should take care to intervene gently
  if one or two people are monopolising the discussion. They should actively solicit views from quieter members
- Group convenors should be clear about the aims of the discussion and the purpose of the research. They should reassure the group of the confidentiality and non-judgemental character of the research
- Groups cannot be random but need to be representative of the larger population of interest

---

Focus/discussion groups are regularly convened in marketing and advertising research to explore broad, open questions and issues. The focus group may be the most popular form of non-digital qualitative data-gathering instrument in the marketing industry, because of its convenience and potential for generating penetrating and action-able insights. In many advertising agencies, getting on a train and 'doing some groups' is the first stage in the creative advertising development process (Hackley and Hackley, 2018a) when the business has been won and the agency wants to understand the relevant sector, segment and consumption practices first-hand.

The composition of the group must be *representative* of the whole population of interest. This means that it must consist of the same kinds of people as the wider population of interest in terms of age, sex, class or other significant variables. With this form of research, sampling is invariably purposive and convenient rather than random or systematic. If, for example, a marketing agency is investigating voter attitudes to local government policies, then clearly the group convened must be local residents of voting age. It would be useful to get a cross-section of ages in this case, but since older people are generally more likely to vote than younger people the groups may well reflect this age imbalance. Advertising and other marketing agencies sometimes use consumer research panels that have a roster of potential interview participants of every demographic. A group of the desired demographic composition can be put together and a room hired within days. Of course, such commercially supplied groups may not necessarily yield the best quality data because the participants are there for money and not for the love of the subject or for the enjoyment of the experience.

It is very important to understand what focus groups are good for, and what they are not good for. Focus groups are useful for exploring topics and generating ideas. They are not usually appropriate for testing concepts prior to going to market. They can be very useful for generating insights that may capture something of the character of a whole group, and there are many examples of noted advertising campaigns that were inspired by a comment in a focus group that seemed to capture the essence of a consumption practice with, say, a powerful metaphor or telling phrase. For example, if a student researcher is investigating advertising ethics, then it can be useful to convene a focus group to discuss the responses of a given demographic audience to particular advertisements. While focus group findings cannot be statistically generalised, they might well elicit a view that prevails more widely across that particular category of people, provided the group was representative of the larger population of interest.

Focus group discussions are typically audio-recorded and/or video-recorded in industrial market research settings. The researchers then replay the recordings to assess which views expressed might reflect more general positions, or which views seem to express a general insight in a particularly succinct or telling way. Contrary to popular myth, the focus group is not an appropriate way to test ideas (as we note above). Brand logos, advertisements, new product concepts, product packaging and even political ideas have all been put to the focus group test by less than rigorous market research agencies. The fact is that since focus groups are not randomised they cannot generate views or opinions that can be generalised across larger populations, hence they are not appropriate for *testing* ideas or concepts. The value of the focus group lies in its ability to generate telling insights and novel ideas at an exploratory stage of a marketing, management or consumer research issue. Focus groups offer stimulating material that can contribute to strategy discussions. The 'voice of the consumer' can then be heard in strategy and planning meetings. In research projects the focus group can offer stimulating perspectives for further discussion and analysis in the research report.

Convening the focus group discussion

Researchers need to follow some simple rules to get the best-quality data. A focus group should ideally be comfortably seated with no noise or other distractions. The researcher needs good social skills to make the group feel at ease and to reassure members of the confidentiality and non-judgemental character of the process. The researcher also needs to have the confidence to gently intervene if discussions are being monopolised by one or two speakers, by asking quieter members of the group their view. The purpose of the research should be clearly communicated to the group. There have been cases of student researchers losing control of the theme of discussion so that the data set was not useful for the project. It is important that the researcher/ focus group convenor stimulates and guides the discussion without dominating it. It can be useful to have stimulus material in the form of storyboards, pictures, role-plays or other stimuli. With focus group discussions, it is often the case that once the discussion gets going little intervention is needed from the researcher. The early stage of the group process is important.

Recording and transcribing the discussion

Student researchers seldom need to video-tape focus group discussion, but audio-recording is always a good idea so that what has been said can be carefully examined afterwards. As with individual interviews, the task of interpreting the data is not straightforward. The transcript, or audio – recording, often needs to be read/listened to many times so that the major themes or insights become apparent. At the time of the focus group the researcher's attention is on many things so he or she cannot form insightful interpretations immediately. Transcription accuracy is important and the use of transcription conventions mentioned above can be especially useful with focus group data because it enables accurate reproduction of interactions and conversations, such as in Box 4.4.

The data extract in Box 4.4 illustrates one way in which a focus group interaction can be reproduced using transcription conventions. Note that the data extract is fully anonymised – none of the participants' names or

---

Box 4.4   A focus group transcription extract

The extract is taken from Szmigin et al. (2011) and the transcription conventions are adapted from Potter and Wetherell (1987). The conversation is about the definition of 'binge' drinking (of alcohol).

Tiffany	Yeah cos everyone's different opinion of binge drinking=
Molly	Yeah
Tiffany	= some people say oh drinking three is going on a binge
DC	Mmm
Molly	See I don't drink for ages and ages and then I'll go out and I'll get absolutely smashed off my face
Melanie	That is a binge but what about those of us that go home and have a drink every night what is that (.) binge drinking?
Dawn	[nah that's not binge drinking
Karen	[that's not binge drinking
Melanie	Well what is that then?
Karen	Just drinking
Dawn	Just drinking

Source: (Rowchester FE College, March, 2006: six white British females, one Black African female; one white male, aged 18–24)

the college name are the real names, they have been changed to protect anonymity. Using made-up names reads better than simply putting 'Participant 1, Participant 3' and so on. Note also that demographic data are important, information such as age, gender and ethnicity help the reader to understand how representative the group was of the wider population of interest. This particular study was a study into the role of alcohol in the lives of young people in the UK at a time when media stories of 'Binge Drinking Britain' were frequently seen, usually focusing on young people. The qualitative method employed in the study (using focus groups, depth interviews, consumer diaries and ethnographic field notes) proved ideal for generating insights into how young people used alcohol in their social lives for purposes of friendship bonding and identity.

The number of groups to convene depends on the topic and the nature of the research design. A master's dissertation research student of the author wanted to investigate the influence of alcohol advertising to teenagers in the UK. She convened four focus groups at three further education colleges in the West Midlands. Each group lasted about half an hour and she used bottles of branded alcoholic drinks to remind the groups of the topic. The groups went very well, all the students had much to say about the role of alcohol, and alcohol advertising, in their social lives. The researcher loosely followed an ethnographic methodological scheme she had seen in published research literature (Ritson and Elliott, 1999) and developed a perspective that reproduced a small-scale but more closely focused version of this study. The focus group discussions were audio-recorded, fully transcribed and placed in the appendix of the research report. In this project, the data-gathering strategy was exceptionally thorough – it is unusual for a student researcher to be so conscientious that they gain access to focus group participants at three separate venues. It is important to note that the number of groups convened is less important than the quality of data elicited. In the above study four focus groups amounted to a very considerable data set for this topic and the participants were highly representative of the wider population of interest, that is, young people aged 18–24. In other projects, the number of focus groups convened might be fewer, or more (although more than four groups would be quite a lot for a student research project as it entails a lot of work).

Textual research and content analysis

Interpretive research traditions are well suited to textual research in which social texts of all kinds can be subject to interpretive analysis. The foregoing data-gathering techniques of research interviews and focus groups have a textual character in that they generate data sets that are converted to textual form in transcription. Other forms of text can include advertisements, emails, in-company records and documents, historical records, newspapers, visual images, television and radio, print media, course internet media, and textual data elicit from research participants (Thompson, 1997; Brown,

1988). In interpretive research, a text is often defined as 'anything that can be described', that is, anything that can be rendered into words or text. For example, in advertising research, the idea of the advertisement as a social text (Stern, 1989, 1993) opened up a (then) new avenue of research that used literary theory (see Chapter 9) to analyse advertising text in order to better understand the ways in which consumers react and respond to advertising (Hackley and Hackley, 2018b). Qualitative research in general has made a major contribution to advertising practice and research (Nuttall et al., 2011).

Content analysis can be used on any kinds of text. It is a crude technique in some ways because the theoretical assumptions underlying content categories may not be specified. It can, however, form the basis for a more careful subsequent interpretation. The technique is quantitative in that it entails counting the number of incidents of particular content in a given data set. For example, in the mission statement research mentioned earlier (Hackley, 1998a) the content analytic framework was based on research that showed many mission statements to have similar features of content. Many made reference to the ethics of the company; many referred to the products or services that the company produced; many also referred to stakeholders in the company such as shareholders, customers or employees. These and other features of content were ticked off as each mission statement was looked at.

In this way a quantitative basis for interpretation was generated. The researcher could say that so many per cent of mission statements in a given data set displayed specific content features. The interpretation of these features is a separate matter: why they were there, what they were intended to accomplish, what motives they implied, how effective they seemed to be are all matters of interpretive judgement beyond content analysis. Similarly, if, say, magazine advertisements are subject to a content analysis by counting the portrayals of sexuality in a given sample and time frame, the results could inform a discussion but the content analysis in itself tells the researcher nothing about the reasons why these portrayals of sexuality were there, or what kind of portrayals they were. The content analysis could, however, provide a basis for further reasoning and informed interpretation.

Content analyses of textual data can be expressed simply as percentages, or more colourfully as bar charts, pie charts or histograms. One researcher examining changing representations of gender in UK magazine advertisements generated graphical representations of the content analytic data set that clearly showed marked changes in the number of advertisements that showed women as independent of, or as socially dependent on and subservient to, men, over a time period. While such analyses can be stimulating and revealing, they clearly depend on a way of categorising textual data that would not necessarily be agreed upon by everyone because a degree of subjective judgement is required in order to decide whether or not a particular ad fulfils the category criteria set by the researcher cannot be agreed on by everyone.

There are two main ways to deal with this subjectivity in content analysis research reporting. One is to make the content categories clear to the reader and to reproduce the advertisements (or whatever data set is being used) in question in the report appendices. In this way, transparency of interpretation can be achieved so that the researcher can argue in favour of their preferred interpretation of text. The reader can then decide for themselves whether the researcher's position seems plausible to them. A second technique is to test content analytic categories to see if another person would make the same interpretation. In this way the researcher can offer evidence as to the *inter-subjective reliability* of their content analytic categories. This can never be an entirely satisfactory approach since the researcher cannot test their categories with every kind of person. It is, however, rhetorically powerful to show that the researcher's position is not purely a matter of subjective opinion but has been supported by another researcher.

Digitisation and textual data sets

There are many variations of textual research, including digital texts, some of which we will look at later in the book, for example in the section on digital ethnography. What we have tried to do here is to look at the basic data-gathering techniques without getting too deeply into the interpretive framing, which we begin to do in the next chapter. In using the category 'textual analysis' to head this section we are trying to begin with the simple principle that words and text can be subject to all manner of analysis purely according to how categories of content are defined. Researchers can look for the repeated use or incidence of single words, of phrases, or metaphors or idiomatic expressions, depending on the goals of the study. Textual analysis cuts across all kinds of text so that imagery can be included (as in the example above regarding print advertisements) but also digital text can be subject to the same search criteria. Indeed, such searches for content can be done with software (Humphreys and Wang, 2018) and there are plenty of software packages (such as nVivo) that are advertised as qualitative data analysis packages. Such software packages are very useful for analysing large volumes of text very efficiently, but they are essentially content analytic programmes. Digital qualitative analysis software misses the nuances of personal interaction that took place within the focus group or interview (Catterall and Maclaran, 1997) and which can be crucial for the interpretation of meaning in the data set. Software analysis tools can only be as good as the categories fed into them, and the categories in interpretive research are framed by the theoretical perspective. We would differentiate between content analysis and interpretive analysis, since the former is a matter of counting incidents (at which software is very good), whilst the latter is a matter of interpreting content according to a theoretical perspective.

Stephens-Davidowitz (2017) refers to several online sources of 'big' textual data, such as Google Trends and Google Ngrams. Cleverly conceived searches can reveal very interesting and often counter-intuitive findings by searching for particular words or phrases in all the digitised text that exists in book depositories, news story archives or social media platforms. Indeed, private emails can also be used for this, but non-Google employees have to scrape publicly available data banks since emails and other personal content are ostensibly private. Stephens-Davidowitz (2017) is undoubtedly correct when he says that Google and other search engine data banks offer unique and intriguing sources of insight into human psychology, and he offers several striking examples of prevailing or conventional opinion being soundly de-bunked by creative use of search terms in Google Trends.

However, powerful as such text-driven studies are, they suffer from two main problems. One is that they tell us little about human psychology as such because they are culturally and demographically specific. Using digital data sets is not the same as practicing digital ethnography (Pink et al., 2016). To be sure, the databases in large search engines such as Google allow for a high degree of demographic specificity when setting the parameters for a search. Nonetheless, they suffer from the sale problem that afflicted one of the most famous market research failures in history, when one of the largest surveys then conducted of 2.4 million readers of the respected US magazine the *Literary Digest* failed to predict the winner of the 1936 US election by a huge margin of error of 19 per cent. The problem was, sampling error.[3] All Google surveys of text will, similarly, suffer from selection bias and non-response bias. Of course, data scientists are well aware of this limitation of their field and carefully couch their findings in caveats and conditionals whilst devising every more fine-grained forms of analysis to try to reduce the margin of error.

The second main problem with digital Big Data sources for text search is that the searches for words or phrases can be very cleverly designed but they lack a theoretical framing, therefore the findings may be stimulating, counterintuitive, provocative and sometimes actionable for, say, health policy or political marketing strategies, but they cannot usually inform a theoretical understanding of the world. *Empirical generalisations* give us intriguing *correlations* but tell us nothing about *causation*. The basis for this book, in contrast, is that theoretical framing for interpretive research can generate insights that can be integrated with other theoretically-informed findings to build scientific knowledge.

Thematic analysis and coding

Thematic analysis (Braun and Clarke, 2006) is a way of analysing textual data sets that is not theoretically driven, but which goes beyond the content analytic search for precise words or phrases and tries instead to code

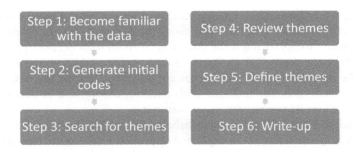

Figure 4.3 Braun and Clarke's (2006) framework for thematic analysis

data searches with more abstract concepts that might be expressed with quite different arrangements of words and phrases. Thematic analysis is often preoccupied with meaning; hence it tends to fall within the interpretive research paradigm, although it is not tied necessarily to specific theories. This makes thematic analysis particularly flexible for qualitative studies (as, indeed, is true of the other qualitative data gathering approaches outlined in this chapter).

One possible process model for doing thematic can be seen in Figure 4.3.

Of course, the model does not capture the qualitative evaluation of the data sets that leads to the generation of initial codes and eventual thematic categories. This is a creative and assimilative process that happens when the researcher becomes immersed in the data sets and begins to see patterns of meaning that structure the data sets. Maguire and Delahunt (2017) differentiate between theoretical coding, in which the researcher looks for particular themes that respond to the research question, and inductive coding, in which the researcher has no presuppositions about what they will find and the initial codes emerge inductively from the analysis of data sets. Some researchers establish initial codes and then use qualitative data analytical software such as ATLAS or Nvivo. This is useful for large data sets but essentially reduces thematic analysis to content analysis by taking out a level of the interpretive process.

Grounded Theory (1967) (GT) tends to use a version of inductive coding for thematic analysis since it seeks patterns of meaning in qualitative data sets. GT 'open' coding[4] is consistent with thematic analysis in the sense that the researcher analysing textual data sets has the license to use some imagination as they look through the data sets and think of abstract categories that capture the sentiments, practices or other aspects of interest in the data sets. This process of coding precedes the development or the emergence of themes as an iterative process.

As noted above, thematic analysis might proceed with an idea of what it is that the data analyst is looking for, driven by a particular research question, while Grounded Theory (GT) seeks to develop creative theoretical themes that 'emerge' inductively from the data analysis. In other words, the researcher looks through the data sets from an a-theoretical perspective in GT. Once the themes or categories have emerged and coding takes place to sift the data sets for incidents that contain the relevant themes, the GT researcher will look for linkages with existing theory and if necessary go back to the literature review to re-position it.

Grounded Theory is a well-established form of qualitative data analysis although it is not really an interpretive approach in the sense that data sets are approached with no theoretical framing. GT findings can consequently sometimes appear rather descriptive, unless they are successfully hooked into a theoretical frame a posteriori. It is very difficult to say that researchers can approach data sets with no presumptions whatsoever about the nature of what they are looking for or what they will find. It could be argued that GT essentially tries to erase the interpretive process that is, inevitably, taking place. The difference between GT and interpretive research is that interpretive research makes its presumptions, assumptions and values explicit by locating a study within a theoretical frame.

Observation as qualitative research data

Naturalistic, participant and non-participant observation

Observation is a research technique that is often implicit, informally, in data-gathering approaches. If we go to a company to interview a manager we observe the manner and style of personnel, we watch the way managers and subordinates interact, we note the quality of the furniture, how good the company restaurant is (and if there is one), we notice whether people seem happy, relaxed, aggressive, defensive, smart, depressed, or whatever. We form implicit and intuitive judgements from these observations. Similarly, if we interview consumers to understand their experience of a category of consumption practice, our interpretation of what they say is influenced by our observations of their manner, tone, gesture and vocabulary. Observation is something that we cannot fail to do as people: we are all expert observers and it makes perfect sense to utilise this social skill as researchers.

When we go shopping, or go to a restaurant, to the cinema or to a nightclub, we observe others and their behaviour in that environment. In commercial contexts we are acting as consumer researchers, forming judgements about the provision of a service or the competence of an organisation that will inform our own future consumer behaviour and that of others with whom we share our experiences and reflections. Informal observation is, then, an integral part of interpretive research. Our observations furnish the context that informs our judgements.

More formal uses of observation in social research include 'naturalistic' observation, experimental observation, 'action re – search' and 'participant' or 'non-participant' observation. Naturalistic observation entails observing people and their behaviour in their natural environment. For example, a study of the night time economy around the drug taking 'rave' club dance scene entailed participant observation as well as interviews (Goulding et al., 2009), as did a study of young people and alcohol in which research assistants were enlisted to make observations on a night out with participants and write up ethnographic fields notes as part of the data set (Griffin et al., 2009). These examples of observation were naturalistic in the sense that the group of interest were observed going about their business as they typically would. In this way, the research was lent a quality of *ecological validity*. Experimental observation, in contrast, would entail setting up an artificial situation in order to watch participants. Setting up an artificial observation for experimental purposes, such as asking participants to respond to questions about an advertisement viewed in a viewing booth, does not observe ecological validity since it is not the way that advertisements would normally be viewed by TV viewers who would typically watch TV in the company of friends or family (Ritson and Elliott, 1999).

Each of these techniques involves the researcher in the process that is being studied. For example, many researchers in the *ethnographic* tradition spend lengthy periods in the company or industry that they are researching. In some cases, they take part in the activities by fulfilling a role in the process. During and after their working day they will make *field notes* that record their observations and impressions. Later they will use these field notes as data from which they will compile their research report.

Formal observation research can sometimes take the form of intervening in a social situation to see what results. Some social psychology students once watched from a window over their street as one of their group said 'hello' to passers-by he had never met before. The observers were watching to count how many of the passers-by returned the 'hello' to the person they did not know. Their topic was social convention in greeting rituals.

Researcher/observers who are not seeking to intervene in a social situation should normally try to be as unobtrusive as possible in carrying out their non-participant observation. If they have been granted access to an organisation to shadow an employee or to watch management processes, they should at all times consider the ethical issues of confidentiality and discretion. It is a privilege to be granted research access to a company. It is inappropriate in reporting such research to report anything that may embarrass the participant. Speakers in reported dialogue should be anonymous in the research report. The company itself should not be named or recognisable unless by agreement. The non-participant observer should act as a 'fly on the wall', present and observant but intervening in the social processes that they observe.

Research diaries

Research diaries can be useful if the researcher is seeking an *experiential* perspective from the research participant. The participant is asked to keep a diary relating to a particular event or experience. The disadvantage of research diaries is that they can generate vast amounts of data that can be difficult to interpret. Their advantage is that they offer an intimate channel into some aspect of an individual's experience, provided that people can be relied upon to fill in the diary conscientiously. If, say, a researcher can persuade a senior executive of a firm to keep a diary during a hostile takeover, this would clearly offer a very different research perspective than any other form of data gathering. It is equally clear that such data would need to be handled very sensitively and discretely by the researcher. Diaries can be kept over varying periods of time. They can be written at any time of the day, or at specific times. They can be detailed and analytical or general and personal. It all depends on the researcher's aims and interests.

The interpretation of diary data takes some skill on the part of the researcher. Comments in a diary can be fragmented and difficult to group into thematic categories. As with all qualitative data analysis, the most penetrating analyses result from having a well-informed interpretive perspective. This will give the researcher the theoretical background to generate supported insights from the data. One study conducted by an advertising agency used a *deprivation study* sometimes used by cultural anthropologists. The agency researcher enlisted music fans and asked them to give up their music playing equipment for a period of time. They were asked to use the diary to articulate their experience whenever they felt the loss of the music equipment. The agency wanted to understand the roles that music played in peoples' lives, and the diaries related how some people missed it most in the mornings when they got ready for work, some missed it most in the evenings when they relaxed after work, others missed it when they were getting ready for a night out, and so on.

Researchers themselves can also keep research diaries. These would be supplemental to field notes and would assist in reflexive analysis of the research process. Research diaries can be useful for recording particular events and times so that the chronology of events can be recorded for later reference. Particular impressions can also be revealing in the light of information received later, so recording them carefully as the research unfolds can be useful.

Case study research

Case study research is well-established at every level of education, particularly in the business and management areas. Case studies are common in qualitative studies (Bryman, 2012), but the case study often uses mixed methods in addition to the case material. The 'case study' is a wrapper for quite a wide range of studies of differing method and ontology, focusing on either single or multiple and comparative cases. The idea of the case is that it should be bounded in some way, focusing on the business of organisation, a problem or issue, or on two or more examples for comparative case studies.

For Yin (2014) the case study is not merely a data-gathering approach but a method with a distinct research design. However, although the case study can be a very useful approach for packaging a research study, particularly a practical study, it is difficult to locate in a sociological paradigm. It is, really, a kind of storytelling (Gabriel, 2017). The case study seems to often be used within an implicitly realist/positivistic framework in the sense that there is emphasis placed on verification of results, as if the case findings ought to be generalisable. Given the limited sample of the case study, generalisability in a positivistic sense is not achievable. Case studies can be used in a research design that includes a theoretical stance and this can be a useful way of organising data sets and structuring the data gathering and analysis.

Case studies are often used in qualitative studies without, necessarily, any theoretical framing. As noted earlier, 'qualitative' research in general is often conducted without an explicit theoretical framing, and whilst there is inevitably an element of interpretation as there is in all research, this does not mean that qualitative research case studies necessarily fall within the interpretive paradigm (see Chapter 5 for more on sociological paradigms). Qualitative data analysis often does apply analytical approaches that are taken from interpretive research traditions (Spiggle, 1994), but the term 'qualitative' by itself does not tell you the implicit assumptions that underpinned the data gathering and analysis. Saying that a research project is a case study leaves much unsaid, since it does not explain the theoretical assumptions that guided the choice of data sets and the analytical approach that generated findings.

Case study analysis has a distinguished pedigree. The world-famous Harvard Business School made the case study the central pillar of their teaching. Originally, students would study the available information on a particular organisational management problem and would also visit the organisation to see first-hand what its methods were and to speak to its managers. In other words, there was an element of naturalistic observation to the case. The students would subsequently return to the classroom, offer their analysis of the business issues and problems facing that company, and debate this with the students and faculty. The aim of this was two-fold. By analysing the case and then debating their analysis with colleagues and professors, student researchers might develop skills of advocacy and critique (Contardo and Wensley, 1999). Through this demanding process they sharpened their understanding of case situated business practices and also their skills of debate and argument.

Many research studies that are labelled as using a case-study method rely on pre-existing information such as company and industry reports and other publications. Some employ an *ethnographic* style if the researcher can gain access to a company to observe processes from within. Others draw on data from depth interviews with company managers. Some case studies use a comparative approach by taking several cases and making comparisons between them of particular managerial issues or processes, while others focus on a detailed analysis of the single case situation. Gerring (2006) refers to ideographic case analyses, which offer detailed analyses of single case situations, and nomothetic case analyses, in which many cases are analysed quantitatively to try to draw generalised conclusions. Some cases are conducted over a specified time period, others over many years, called *longitudinal* case studies. It can be very instructive to return to particular cases over time to see how the data change. Case study research can use interviews, surveys, observation and participant observation and any other of the range of qualitative data-gathering methods, they can use a sample of one case or many, and they can use descriptive forms of data analysis, or they can be used with any of the interpretive theories discussed in the latter half of this book. The flexibility of the case method is its great strength for application to a huge range of situations with a variety of methods.

This chapter has taken a mainly practical perspective and has pointed out particular difficulties and advantages of the various qualitative data-gathering techniques. In keeping with the theme of the book as a whole, the chapter has taken the view that data-gathering techniques are implicitly theoretical in the sense that they carry assumptions about the nature of their subject of study and the kinds of analysis that are useful and appropriate. The next chapter will look in more detail at some key concepts of interpretive research before moving into the second half of the book with an introduction to some of the most influential theoretical approaches for theoretical framing of interpretive research.

Glossary

Convenience sampling A sample frame that is convenient in the sense that participants should be relatively easy to access..

Correlation A statistical relationship between two things. Correlation does not imply *causation*, that is, just because there seems to be a prima facie statistical link between two phenomena, this does not mean that one causes the other.

Deprivation study An approach used in cultural ethnography and sociology, which entails asking a participant to go without something, an activity or an object, and then record how they feel in its absence. It is a way of generating insight into the symbolic role of a practice or object in the life experience of participants.

Ecological validity A research method that allows participants to act as they would in their everyday lives is said to have ecological validity, whereas a method that sets up an artificial situation for the purpose of research, does not.

Empirical generalisations A statistical relationship between two or more variables.

Ethnographic research Ethnography is a research technique made popular in anthropology. It entails trying to see the world through the eyes of a particular group with reference to their own cultural values and symbolic practices. Anthropologists have often lived for up to two years with the group they are researching. Management researchers tend to use quasi-ethnographic studies based on much shorter data-gathering periods (i.e. a few days).

Experiential The *experiential* perspective has evolved from humanistic psychology and phenomenological philosophy. It values the experience of the research participant and often seeks to empower research participants by facilitating constructive reflection and informed reasoning.

Field notes Term from anthropology referring to notes, observations, reflections, details and questions written down by the researcher during their period of 'field' research. Management researchers conducting ethnographic research in host organisations would usually make use of field notes.

Idiographic   Research approaches that do not seek universal generalisations but, rather, seek insight into a subject's experience by taking into account all their biographical detail.

Inter-subjective reliability   Reliability refers to research approaches that generate the same findings in different cases; inter-subjective means agreed upon by two or more people, so inter-subjective reliability means that an interpretation has been agreed upon by the subjective evaluation of two or more people.

Longitudinal research   Data-gathering phases that are repeated over time so that a long term picture is taken of a situation.

Nomothetic   Nomothetic research seeks truths that are universal and can be statistically significant.

Observation and participant observation   (discussed in Chapter 7): entails the researcher being immersed in a social group and observing the practices, behaviour and interaction of the group, either as a 'fly on the wall' non-participant, or as an active participant and member of the group.

Pilot studies   A pilot data-gathering exercise is conducted prior to the main study. A pilot interview or focus group can be useful to ensure that the sample and interview agenda are right, and also to practise interviewing or other qualitative research skills.

Practice theory   (see also Chapter 9) A theoretical stance on symbolic social practices that can be employed in qualitative research studies.

Purposive sample   Used to describe a sample frame, purposive means the same was generated according to set criteria to suit a particular purpose or objective.

Representative   Interpretive researchers seek samples that are not statistically random but are analogous to the larger research population in significant respects.

Transcription conventions   A system of indicating the pauses, tone and other quirks of natural conversation in written text.

Universalised   Research that is often categorised as 'positivist' or 'realist' seeks nomothetic insights that are universally true and can be formulated into hypotheses for testing across very large populations.

Notes

1 The word data is a plural. Datum is the singular. However, it has become so common to hear people saying 'I analysed my data' or 'the data was clear' that the word data seems to be becoming a plural as well as a singular through common usage. But beware, academics can be grammar pedants.

2 Some of these stories are related in Hackley, 2000; Hackley and Kover, 2007.

3 www.math.upenn.edu/~deturck/m170/wk4/lecture/case1.html

4 http://groundedtheoryreview.com/2010/04/02/the-coding-process-and-its-challenges/

Sociological paradigms and research philosophy

Chapter outline

Theoretically informed qualitative research studies need to be 'set up' in the sense that key assumptions about the nature of the social research task need to be clarified at the outset because they influence the way that research questions, method, analysis and findings are all conceived. Some of the key concepts and methods of qualitative/interpretive research have been introduced in Chapters 1–4. Chapter 5 gives deeper consideration to theoretical framing for interpretive studies, particularly with regard to the location of interpretive studies within a sociological paradigm. The chapter then goes on to discuss interpretive data analysis.

Chapter objectives

After reading this chapter students will be able to

- grasp the key assumptions of the main sociological paradigms
- understand more of the technical vocabulary of interpretive social research
- frame a research study in the appropriate paradigm
- understand more of the philosophical principles of interpretive data analysis

The interpretive stance and empirical knowledge

We have noted earlier in the book that interpretation in and of itself is not a matter unique to qualitative research. It is an element of all research and all knowledge (O'Shaughnessy, 2009). For Holbrook and O'Shaughnessy (1988) 'all knowledge and all science depends on interpretation' (p. 398). It can be useful sometimes to ground the activity of research by standing back from theoretical perspectives to ask naïve philosophical questions, such as what, and how, can we know about the world? One traditional 'problem' of Western epistemology is that we cannot know 'the world as it is': we can only know it through our sense perceptions, that is, empirically (David Hume's work, *A Treatise on Human Understanding*, is a famous expression of this idea). We have no way of knowing if our sense perceptions are deceiving us. You could be dreaming that you are reading this book. You have no way of being absolutely certain that you are not. There is a further problem with this truism. We cannot 'know' the electronic impulses that are our senses. We can only interpret them, that is, we can ascribe meaning to them by finding words that seem to express what we feel or see. This problem gave form to the contrasting philosophical positions of empiricism and rationalism, empiricism being the knowledge of the world we gain through our sense perception, and rationalism being the knowledge we gain through our internal thought and reason. For interpretive researchers, knowledge of the world is gained through a combination of both empiricism and rational thought. Through our senses we gain knowledge of the world, which we have to interpret using our reason.

For most interpretive researchers, knowledge of the social world requires a different method of interpretation to knowledge of the natural physical world, because the nature of reality in each is different. Empirical social research on a realist model assumes that social reality is just as concrete and stable as physical reality, so social reality can be investigated using the same methods as physical science. This is the realist/positivist ontology of social science to which we have referred earlier in the book. As we have also noted earlier, the 1959 Ford and Carnegie reports[1] on American business school research lamented its un-scientific character and called for a far greater emphasis on the scientific study of business and management. This has been interpreted as a call to use the research methods of natural science and American University Business Schools have prioritised such methods ever since. In contrast, most interpretive researchers agree that the social world is different from the natural physical world. Social reality is seen as being constructed through social interaction in a far-reaching sense: social reality is a social construction (Berger and Luckman, 1966). This social constructionist ontology of social life is of course very different to the realist ontology, and each leads to different epistemologies of knowledge. In particular, socially constructed reality has to be conveyed through rich analytic descriptions of social situations, it cannot be conveyed through generalised propositions.

Interpetivism and big data

We touched upon the issue of digital data scraping in the previous chapter. In the age of Big Data, it is tempting to suppose that questions of social research can be answered simply by finding the right Big Data banks to scrape, and by asking the right questions. Importantly, the seductive and undeniably fascinating potential of Big Data as a research resource (Stephens-Davidowitz, 2017) does not mean that interpretation is not necessary. Some things are even beyond AI and algorithms, as Professor Russ Belk has elucidated[2] and Thompson (2019) argue that Big Data myths lead to ontologically confused opportunism;

> I argue that culturally oriented marketing researchers should promote a different ontological frame – the analytics of marketplace assemblages – to address how big data, or more accurately its socio-technical infrastructure, produces new kinds of emergent and hybrid market structures, modes of social aggregation, consumption practices, and prosumptive capacities.
>
> (Thompson, 2019, p. 207)

Thompson (2019) points out that data scraping and algorithm-driven analytics lack the critical interpretation that is made possible by theoretical framing, and he suggests a particular approach, assemblage theory (Deleuze and Guattari, 1987). While assemblage theory is beyond the scope of this book, Thompson's (2019) point that taking a naïve empiricist approach to Big Data is potentially dangerous is clear. Digital data-gathering techniques and analytics have biases built into them, while as referred to earlier, they suffer from sample error and, crucially, non-response error, so the kinds of behavioural conclusions drawn from Big Data referred to by Stephens-Davidowitz (2017) lack a theoretical grounding and are sharply constrained within a narrow cultural context. Rather like the 'nudge' theories of behavioural economics (Thaler and Sunstein, 2008), Big Data analytics can generate facts that lead to predictions, such as the fact that the pre-eminence of racist terms in Google searches by region seem to predict political affiliation and voting behaviour in the USA. However, they cannot explain the underlying reasons for the behaviour. Thompson (2019) is calling for a critical interpretive standpoint somewhat overlapping with the Radical Humanist paradigm (of which more below) and warning of the naïve reliance on Big Data without theory to guide its interpretation.

Theoretical 'framing' of interpretive research

Framing a research study means to acknowledge and be explicit about the deep assumptions upon which it is based, and being aware of the implications these assumptions have for the interpretation of findings. To put this another way, framing research studies means demonstrating that the researcher understands the ontological position they are taking with their research questions and method, and that they are also aware of the epistemological implications for their analysis. Certain research philosophies fit better with one paradigm than with others. Framing a study plausibly, that is, understanding what the main paradigmatic assumptions of the research question and research design are, helps an enormous amount in interpretive research because it enables the researcher to pull together the various stands of the study into a coherent whole.

Interpretive research traditions do overlap each other, distinctions blur, there are tensions and disagreements (Hudson and Ozanne, 1988; Alexander and Smith, 2001) even though, or because, many interpretive research traditions share similar positions on epistemology, method and scope. Some published researchers take a broad stance and frame their work as 'interpretive' (e.g. Hirschman, 1989; Szmigin and Carrigan, 2001) or 'qualitative' (Spiggle, 1994). This does not mean that their work is a-theoretical and merely descriptive, but it does mean that they have chosen not to frame their research within a specified theoretical approach. For student researchers, too, it is fine to do this. However, it is best to also be able to defend the position of interpretivism by knowing what is implied in it, and likewise if the study is labelled as a qualitative study. Many other published academic authors frame their work in terms that emphasise specified theoretical traditions and/or data-gathering approaches, such as naturalistic research (Belk, 1991; Belk et al., 1988), existential phenomenology (Thompson et al., 1990; Askegaard and Linnett, 2011) semiotics (Chandler, 2002; Holbrook and Grayson, 1986), discourse analysis (Ardley and Quinn, 2014; Hackley, 2000), literary theory (Brown, 1999, 2016a; Hackley et al., 2013), poststructuralism (Elliott and Ritson, 1997), subjective personal introspection (Brown, 1988; Shankar, 2000; Holbrook, 2018), postmodernism (Brown, 1994), rhetoric (Scott, 1990; Brown et al., 2018; Miles, 2014), critical marketing (Tadajewski, 2014; Tadajewski et al., 2019), humanistic research (Stern and Schroeder, 1994), narrative analysis (Shankar et al., 2001; Stern et al., 1998), ideology (Thompson and Coskuner-Balli, 2007), practice theory (Ghaffari et al., 2019; Skålén and Hackley, 2011), social phenomenology (Svensson, 2007), assemblage theory (Preece et al., 2019) and many more.

Specifying the research tradition(s) in which a research project is located can be useful because of the different emphases and assumptions of each tradition about data gathering, interpretive process and epistemology. A student research project that explicitly states that it draws on a particular theoretical perspective immediately makes favourable signals to the person reading and assessing it. A defined theoretical perspective implies that the researcher has attempted to think through the implications and scope of their research questions. It also implies that the researcher is aware of the need to make assumptions explicit and to refer to previously published research. Finally, it suggests that the researcher will attempt to write a research report that is coherent: its aims, method and analysis will all 'hang together' and make sense in terms of each other.

It was mentioned earlier in this book that multi-method approaches, combining useful features of more than one approach, can be fruitful. Many research studies are innovative in adapting data-gathering methods that are typically used in one research design, for use in another. However, all such adaptation requires some understanding of why particular aims, methods and analyses seem to fit together while others do not. The theoretical coherence of the research study is important. Mixed method studies can be located within single paradigms and this can give the whole a sense of coherence even where the element of the study, the data-=gathering approaches and analytical methods, may be quite diverse.

Figure 5.1 indicates the inter-connectedness of research paradigm, research questions, data-gathering method, analytical approach and the implications for findings. If the student researcher has a basic grasp of the key paradigmatic assumptions discussed below, then the research design falls into place as a coherent whole. It can be particularly useful to combine two theoretical traditions if they fall within the same broad paradigm. For example, in Ghaffari et al. (2019) the practice theory approach was embedded within an ethnographic study. The lead researcher spent more than a year in an

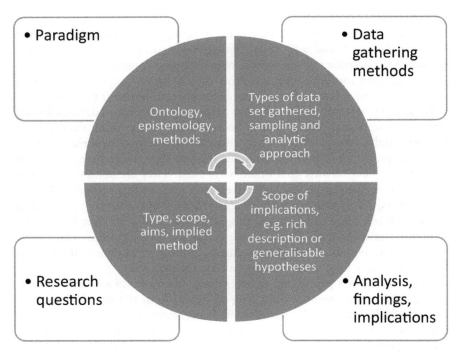

Figure 5.1 The role a theoretical perspective plays in 'pulling a research project together'

advertising agency as a non-participant observer, conducting interviews, sitting in on meetings and making field notes. Ethnography informed the data-gathering stance whilst practice theory informed the theoretical lens through which data analysis was conducted.

Research paradigms for physical and social science

A scientific 'paradigm' is a term popularised by Kuhn (1970). A paradigm is a set of explicit and implicit assumptions about how research should be conducted in the pursuit of scientific knowledge. A paradigm entails a 'world view', a position on the very nature of the phenomenon being studied. Academic management and marketing researchers often argue that certain 'paradigms' or sets of assumptions are more correct or better in practice than others. For example, there has been a widespread assumption that questionnaire surveys subjected to statistical analyses closely approximate natural scientific methods. This is by no means agreed upon by all researchers. Many have argued that 'natural' science, that is, research that investigates the physical world of atoms and molecules, has its own set of interpretive methods. It can be argued that research investigating the social world of human activity demands particular data-gathering and analytic methods that reflect the special character of social life. As one argument goes, life does not have to mean anything to an atom. In contrast, seeking meaning is a defining characteristic of human beings. Social research is concerned with people and their activities, including the activities of organising, managing and consuming. As such it is concerned with meaning since the primary activity of humans in any given context is to make sense of their lived experience, to render it meaningful.

Kuhn's (1970) book drew attention to the way that certain data-gathering techniques and analytical methods become taken for granted over time as the only right way to do scientific research in a particular field. What is taken for granted can become so dominant that new researchers in the field are often not even aware that other ways exist. They are simply tutored in the way that their supervisor does research and don't necessarily have a critical grasp of alternative methods. Alternative ways of understanding and doing research cease to be part of taught courses and texts over time. Consequently, as Kuhn (1970) suggested, it takes a 'revolution' in knowledge to make people realise that what seemed a good way of conceiving of new knowledge for a long time was not, in fact, the only way.

There have been protracted debates about the relation research in marketing and management should have to research in the physical sciences (Hunt, 2003; Arndt, 1985). Arndt (1985) suggested more than thirty years ago that marketing was "dominated by the logical empiricist paradigm stressing rationality, objectivity, and measurement" (p. 11). Arndt's (1985) logical empiricist paradigm broadly falls within Burrell and Morgan's (1979) functionalist paradigm, in Figure 5.2 below. Arndt (1985) called for

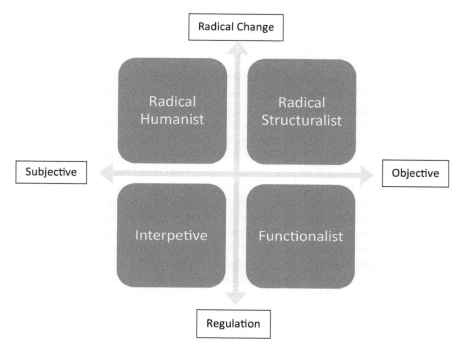

Figure 5.2 Burrell and Morgan's (1979) Sociological paradigms

a wider understanding of other paradigms, which would benefit the academic field of marketing research. In spite of regular outbreaks of similar calls in the marketing journals, the same domination remains today, even though there is a tokenistic plurality of methods that allows occasional consideration in the top journals of research publications from alternative (including the interpretive and radical humanist) paradigms. Arguably, the consumer research field, which strangely, is distinct from the marketing research field in many faculties, has demonstrated a greater degree of plurality in its top journals than has marketing, and regularly publishes articles based on qualitative anthropological and sociological studies (e.g. Weinberger et al., 2017).

The philosophy of science debates have more or less died out in the top marketing journals but still have passionate advocates on all sides. This book takes the position that research is served by many differing approaches. Most importantly, it takes a pragmatic view on research: student researchers do not have to be experts in philosophy of science in order to understand some of the philosophical issues that are debated. If student researchers can demonstrate some understanding of the basic principles of differing paradigms this will be of great help to them in devising creative and coherent research designs that are paradigmatically coherent.

Sociological paradigms revisited

When we write of interpretive research we are referring to a paradigm of research, roughly mapping onto Burrell and Morgan's (1979) sociological paradigms (outlined in Chapter 1). Foxall (1995) suggested that no single model of science can capture the interrelation of different assumptions that act together in scientific research (p. 8). This is fair, but, nonetheless, Burrell and Morgan (1979)'s scheme is still referred to as it captures some key assumptions of the different paradigms in a way that can apply broadly to many examples of research in each paradigm. Burrell and Morgan (1979) were organisational researchers who argued that all the different ways academics research organisations were characterised by assumptions that each made about the nature of knowledge (epistemology) and the nature of society. These different ways of looking at organisations theoretically they termed paradigms. For an academic researcher, working in a particular paradigm is to work from the basis of a particular world view. Many researchers have perfectly good careers in academic work neither knowing nor caring very much about the world view implied in their approach to research. Indeed, many would simply reject the idea that their work conforms straightforwardly to a paradigm, the world (and social research) being both too complex and too pragmatic to fit neatly into a paradigm. Burrell and Morgan (1979) felt that it was important to make the deep assumptions implied in research approaches explicit, not because every study has to take sides in a philosophy debate, but because it is only by making the deep paradigmatic assumptions explicit in research that the coherence of the research can be fairly judged and assessed. Understanding something about social scientific paradigms is therefore essential for people who want to read social research and scholarship critically – doing so means they can see the paradigmatic assumptions made in the work they read, and they can then make judgements about how plausible and coherent this seems judged against their own preferred world view.

Figure 5.2 is Burrell and Morgan's (1979) graphical representation of their sociological paradigms. It is useful to understand interpretivism as they saw it by contrasting it with the other paradigms. The functionalist paradigm generally aims to improve and optimise systems, it sees the world as something that is exterior to us, knowledge is 'objective' and 'out there', waiting to be discovered. This increased knowledge can help to solve more problems. A lot of management (and managerial) and marketing research is functionalist in this sense, being based on a realist ontology (the social world can be understood in much the same ways as the natural world). The radical structuralist paradigm similarly feels that knowledge is objective, there is an underlying reality to the social world (structures of reality), and the *axiology* of research, its guiding purpose, is to generate knowledge that improves existing systems. However, radical structuralism is focused more on changing policies and institutions in order to improve the distribution of power and equity in the world.

The radical humanist paradigm also aims to change the world and re-order power structures through its research, but it assumes that social real-ity is created by the thoughts, language and communication of individuals, acting collectively, hence its methods and focus of research differ from those of the radical structuralists. Radical structuralism and radical humanism could both be labelled as critical research paradigms in the sense that they believe that radical change is needed in the world, and that one way of moving toward such change is through politically aware social research and education. Politically aware in this sense refers not to party political advo-cacy but to research that focuses on power and how it plays out in social relations. So, for example, radical structuralist research might focus on, say, the laws around industrial relations and worker's rights in order to improve fairness in the workplace and in society, while radical humanist research might view unequal relations of power as things that are reproduced in micro-interactions to focus on, say, an ethnographic study of power and gender relations in school classrooms.

The interpretive paradigm holds that the social world is created by indi-viduals, acting collectively: in other words, there is no underlying mech-anism of causation for social life, it is produced through language and discourse, and through symbolic communication and interaction. The axiology of the interpretive research paradigm tends to be focused on rich explanations of the world to promote deeper understanding and greater individual liberty and autonomy, rather than on radical change. One criti-cism sometimes made of research studies in the interpretive paradigm from the point of view of radical humanists is that it sometimes pays too little attention to power structures. Interpretive researchers might counter that there is a need for greater understanding of human culture which in itself can act as a liberating force for individuals to empower themselves intellec-tually, to some extent. Of course, this example highlights the fact that these paradigms are logically incompatible. For example, counselling psychology aims to empower the individual by promoting greater control and insight into their own thoughts and behaviour, but the criticism is that people who seek out counselling for personal problems of depression and mental health my often be subject to structural unfairness (such as being poor, having an unfair employer or being in an abusive relationship) that counselling can do little to address.

Many researchers would say that whilst these sociological paradigms are useful in clarifying the key assumptions of various differing research approaches, they have to be treated pragmatically. It seems intuitive that the personal situation we find ourselves in life arises because of a mixture of our own personal qualities and character, and our position in structures and institutions of social life such as class, race, gender and sexuality, ethnicity, nationality and so on, over which we have no control. Interpretive research tends to occupy a space somewhere on the left of Burrell and Morgan's (1979) graphic reproduced in Figure 5.2, with some pieces focused more on describing social reality as it appears to be in that moment, and others focused more on the conditions that caused the social reality of a given situation to arise. There are tensions between the various paradigms and Burrell and Morgan's (1979) framework does oversimplify these (Alexander and Smith, 2001). Nonetheless, it is a very helpful framework for an introduction to interpretive research for student researchers. One thing that interpretive and humanist researchers tend to agree on is the assumption that social reality is produced through social interaction, and is not the result of underlying and invisible structures of reality, hence the framework does offer a guide to the major ontological basis for interpretive research as a whole.

Philosophical issues in interpretive data analysis: 'rich' description, agency and meaning

Interpretation and research 'method'

Research findings are invariably framed and constrained by the methodological assumptions researchers bring to the study. The spirit of research followed in this book is better expressed by phrases like research 'perspectives' or 'approaches' than method. In interpretive research, the researcher's reflexive and philosophically informed interpretation of the data generates findings. The findings are not cranked out of a machine: they are not generated impersonally by a research 'method'. There is room in interpretive research data analysis for findings that are not mechanistically produced but which are creative and emergent.

Interpretive data analysis and 'rich' descriptions

It was noted above that while interpretive research traditions hold differing emphases on data gathering and analysis, there are also many commonalities and overlaps between the various traditions. The interpretive stance is that social accomplishments of every kind are complex and enigmatic phenomena that cannot be represented by direct causal relations or boxes-and-arrows models without employing an extreme order of *reductionism*. Reductionism refers to the over-simplification of explanations. Such research tends to ignore contrasting perspectives in order to produce a simple, and simplified, process model of a far more complex process. This can be useful where models and theories provide elegant and concise representations of particular phenomena or relationships. However, interpretive research is more often characterised by 'rich' (Geertz, 1973) descriptions of social phenomena that attempt to confront and represent, rather than erase, the deep complexity of social worlds. These rich descriptions tend to focus on the particular social context (Askegaard and Linnet, 2011) rather than the world in general.

The idea of the rich description should not be confused with the earlier comments about academics judging student work on a continuum from descriptive to analytic. The genuinely rich (in an ethnographic sense) description is analytical, such is the complexity and nuance with which the description is invoked. For example, Ghaffari et al. (2019) (referred to above) generated findings that fell into three broad categories of social practices around the creative advertising development process. These social practices described how power over the creative output was constituted and represented a new way to understand advertising that could have implications for how advertising agencies organise their work and assess creative output.

Meanings in interpretive research

Another important feature of interpretive research is a focus on meanings as opposed to a focus on facts (e.g. Puntoni et al., 2010). Interpretive researchers seek to understand how social life is actively produced by people's language, behaviour and social practices. Particular social worlds are understood from the point of view of participants. Ethnographic researchers (and qualitative 'street' sociologists) have tried to understand consumer sub-cultures by, for example, becoming a member of a crack-dealing gang[3] (Venkatesh, 2009) and by becoming members of a bike gang (Schouten and Alexander, 1995) in order to become part of the social process they are investigating, thereby enabling them to understand it from the perspective of the group being investigated. In other words, the goal is to understand the meaning of this lifestyle for participants rather than trying to understand the phenomenon through questionnaire surveys or government statistics. Understanding meaning demands a first-hand, theoretically informed, qualitative engagement with the subject matter.

Interpretive researchers do not seek to impose preconceived values or concepts on the people they are focusing on in their research. Researchers must seek to accept the world as it is produced by participants. Ethically, this does not mean that the researcher must agree with or encourage behaviour they think is ethically wrong. It simply means that the integrity of the research process is best served if researchers seek to empathise with research participants. The emphasis on meaning results in a focus on meanings as they are constructed by research participants, rather than imposing the meanings and values of other groups on to the group that is being studied. In this way researchers can stand back from their research to try to understand why particular meanings become constructed and valued in a particular social setting. For interpretive consumer researchers, buying products and services and understanding advertising and branding are all activities that people make meaningful by projecting symbolic values on them. These symbolic values play into consumers' senses of identity, their (and our) identity 'projects' (Elliott and Wattanasuwan, 1998). Understanding the meanings consumption practices have for consumers is considered to be the key to understanding consumer motivation and behaviour. Importantly, in the interpretivist approach, these meanings are produced by consumers in interaction with each other and the social world, they are not imposed from above by brand managers (Gabriel and Lang, 2015) or driven from within by individual consumers' attitudes or personality.

Interpretive management researchers are similarly concerned with management processes as aspects of human interaction in organisations. Managers are seen as thinking, feeling individuals, as are the people they manage. Work is an important site of meaning for human beings. Management is a class of organisational authority but it is also, colloquially, something all workers do: we 'manage' our lives, our relationships, our time and our activities. In managing our work, we bring meaning to it and it is this meaning that interpretive researchers seek to tap into and use as a source of insight and understanding when they research organisational work and management (Watson, 1994).

Agency and situated freedom

Agency refers to the power of individuals to act and behave independently of social structures. Are your beliefs, likes, dislikes, manner and attitudes unique to you? Do they reflect your own personality? Are your decisions and accomplishments your own and no one else's? Or are they the result of the influences under which you grew up, your social class, the culture of which you are part, the kind of family you have? Are your actions, behaviours, your very thoughts, the result of the social structures within which you exist?

Such questions as these have been the cause of much debate among social theorists and are usually referred to collectively as the agency–structure debate. The debate is important to researchers because it influences the kinds of findings that can be produced. So, for example, researchers inclined to structuralist explanations of social life would be inclined to work in the right hand side of Burrell and Morgan's (1979) sociological paradigms. Structural explanations of social behaviour focus on the institutions and social structures that frame and constrain the behaviour and thinking of individuals, including class, ethnicity, income, education, gender and so on.

If people behave because of the forces that are imposed on them through class, culture and other outside (structural) influences, then change can only come about through large-scale social change whereby these social structures are fundamentally changed (the radical structuralist paradigm in Burrell and Morgan (1979)).

If, on the other hand, people are thought to have the power, however curtailed and limited, to act, think and behave independently of the social structures around them, they are said to possess the power of agency. Some interpretive research traditions (such as the phenomenological/existentialist) make this very assumption. They assume that people have some power, some limited or 'situated' freedom, to define their own existence and to determine their own course of action. Their freedom is situated because it is framed by the social structures and institutions within which the person lives, and which both influence and constrain their thought and behaviour. The idea of agency is important in interpretive research because studies of how people produce meaning within certain social situations would have little value if the people were merely playing out destinies that have been imposed on them by their social circumstances. The very idea of interpretation implies that there is some creativity and independence to the researcher's stance: he or she has the freedom to place creative interpretations on the research they conduct. This is important because it is assumed that the actions of consumers, marketing managers and other research participants are, similarly, not simply determined by forces outside their control, but are the result of their agentive action (consistent with the interpretive paradigm in Burrell and Morgan's, 1979 model).

Much interpretive work assumes that the individual's power of agency is sharply constrained by institutional forces and social structures. This tends to be a standard assumption in sociological as well as functional approaches to social research. As a result, quite a lot of published qualitative work today is not easy to fit into Burrell and Morgan's (1979) framework. One could also say that some qualitative published work today ought to have read Burrell and Morgan (1979) because it could help achieve greater ontological clarity in the work. There is sometimes a disconnect when studies that focus empirically on a qualitative investigation of agentive individuals and their socially constructed meanings then offer structuralist explanations and solutions. But, then, academic work is all about debate and critique, and the more the student researcher knows about interpretive theory, the better they can defend their work, like academics, even when they are wrong.

Replicability and validity in interpretive research

We have touched on the notion of objectivity earlier in the book. An important principle of experimental research traditions has been that the researcher stands apart from the research. The people who are in the research study are called research 'subjects', denoting the authority of the researcher (the scientist) to determine what they should be told, to control how they are used in the experiment and also to interpret their motives, actions and behaviour. The researcher, on this experimental model, stands outside what is being researched and attempts to generate 'objective' findings. 'Objective' here means findings that are independent of both the researcher, and of the research design. In principle, if objectivity is achieved, then findings should be *replicable*, that is, other researchers should be able to do the same study, using exactly the same method, at another time and in another place, and replicate the original findings.

Social research is notorious for the low replicability of its findings. There has been recent publicity around the failure to replicate major findings in psychology, called a replication crisis.[4] There can be many reasons for the failure to replicate findings, including researcher fraud. The point we make here is that replication is only a thing in experimental science, partly because of the key role that the idea of objectivity plays in experimental and quantitative (and realist) social science research. Interpretivists assume that, in social research, findings are invariably contextual – they may, and should, resonate with wider themes and with other studies, but no one would try to replicate, say, an ethnographic study expecting to generate the same findings as in the original study. Physical science has been shown to be a very human affair with elements of subjectivity, judgement and culture-specificity (e.g. Woolgar, 1981, 1988, 1989; Knorr Cetina and Mulkay, 1983; Billig, 1987; McCloskey, 1983). Interpretive theorists would hold that objectivity is 'worked up' as a textual production – science isn't objective, but objectivity is an aspect of the writing conventions of science.

Ethnographic studies in management, for example, seek to understand the ways in which a particular, specified, organizational social milieu is produced. There is no attempt to reduce findings to direct cause–effect relationships or statistically supported correlations. Such studies do generate general findings in the sense that they contribute to the proposal that organisational management is a human enterprise that is produced by thinking, feeling actors who are idiosyncratic and emotional. The major emphasis of ethnographic studies is on rich description, not testable cause – effect relations or the generation of generalisable facts or relationships, hence replication is not relevant.

Language and the social constructionist ontology

The concept of 'bias' is sometimes invoked to distinguish between the way events are reported by interviewees or survey respondents, and the way the events 'really' happened. In much interpretive research no such distinction is acknowledged. This is because the researcher is not in a position to speculate about a reality that lies beyond the accounts of research participants.

All the researcher can do is to analyse the data sets they can obtain with as much care as possible so that the reasoning and evidence that give rise to their findings is derived systematically and presented clearly. This is not a matter of being excessively credulous toward participants who might exaggerate or have a particular agenda. For interpretive researchers, using qualitative data approaches to language is not, necessarily, an unproblematic window to underlying events and causes. Language itself is the reality that can be studied.

There are techniques that can be used to sift the data sets to arrive at a view on the integrity of reports of events and mental states, such as variability and action-orientation in discourse analysis (Elliott, 1996), discussed in Chapter 8. In brief, variability in accounts refers to variation in the way people describe or account for things over time. For example, some studies of racist discourse have used the technique to highlight how some people who deny that they are racist then revert to racist tropes in different circumstances (Wetherell and Potter, 1992). Another technique used in discourse analysis is to look not only at the content and meaning of words used by participants, but also to consider the function of the words (also called action-orientation), that is, the purpose expressing a particular position in a particular way might have for the speaker. Self-presentation is always an element in discourse (as it is in questionnaire surveys) and words do things as well as say things (Austin, 1962). Using concepts such as variation and action-orientation enables interpretive researchers to apply nuance and sensitivity to the interpretation of textual data sets.

This general position implies a social constructionist ontology. The *ontology* of a research study (also referred to in the previous chapter) refers to deep assumptions about the nature of the reality being studied. A social constructionist ontology regards social reality as something that people construct in interaction through their use of language and other symbolic social practices. This contrasts with the assumption that social reality is fixed, given and prior to language and social practice.

Not all interpretive research approaches assume a social constructionist ontology. For example, some traditions of *semiotics* assume that there are communication codes underlying the construction of meaning. These codes are seen as relatively stable, fixed and unchanging. However, not all semiotics researchers will agree that this is an important issue. The ontological position adopted by a researcher is an intellectual requirement, since high quality intellectual work demands that implied assumptions made explicit are consistent with the implications claimed for the research. The ontology of social research is a working assumption, not a fully worked-through and defensible argument about the nature of reality. Social researchers state assumptions because these have implications for the kinds of findings and conclusions that can be generated from research. They do not assume that assumptions are shared or taken for granted by all.

As noted earlier, the social constructionist ontology contrasts with the *realist* philosophical position. Social researchers invoke the philosophy of realism to support the contention that the social world of managers, organisations and consumers can be regarded as if it were like the physical world of plants, bodies and cells. This can be a rather oversimplified contrast: *realism* is a sophisticated philosophical stance that has many shades and subtleties, as does positivism, another philosophical position that is often identified with realism (hence the realist/positivist assignation sometimes used in this book). For example, *critical realists* hold that the world can and should be regarded as real in a material sense but only as a working assumption. Critical realists are agnostic on many a philosophy of science questions. They take a pragmatic viewpoint. For some critical realists, social constructionist approaches to research lack a sufficiently strong sense of the *materiality* of social life. Human beings are embodied beings, we live in a world of materiality, with material goods, physical impulses and sensory experience – all is not text. Some who adopt a social constructionist approach might counter that social constructionism (Berger and Luckman, 1966) does not preclude an account of the materiality of a social situation.

Interpretive research and power

A final concept that deserves introduction in this chapter is the idea of power, which is discussed in more detail in Chapter 8. Interpretive research does not necessarily seek to uncover the relations of power that frame social interaction (think of the contrast between Burrell and Morgan's (1979) interpretive research and the radical humanism in the quadrant above). Interpretive studies are more typically concerned with revealing how social life is produced and sustained as a 'normal' thing through language and social practice in a given context. However, an awareness of how power is reproduced and played out in social situations is implicit in much interpretive research. If researchers ask the question 'why do these meanings seem to be important to this community of people?' then they must allow that one possible answer is that particular meanings serve particular interests, that is, they support the power of particular interests in some way. It is increasingly common for interpretive approaches to research analysis to be conducted within a 'critical' focus on power and interest.

Power has two broad meanings in social research. These are defined in the glossary for Chapter 8 but are worth mentioning initially here. *Structural power* refers to the ability of one person or group to coerce another person or group. This kind of power is commonly understood since it is usually very apparent, being vested in economic, class, law or other social institutions. It is extrinsic to social action, being imposed from outside a given social interaction. A teacher or parent holds structural power over children (in principle) since they have the authority to wield sanctions for non-compliance (such as giving detention, or withholding pocket money). *Constitutive power*, on the other hand, is often less apparent since it refers to the ways in which we unwittingly reproduce *ideologically* imposed values through our everyday talk and action. For example, in the above situations with children and parents, a child might complain about a proposed sanction by referring to their 'rights' or perhaps by emotional manipulation of the parent. Constitutive power is intrinsic to a given social interaction because the language and social practice of people in interaction does not merely reflect relations of power, it actively constitutes those relations of power.

For example, in many countries a way of speaking can categorise the speaker into a particular social class. This might be supported by the use of a particular vernacular and certain grammatical patterns, as in British 'working-class' or 'middle-class' speaking. Hence any interaction with a person of a different social class is immediately framed within pre-existing ideological norms that set the terms of reference for the interaction. In Britain, a regional accent was once a barrier to social and career advancement because it signified membership of a 'lower' class less worthy of responsibility and opportunity. While this is less true today (arguably), some would argue that it can still be the case in some circumstances, perhaps in certain professions. Within interaction and dialogue, people will draw (consciously or unconsciously) on ideological norms that pre-exist the interaction and they will reproduce these through language and social practice. Ideas of class membership (or ethnicity, gender, religious affiliation and so on) reflect the economic and political dominance of particular groups at certain times in history. Constitutive power often takes the form of an ideology in the sense that it is apparent in implicit assumptions and values that come to be regarded as normal, given and beyond question.

In micro-analyses of social life, researchers can look at how language and social practice confers power on individuals. For example, a study of the construction of authority in a professional relationship such as management consulting might look at the ways in which rhetoric, gesture and language produce the effect of authority in particular relationships. A study of management on the shop floor might study the play of power and authority between management and 'workers' or staff. This could be seen in terms of factors affecting the credibility of the manager, such as personal style, use of language, negotiating skills and so on. Such a study would also look at the ways in which power and authority are resisted in management–staff relations. Published studies have focused, for example, on the disconnectedness of managerial power (Munro, 1997) and on the constitutive character of managerial power in a knowledge-based, professionalised industry such as advertising (Hackley, 2000).

Micro-studies can also employ another dimension of analysis. If particular gestures, bodily rhetoric (managers wear lounge suits, shopfloor workers wear jeans, etc.), sanctions and rewards characterise the relations between management and the workforce, then there may be historical reasons for this. In other words, there may be wider historical influences at work within the *micro-sociology* of particular relationships and groups. Power is clearly important in many organisational contexts. The power of large organisations to change or maintain certain market conditions through the use of large advertising budgets is highly evident in fmcg (fast-moving consumer goods) markets. Some retail organisations have considerable power over suppliers to define price and quality specifications. On a micro-sociological level, formal management meetings are sites of the play of power from board level to shopfloor quality circles. Commercial organisations self-evidently have greater power over resources than individual consumers, but there is resistance to this power through consumer law, pressure groups and other means. Some commentators argue that the internet has changed the power balance, shifting it towards consumers who can express their wants and dislikes directly. However, as some critical theorists point out, it is clearly in the interests of commercial organisations to claim that consumers have the power of choice. To what extent is this choice constrained or framed by commercial power? These questions and many others concerning power offer potentially fruitful lines of discussion for students doing research projects.

One very important aspect of the study of power concerns studies of gender and gender relations in organisational and consumption settings (e.g. Alvesson, 1998; Hirschman, 1993; Stern, 1993). Many student researchers have found that studies of the representation of gender relations in magazines and other media forms can provide fruitful material for speculation on the state of gender relations. Studies that, for example, content analyse advertisements and editorial of magazines from differing time periods tend to reveal striking differences in the ways that relations between genders are represented. In turn, the forms of representation reflect changing values and norms in the social world beyond magazines. What changing media representations of gender imply about the wider social world is a matter for the informed speculation of the researcher. Many other kinds of study focusing on power and gender have looked at career and promotion routes for women and men in different organisations and occupations.

A focus on power, then, implies that many aspects of social action and interaction, such as language, the rhetoric of gesture and dress, the rhetoric of gender relations, can be understood in terms of the power such behaviours confer on individuals. For researchers who draw on the Frankfurt school of critical theorists, power is a ubiquitous feature of social relations (e.g. Horkheimer and Adorno, 1944). For some researchers no interpretive study is complete without a focus on the ways in which wider structures of power, such as institutions of class, gender and economics, are reproduced at the level of everyday social interaction. Interpretive studies that are truly critical in this wide-ranging sense may be beyond the scope of most student researchers. In many cases, the aims of student research projects will be primarily managerial or interpretive/descriptive rather than truly critical. Nevertheless, the link between interpretive research traditions and critical studies that focus on power is too important to be ignored (and developed further in Chapter 8).

Chapter 6 will begin the introduction to some of the most important and influential theoretical traditions that are used for qualitative research studies.

Glossary

Agency The power of the individual to control his or her own actions, thoughts and behaviour in spite of the influence of social structures and institutions.

Critical realism Put simply, the position that the social world can be assumed to be real in a material sense for the sake of convenience. It is a pragmatic position that takes realism as a working assumption and a point of departure for research.

Ideology In a general sense, implicit values and norms that are carried within given modes of speaking, writing and thinking. Ideology is normally regarded as having a centre from which it emanates in support of particular interests and groups. This centre is often obscured from view as ideological influences become widely taken for granted as the definitive way of regarding a subject or idea.

Materiality The material world as an aspect of sociological thinking and research, taking account of human embodiment and the inevitability of material reality.

Micro-sociology The detailed study of how social life is produced within a specific group. It would normally entail a close examination of language, gesture and other social practices. Micro-sociological studies are often connected to larger-scale issues through consideration of the influence of ideological norms in the wider social and historical context.

Ontology A set of basic assumptions about the nature of social and/or material reality. The social constructionist or relativist ontology tends to be contrasted with the realist ontology in social research.

Paradigm A set of assumptions about the best way to pursue knowledge in a field regarding data-gathering methods, philosophy of knowledge (epistemology) and analysis of data. According to Kuhn (1970), paradigms tend to become dominant and taken-for-granted until displaced by a revolution in understanding leading to a new paradigm.

Phenomenological/existentialism Phenomenology was a branch of European philosophy associated with Brentano and Husserl that focused on the direct apprehension of experience. In modern psychology this tradition was developed into the experiential psychology perspective. In its modern form it has also been influenced by existentialists such as Camus and Sartre.

Realism In social research, realism is often invoked to mean that the social world can be assumed to be as solid and material as the physical world, at least for the purposes of research.

Reductionism Reducing complexity to simplicity by applying a particular form of explanation. The term is usually used in a pejorative sense to imply that the economy of a given form of explanation has been achieved at the expense of important detail.

Replicability The ability to replicate a research study, that is, to do it again within a different set of circumstances to see if the original findings re-occur.

Representation Social researchers can only represent the worlds they investigate, using what media are at their command (words or other representational devices). They cannot reproduce those worlds, hence what they produce is a representation of the events they investigate.

Representative Referring to sample choice in qualitative research: if a small group has similar characteristics to a larger group it is representative of that group. Findings from research with the smaller group may, therefore, reflect the views, behaviour or norms of the larger group.

Semiotics Simply, the science of signs. In the tradition informed by C.S. Peirce, semiotics is the study of how signs come to have meaning in a given context. The task of the semiotician is to uncover the codes through which we interpret the meaning of signs.

Social constructionism An ontological position that holds that social reality is not fixed and given but constituted by and through language and social practice.

Notes

1 www.economist.com/business/2009/06/04/the-more-things-change
2 https://m.youtube.com/watch?v=QM67hGqNAZU
3 www.youtube.com/watch?v=yRq1AhFAN-4&feature=youtu.be
4 www.apa.org/science/about/psa/2015/01/replicability

Part 2

Working in theoretical traditions of interpretive research

Practical existential phenomenology for student researchers

Chapter outline

This chapter begins the discussion of specific interpretive research perspectives by drawing on two linked traditions: phenomenology and existentialism. It illustrates possible applications with research studies that could be adapted for use by student researchers. It also develops some of the major ideas, themes and techniques normally associated with each perspective.

Chapter objectives

After reading this chapter students will be able to

- explain the major principles of phenomenology and existentialism
- understand the application of both to social research that focuses on apprehended experience
- apply these themes and concepts in a phenomenologically informed student research project

Theoretical framing for interpretive studies

Chapters 6–10 will offer introductions to a selection of theoretical traditions in order to make more clear to student researchers just how they might frame their work theoretically. Student researchers should note that many of the works cited in these chapters will be much more detailed sources for advanced work in specialist theoretical traditions at master's or PhD level. Chapters 6–10 are designed to offer a route into these theoretical traditions, which is not simplified but is a rather generic introduction. In practice, advanced studies tend to adapt these traditions, bearing in mind that there are often debates and opposing camps within them.

Some scholars use the term paradigm to refer to a theoretical tradition (or to a combination of two theoretical traditions (as in Thompson et al., 1989,

1990). In this book we are treating the paradigm somewhat in the way that Burrell and Morgan (1979) treat it, as an overarching set of assumptions about epistemology, method and ontology that embrace a range of intellectual traditions. Put another way, there are quite a number of theoretical traditions of social research and social theory that can, roughly, be placed in the same paradigm. In this book we are taking the view that the theories discussed in this and the following chapters *can* be placed in the interpretive paradigm, although with the two important caveats that a) they can all be used with differing assumptions that could place them *also* in the radical humanist or even the radical structuralist paradigms, and b) Burrell and Morgan's (1979) framework is useful for researchers, but it is a simplification of paradigmatic nuances and some scholars argue that the way they use qualitative methods does not fit precisely into any of Burrell and Morgan's (1979) paradigms.

The main focus of this book, management, marketing, organisation and consumer studies, is a derivative area in the sense that the research methods and philosophies it uses are derived from other areas of social, scientific and human studies. For example, the techniques of phenomenological interviewing were developed in philosophical psychology before they were applied in consumer and marketing research, the questionnaire survey was developed by anthropologists before being enthusiastically embraced by marketers, the approach to discourse analysis adopted later in this book was mostly influenced by its use in discursive psychology, while the psychologists adapted it from the sociologists, and so on. This is to say that disciplinary areas *adapt* social scientific methods. Management and related areas are somewhat new in historical terms, many marketing departments in universities for example have only existed since the 1990s, so the derivative character of theory in marketing isn't perhaps too surprising. The point is that it is quite difficult to find universal agreement on a definitive account of any methodological or theoretical area in social studies. They are all contested, revised, evolving entities. This is why academics value the acquired skill of critical reading and critical evaluation so highly in students. So, the accounts in this book are interpretations aimed at a particular level of student researcher, they are not definitive (no account is) and they are invariably provisional.

Figure 6.1 offers a simple diagrammatic of the relationship assumed in this book between the paradigm, the intellectual tradition or theory, and the methods. As a working model it can be useful for helping student researchers to think about the basic assumptions they make in their research design, and to adapt their data analytic approach accordingly.

The kind of theoretical framing referred to in this book is seen as a way to raise the level of a qualitative study by adding a theoretical perspective to the research design. It is also a way for student researchers to achieve clarity in pulling together their research questions, data-gathering method and analytical approach into a coherent whole under the umbrella of a paradigm.

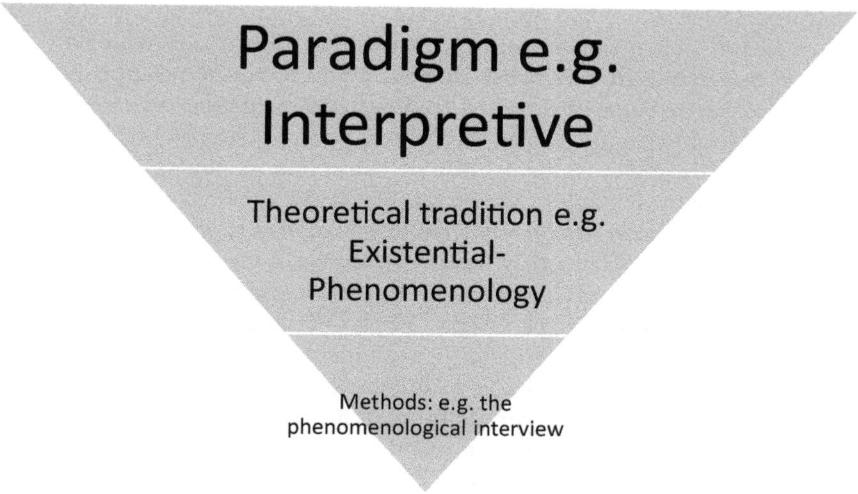

Figure 6.1 The relationship of paradigm to theoretical tradition

Many first-time student researchers make basic errors in mixing research questions, methods and data analysis in ways that immediately strike the person reading and marking the work as incoherent and confused.

The phenomenological perspective – an introduction

Social researchers of every persuasion have adapted philosophical systems and ideas for use in their own research. One particularly important philosophical theme that has been used in many social research studies is phenomenology, often allied with existentialism, although the two originated as distinct traditions of theory. Phenomenology has served a political purpose in academic research because it has been used as an intellectual justification for qualitative and interpretive research approaches for social researchers in marketing, management and consumer research. Specifically, researchers have used phenomenology to argue that, rather than accessing research participants' inner states, reasoning and motives through experiments or questionnaires, researchers should try to find methods to access participants' direct (phenomenological) experience. Hence, terms such as the 'phenomenological interview' are used to refer to, well, an interview that regards the participants' expressed experience as valid research data rather than using an interview to try to access deeper, hidden motivational drives, as in, say, psychoanalytic approaches or laddering (Gruber et al.,

2008) techniques. Philosophical purists might say that phenomenology is used in a rather simplified and, at times, perhaps misappropriated way by business and management researchers. Student researchers who find this chapter interesting (if somewhat simplified and at times misappropriated) should follow up some of the cited readings and form their own view.

Phenomenological principles have been used in management research areas to, for example, frame a study of marketing managers' lived experience of their working roles (Ardley, 2009, 2011), they have been the basis for the use of literary theory that has been applied in consumer research (Iser, 1972; Scott, 1994a), they have been the basis for a renewed focus on consumer experience as a counterpoint to the focus on consumer's attitudes and behaviour (Wilson, 2012; Sherry, 1991; O'Guinn and Faber, 1989) and phenomenology has been particularly prominent in consumer culture theory (Askegaard and Linnet, 2011). For Thompson et al. (1989) existential-phenomenology amounts to a paradigm in itself, blending the philosophy of existentialism with the methods of phenomenology.

As with any philosophical traditions that have been adapted for social research, there are differing interpretations. Edmund Husserl's (1931, 1970) ideological phenomenology was adapted for social research by subsequent writers (Gurswitch (1974), such as Heidegger (1962), Sartre (1943, 1946) and Schutz (1932). Other strains of phenomenological research were developed, such as Habermas's (1970) interpretive sociology and the phenomenological social constructionism of Berger and Luckman (1966). These writers generally emphasised the embodied, agentive character of lived experience, placing phenomenology squarely within Burrell and Morgan's (1979) interpretive paradigm. Phenomenological social research takes the embodied, experiencing agent as a starting-point and explores the mutually constructed 'lifeworld' of participants, the world of lived experience from which all others derive. The phenomenology of Merleau-Ponty (1962a, 1962b) advocated a return to that experiential world that pre-exists science and knowledge.

Philosophical phenomenology was a development of Hegel's philosophy of knowledge: phenomenological knowledge was knowledge as it appeared in consciousness. The emphasis is placed on how people can access and describe their directly apprehended, lived experience. There is, therefore, an acknowledgement of the role of intuition, recognising that much of our understanding is not articulated but, rather, is 'felt' or intuited. Phenomenologically informed researchers attempt to draw out this understanding by being open to the various personal ways people might describe this kind of experience (see Box 6.1).

For example, within organisations, managers are a category of person charged with particular responsibilities. 'Management' has, since the 1960s, been rather mythologised in that the skills, personal attributes and tasks of individual managers are held to be the reason for organisational success

---

Box 6.1   Major concepts of phenomenological/ existential research

Themes
A focus on the lived experience of actors
An emphasis on meaning, language, intentionality, agency and reflection
An empathetic stance from the interviewer as research participant
A focus on intentionality, the lived experience of people as they express it themselves as a valuable source of research data.

Assumptions
People are experiencing, reflective and agentive actors who collectively produce social events
The experience of existence, time, and death, are major aspects of what it means to be human
The integrity of the research data is paramount: there is no 'bias', only differing possible interpretations
The researcher is an active part of the construction of the research

Methods of data gathering
Qualitative, especially the audio-recorded, transcribed depth interview. Use of research field notes

Approach to data analysis
Focus on descriptions of experience, use of metaphor, the subjective construction of meaning, existential issues

Approach to research reporting
Direct quotes used as exemplars of important themes to support findings

---

or failure. Phenomenological research can reveal how managers themselves experience this role (Ardley and Quinn, 2014). Do they recognise the heroic picture drawn in many popular management books (such as Peters and Waterman, 1982)? Do managers themselves feel that they have the skills, the knowledge and, in particular, the power to enact this role? Phenomenological research approaches would seek to access the subjective experience of managers to gain intimate insights into this experience. This results in what can be a distinctive and penetrating research style when the study is executed well with participants who are willing to be (and who are enabled to be by the researcher) candid.

Phenomenology has been placed in opposition to realism/positivism in social research (Anderson and Ozanne, 1988) since the two research perspectives are

usually characterised by assumptions that are mutually exclusive. Most notably, where phenomenological research assumes a socially constructed reality,
positivism assumes that reality is external and objective (Easterby-Smith et al.,
1991; Morgan and Smircich, 1980). As we have noted in the previous chapter,
the contrasting ontological positions of different paradigms imply considerable differences in the conduct and analysis of research projects.

Existentialism and phenomenology

Thompson et al. (1989) point out that interpretive consumer research was,
then, most closely identified with ethnography, semiotics, and structuralism
(Hudson and Ozanne, 1988). Thompson et al. (1989) labelled their contribution to the interpretive 'turn' (Beckman and Elliott, 2001) in consumer
research existential-phenomenology. They point out that the dominant
paradigm in research in marking was then (and arguably remains) "logical
positivism" (Thompson et al., 1989, p. 134). Arndt (1985) referred to the
dominant marketing research paradigm as logical empiricism. In the philosophy of positivism (Ayer, 1936), anything that cannot be observed and
measured is treated as metaphysics. In other words, the un-measurable is
outside the realm of social science. The universe is treated as if it is a mathematical whole, and the goal of science is to measure everything until we
have a complete mathematical picture of the universe.

Insights about the human condition can, of course, also be gained from
art and the humanities, and interpretivism in social research springs partly
from this sentiment. The argument does not need to be labored today, but
Thompson et al.'s (1989) paper was part of a movement to find a place for
meaning in consumer research, alongside the research that sought observa-
ble and measurable social facts. Existentialism-phenomenology represented
a new contribution in interpretive consumer research as a(nother) counterpoint to the logical empiricist/logical positivist research enterprise that drew
no distinction between research in the physical sciences and social science
research. The philosophy of existentialism focuses on the undeniable fact
that human beings are here in the world, we live, and we will die, and in
between we think and reason and make decisions about our lives that shape
them. We have consciousness, unlike many of the objects of physical science. This is why, for interpretivists, social research has to be different to
research that studies the physical world. Our conscious experience of life
matters, since it is our medium for seeking a sense of meaning in our existence. Consumer choice can be seen as an expression of existential freedom
(Elliott and Gournay, 1996), that is, our freedom to make decisions, however constrained that freedom may be. Consumer research that explores the
fact that we humans are thinking, feeling beings who are compelled to try to
make sense of our conscious experience clearly falls within the interpretive

paradigm (Burrell and Morgan, 1979) and constitutes an alternative to the dominant paradigms.

Phenomenology fits well with existentialism with its emphasis on the conscious experience of life as lived in the moment, in a given context. The fact that we always occupy a context is important. Logical empiricism/logical positivism focuses on decontextualised knowledge, knowledge that is distinct from the researcher, the participants and the context in which they all operate at that time. Interpretivists are agnostic on whether or not such decontextualised knowledge is viable at all in social research. As interpretivists, they wish to do social research that acknowledges the human condition, with its sense of constrained agency, the fact that our existence consists in a stream of consciousness that responds to changing contexts over time, and the fact that we strive to make sense of this conscious experience. Hence, in phenomenological research, researchers seek to acknowledge the integrity of the participant interviewee's verbatim (Thompson et al., 1989) personal expression. Research participants' expressions of their lived experience are interpreted, but they are not taken to be consequences of other, deeper, impulses driven entirely by biology or other deep structures of causation.

Interpreting the phenomenological interview

Thompson et al. (1989) refer to three criteria for interpreting phenomenological interviews – "the *emic* approach, the autonomy of the text, and bracketing" (p. 140). The emic approach requires the researcher to understand the interview participants' expressions from the participants' own frame of reference, and not from that of the researcher (in contrast to *etic* research approaches which understand groups from the outsider's perspective). The need to understand the meanings of a section of social life as the research participant understands them echoes the priority of ethnography, which also emphasises emic understanding.

Second, the transcribed interview text is the focus of the analysis, and the text is regarded as 'autonomous' in the sense that there is no attempt to ratify the veracity of factual assertions by the participant. This does not mean that aspects of the context outside the interview text are not taken into account – the default data gathering method of existential phenomenology is the interview, but there is also room for the researcher take a reflexive consideration of the wider context of the situation through field notes. The autonomy of the text refers to what in positivistic research is called reliability, that is, the idea that the research data are clues to an underlying reality. The autonomy of the text is a principle also applied in other textual research approaches such as discourse analysis. The text is the reality being investigated, and the important thing is not necessarily the accuracy of participants' recollection of events and processes but the meaning the expressions of these events had for the participant. In order to focus on the text,

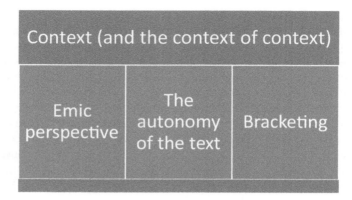

Figure 6.2 Thompson's (1989) three criteria for interpreting phenomenological interviews with Askegaard and Linnet's (2011) context of context

any ideas that the researcher has about the phenomenon being investigated must be 'bracketed' or set aside as the focus is solely on the phenomenological expression of the participant. For these to be fully apprehended by the researcher, the researcher must not approach the task of interpretation with any prejudices or stereotypical notions about the participant or the subject matter.

Figure 6.2 reminds us that the context in phenomenological interviews has two elements, according to Askegaard and Linnet (2011). The first is the context in which the speaker apprehends their lived experience, which they might refer to in their interview. For example, an interviewee might express sadness in connection with a recent experience and then mention the reasons why they are susceptible to sadness because of events in their life history. Or, an interviewee might talk about a consumer service experience and how they enjoyed it so much partly because it was a reason for their family to get together. These examples illustrate that there are contextual factors that are pertinent in the way that lived experience apprehended by the subject.

The second kind of context which Askegaard and Linnet (2011) ask phenomenological consumer researchers to consider is the more subtle yet powerful influence of social structures and institutions. These, they argue, can profoundly influence the way that a subject apprehends their experience, often without the subject being aware of the influence of these social structures and institutions. For example, a minority ethnic person might rationalise their failure to get a better job as a result of their personal failings in character and ability, until one day an event occurs that makes them realise that, in fact, they may have been rejected from some jobs not because of any personal inadequacy but because of racism. In that event, their phenomenological experience was being framed by their minority ethnicity and, for some time, they didn't realise that was what was happening therefore they couldn't articulate it as part of their phenomenological experience. Askegaard and Linnet (2011) advocate that phenomenological consumer research should also embrace the structural and institutional influences on individual lived experience which may often not be articulated or felt but which, nonetheless, powerfully impact that lived experience and circumscribe the individual's subjective sense of agency.

Askegaard and Linnet (2011) make the point that Consumer Culture Theory (CCT) made a major contribution to consumer research by bringing existential-phenomenology into the field (Thompson, 1989). As we have noted, existential-phenomenology occupies the interpretive paradigm of Burrell and Morgan's (1979) matrix. However, Askegaard and Linnet (2011) suggest that there is a tension in CCT research between the grounded interpretive approaches to consumers' lived experience of consumer culture influenced by anthropology and ethnography, and the more sociologically informed examinations of the structural relationships of consumers to class, education, ethnicity, gender and other social structures and institutions. Askegaard and Linnet (2011) then argue for CCT researchers to embrace a micro-macro perspective. In effect, they are reminding readers, as Arnould and Thompson (2005) asserted, that CCT is not a paradigm, and not necessarily an interpretive paradigm, but a collection of qualitative research studies that cut across the interpretive and radical structuralist (and arguably also the radical humanist) paradigms of Burrell and Morgan's (1979) framework. A lot of interpretive research, though, regards a consideration of constitutive power as it plays out through the experiential perspective as a basic principle of critical interpretive research, and thereby does take account of wider social structures and ideologies (as discussed in Chapter 8). We will discuss CCT a little more in the subsequent chapters.

Returning to the philosophy of existential-phenomenology, Box 6.1 offers an overview of key themes, assumptions, methods of data gathering, data analysis and research reporting that can be deployed in doing phenomenological research studies. Much of this is self-explanatory and it is intended as a checklist for student researchers. Some of the concepts receive a little more explanation and discussion below.

Intentionality and phenomenological research studies

Phenomenology focuses on intentional human experience. *Intentionality* concerns the sense in which experience is directed onto objects or phenomena, real or unreal. Literally, phenomenology refers to the study of appearances. Husserl was concerned with the way objects or phenomena appear to people. For researchers in management such 'objects or phenomena' could include marketed products, brands, services, consumer experiences, managerial actions and interventions, marketing communications or any other aspect of consumption, management or organisational activity. Researchers drawing on this perspective are interested in accessing the emotions and subjective reflections of research participants in order to better understand the processes of management and/or marketing/consumption in which they are involved and which they jointly produce.

In phenomenological research, the route to knowledge is to examine carefully what is felt, thought and perceived by the research participant(s) as expressed in phenomenological interviews (Kvale, 1983). Interpretation of phenomenological interviews is a nuanced process – it cannot be reduced to a "cookbook" (Hycner, 1985, p. 297).[1] People ascribe meaning to the objects that present themselves in consciousness. The task of the researcher is to explore events or processes by gathering first-hand descriptions of these feelings, thoughts and perceptions. Consequently, the depth interview is an ideal data-gathering method for phenomenological research. Through this method, researchers can generate insight and understanding into marketing, management, policy and consumption issues and processes from a human perspective by acknowledging that these processes and issues are done by thinking, feeling, reflecting people.

This last sentence calls to mind the section in the previous chapter that emphasised agency and meaning in interpretive research. In phenomenological research, people are active participants in social processes. They are not merely bodies that 'behave' according to external stimuli. Phenomenology emphasises the human urge to derive meaning from experience. People are seen as actively interpreting their social worlds. Their interpretations and the meaning they ascribe to their experiences are seen as the key to understanding social events and processes, such as consumption practices, management and organisational activity. Most importantly, phenomenology sees people as independent thinkers with the power of agency. That is, people are thought to be able to initiate words, thoughts and actions. People's lives and thoughts are not simply determined by social structures and other forces.

Humanistic influences in phenomenological interpretive research

Humanist influences in social research are important to the phenomenological tradition. Humanism in itself is an intellectual tradition that is referred to in management research. For example, Hirschman (1986), among others, has written of the humanistic influence in phenomenological consumer research, while Stern and Schroeder (1994) invoked humanism in their study of advertising imagery. Humanistic social research can be seen, historically, as a reaction to the dominance of experimental and statistical social research in the 1950s. As we have already discussed, the positivist, realist and experimental research designs place the emphasis on people as organisms that learn from and behave in response to, external stimuli. In contrast, humanism emphasises the ability of people to be aware of how their action and behaviour is based on their own reflections and reasoning. Many researchers wanted a more human level of understanding in social fields such as psychology, sociology and management studies. They felt that the model of the person in experimental research was flawed since it reduced the human being to an unreflexive organism without agency or reflexive awareness (although researchers using positivistic traditions would say that they don't minimise the agency or reflexive awareness of humans – they just don't think these capabilities are relevant for research).

The man-machine model of the person assumed in positivistic research (as a working assumption) also assumed that humans 'process' information much as computers do. For example, popular theories of mass communication are based on the transmission model from electronic engineering, that is, communication is modelled as if it were data being transmitted into a processor. This assumption is influential, for example, in marketing communications textbooks that emphasise linear models of mass communication involving encoding from the sender and decoding by the receiver (Hackley and Hackley, 2018b). By implication, the man-machine model assumes that humans have a strictly limited or zero capacity for reflecting on their circumstances and behaving creatively in response to reasoning and emotions. In contrast, humanism emphasises the agentive capacity humans have to define our own existence and influence our own fate.

To repeat, the fact that theories and their models have assumptions that are not realistic does not necessarily invalidate them, as economists are always quick to mention. In some disciplines, the value of a theory is not in the realism of its assumptions but in the quality of its predictions. Of course, some would suggest that economics does not have the greatest track record in prediction either, but that is by the bye. The point is that humanistic researchers (working, as noted, in psychology) decided that, for them and their clients, having a more realistic model of the person does matter. For humanistic psychologists such as Carl Rogers (1945), the phenomenological interview enabled people to reflect on their experience and, by doing so, change their perceptions and behaviour. The goal of humanistic psychology was, and is, self-realisation. People are thought to have a capacity for reflection so that self-awareness can be increased and behaviour changed. This is the basic premise of humanistic counselling psychology.

In social research in management and marketing and related areas, the same assumptions are made but the ends are, usually, somewhat different to those of psychology. While management researchers wish no harm on their research participants, the primary goal of the research is to generate insights and understanding about a particular issue or process, not to empower individuals with the ability to change their lives (although the happiness of research participants is certainly a part of the rationale in some consumer research studies that focus on consumer disadvantage, fairness and/or unhappiness e.g. Thomas and Epp, 2019; Husemann and Eckhardt, 2018; Labroo and Patrick, 2009). The important thing for researchers (as opposed to therapists) is the assumption that people can stand outside their behaviour, so to speak, and reflect on it. This unique ability means that humans are more than bundles of learned responses and reinforced behaviours. We are more than machines. We are actively interpreting our experience in a search for meaning. This means that researchers must understand our experience from an emic perspective, as it appears to us, in order to fully understand the dynamics behind behaviour and social practices.

Experience and existence in phenomenological research

The title of one study in the *Journal of Consumer Research* shows exactly what this theme emphasises for consumer researchers: 'The experiential aspects of consumption: consumer feelings, fantasy and fun' (Holbrook and Hirschman, 1982). These researchers argued that consumption, or buying things, are not only done on the basis of a careful and explicit comparison of product or service features in the light of rational needs. They suggested that consumption can also be indulged in for fun. This insight may seem profoundly obvious to student researchers reading this book who have recently enjoyed a shopping trip, a meal in a restaurant or a night out dancing. The need for researchers to draw attention to the experiential reality of consumption arose because of the dominance in academic marketing research of theories which emphasised the economic rationality of consumers. This, in turn, arose because of the dominance of quasi-experimental and positivistic research methods which assumed a non-agentic and non-reflexive human organism responding to biological or evolutionary impulses. The publication of articles such as Holbrook and Hirschman, (1982) represented a challenge to accepted research orthodoxy in consumer and marketing research.

The experiential perspective offered a radically new departure in academic business school research into buyer behaviour. Interpretive consumer research contributions developed approaches that acknowledge the emotionality (Holbrook and Hirschman, 1982; Elliott, 1998) and symbolism (Mick, 1986; Belk, 1988) of many buying decisions and consumer experiences. Much consumer research then and now has focused on the measurement of attitudes through surveys or experiments. In contrast, phenomenological consumer researchers wish to tap into consumer experience as it appears to consumers, without the mediating influence of attitude scales or survey questions. They wish to understand the buying process as a phenomenon, as it appears to consumers. In this way, phenomenological social research seeks to understand what consumption *means* for shoppers, for example, by articulating the meaning of shopping experiences by drawing on myth (Brown et al., 2017).

Phenomenology, then, was adapted in social research as part of the humanistic movement to find research perspectives that employed a richer model of the person and acknowledged the influence in social events of human emotion and agency. It acknowledged the human need to make experience meaningful, and hence conceived of humans as seekers after meaning. One important part of what it means to be human is the experience of time and the certainty of death. This emphasis was incorporated into phenomenological research from existentialist writing.

Death in consumer research

Existentialism is, broadly, the study of being. We are thrown into existence and have to face the reality, temporality and finiteness of our own finite existence. Death, in fact, has been a topic of consumer research, not focusing on the fact of it but on the consumption practices and symbolism around it (e.g. Dobscha, 2016; Hackley and Hackley, 2015a). However, in the context of existential phenomenology, it is the fact of the inevitability of death that is important rather than the symbolism and social practices around it.

As agents of our own destiny, we make decisions about our lives. For existentialists, we are often unaware of our power to determine our own fate. Indeed, we are often scared by this power and escape from this knowledge by busying ourselves with trivial, everyday concerns and worries. This can represent a 'flight from freedom' whereby we deny our right to choose our destiny. Existentialist philosophy dwells on this extreme position on agency, suggesting that we live with choice and every moment we experience is governed by our willingness, or reluctance, to acknowledge this power of choice to ourselves. Incidentally, it is not only trivial consumption that might divert us from the terrible reality of our existential freedom. For psychoanalytic psychologist Erich Fromm (1941), those who cannot cope with existential freedom sometimes embrace the authoritarian certainties of fascism. Fromm (1941) could be writing about 2019, 80 years ago.

The themes of being, existence and death may seem out of place in a research project about, say, the marketing of garden tools or the management of fast-food service operations. The existentialist influence is important for the analysis of qualitative phenomenological research data because of the interpretive position taken by the researcher. It is a subjectivist position that focuses on our immediate experience of being and the ways in which we attempt to make sense of this experience. The ways we interpret our experiences as managers, consumers and workers can, then, be seen as ways in which we reconcile ourselves with the reality of mortality and the enigma of human existence.

Data gathering in phenomenological/existential research

Phenomenological researchers must generate verbal reports and/or written accounts of experience as their data. They must then organise and interpret this data. Clearly, the focus for research analysis here falls on language, since the route to inner thoughts and feelings lies in the accounts and descriptions that people give of their experiences. Language, written or audio-recorded, is the research data. Video and other texts (emails, letters) could also be used. This means that data-gathering and analysis have a 'messy' quality, as qualitative data sets invariably do, the data do not neatly 'fit' into categories and can be unwieldy to collect and collate. On the other hand, the value of these kinds of data set is that they can yield novel, striking and creative accounts that stimulate the researcher's interpretative imagination.

This kind of data set is also, often, intrinsically interesting in itself. When people feel relaxed and safe enough to talk about their experiences, the results can often be very engaging. When it is 'safe' to do so, we often reflect on our experience in ways which are new to us, we see things in new ways. The phenomenological interview has this quality in that it enables inter-viewees to access their experience in ways that may not have been clear to them before. The phenomenological interview is not designed to be a therapeutic intervention, it is intended as a data-gathering device. However, many research participants find that the interview process, conducted sensitively by the researcher, can prove to be a deeply reflective experience. People rarely have the psychological space to reflect deeply on and share their own lived experience in a non-judgemental and supportive situation. Doing phenomenological interviews can be a rewarding and sometimes surprising experience for both interviewer and interviewee.

As mentioned earlier in the book, depth interviews can have varying degrees of formality. The researcher can use a predetermined script to list topics, or they can allow the interviewee greater scope for setting the agenda of the interview. However, it can be very useful for researchers to work to an interview guide which sets out the major themes of interest. This can be useful for remembering what topics to raise and for helping to jog the memory. It is a good idea to give the interviewee some advance knowledge of the topic or issues that will be the focus of discussion. On the other hand, it is important not to be too prescriptive. Part of the excitement of qualitative research is that the researcher does not know what they will find. People are interesting, creative entities and in phenomenological research studies, the interviewee is always the expert. They have had the experiences to which you, the researcher, need to gain access. A researcher cannot know for sure what will arise; interview agenda or guides should allow for this. This implies that phenomenological and existential research principles are not usually useful for testing theories. They are useful for exploratory research designs that set broad terms of reference and set out to discover things about a particular issue or process. Phenomenological researchers do know what they are interested in before they conduct an interview, but they do not know exactly what they will find out about it.

The degree to which the interviewee can set the interview agenda depends to some extent on the kind of topic or research question being addressed. It also depends on the scale of and stage in, the research process. If a study entails a number of interviews then it is likely that the researcher's interests and understanding will grow as the research progresses. This will influence the interview agenda. In many cases research interviews become shorter as studies progress because the researcher has narrowed down the topics of interest. In many more cases the interviewee can raise unexpected and fruitful lines of thought and investigation.

Interviews that have no strict agenda have been used for many years in anthropology and sociology, and also in clinical and counselling psychology. Their history in marketing and management research is somewhat shorter. In humanistic psychology the open-ended interview was devised as a therapeutic intervention by Carl Rogers (1945). In management research the aim of the interview is not client therapy, although as we note above in most cases the interviewee does find the experience fulfilling and enjoyable. The interviewer might intervene at times to help the dialogue along, or to probe particular responses to get at more specific themes. They might also need to gently redirect the interviewee back on to the topic of interest at times. However, in general, phenomenological research gathers better-quality data if the interviewee is made to feel comfortable to that they get into a flow of uninterrupted talk in which they can be frank and insightful about their own feelings and thoughts concerning their working experience. In many cases they will not have had such an opportunity before: good interview researchers are capable of creating a rapport or empathy with interviewees which can help to generate striking and novel research data in the form of original and creative insights.

The phenomenological researcher stance

Conducting a phenomenological interview well is a subtle research skill. It is important that the researcher can empathise with the interviewee's perspective. The researcher must try to see the interviewee's world through their eyes (the emic perspective mentioned earlier). He or she must create a safe, open and confidential 'feel' for the interview. Many of the best qualitative interviews become like friendly chats: the interviewee becomes absorbed in their topic and forgets that the situation is, in fact, a relatively formal one. It helps if the interviewer has a specific interest in the topic, and a general interest in people and their thinking. It should be remembered that one-to-one interviews of this kind can be a powerful, moving and even sometimes a threatening experience. Some sensitivity is demanded of the researcher so that they know when to probe for deeper answers, and when to leave alone. Of course, at all times the interviewee is free to terminate the interview, and they must be made aware of this at the beginning as a matter of ethical research conduct.

Ideally, the researcher should be in a position to maintain eye contact and to attend to what the interviewee is saying (or to 'listen actively' as discussed in Chapter 4). They might find it useful to make occasional notes, but this should be done with subtlety because it can make the interviewee feel uncomfortable. It is best to ask the interviewee for permission to audio-record the interview, then place a microphone in an unobtrusive position to pick up the dialogue. Later, the whole interview can be carefully replayed, listened to and transcribed. As a note of caution, it should be remembered that one interview can generate a vast amount of data. Fifteen thousand words is not unknown for one interview transcript. It is wise to keep interviews as short as reasonably possible; 30 to 60 minutes is more than adequate for most circumstances.

The interview tone

Good phenomenological interviews do develop their own momentum. It is important for the researcher to be sensitive to the tone of the interview. Some interviews seem to be socially difficult, the interviewee seems uncomfortable with giving responses. This is entirely natural, it can be difficult to create a rapport. Some interviewees are simply not comfortable with the directness and intimacy of the phenomenological interview. In such a situation the interviewer will have to work a little harder to generate good quality data by (gently) asking more questions and generally leading the interaction. At the other extreme, some interviewees take some stopping once they realise that the situation is non-threatening and they have a captive audience to whom they can relate their entire life story. In such cases the interviewee might need to gently redirect the interviewee back onto relevant lines of discussion.

At the end of the interview the researcher/interviewer should thank the interviewee for their time and co-operation. They should be reassured that everything said in the interview will remain strictly confidential. Only the researcher and the readers of the research project will have access to the data. The interviewee's name will not be placed in the report unless they specifically agree to being named in the report. In most qualitative research interviewees are not named, either a pseudonym is used or interviewees are referred to by a number or letter (interviewee A said this, interviewee B said that). Many phenomenological researchers allow the interviewee to see the typed-up transcript of the interview to ascertain that it is a fair representation of the conversation. Some allow the interviewee to read the final research project report so that the interviewee can see how their comments were interpreted.

Analysing the interview transcript

When analysing data sets, researchers should bear in mind the kind of research report they must produce. All qualitative research relies heavily on direct quotes to support arguments or to illustrate particular points in the research report. The direct quote is important research material for qualitative researchers of all kinds. The direct quote might be indicative of a general theme that emerged in interviews. It might be a particularly pithy expression of an important issue or concern. It might illustrate something about the research issue that requires explaining to the reader of the research report.

A direct quote from the transcribed interview can often be important in showing how particular metaphors or tropes of speech are used to describe or account for particular actions or events. Whatever their particular purpose in a research report, direct quotes make the research tangible for the reader and they are an important part of the scholarly goal of making the research transparent so that the reader can make a judgement on the interpretation.

Description, empathy, metaphor, existential dimensions

The analysis of phenomenological/existential interviews emphasises several major issues. In the research interview there is a description of the interviewee's experience in relation to a particular object, process or event. The researcher must be careful to interpret this description with integrity by adopting an emic 'insider perspective' informed by an empathy with the interviewee's point of view. The initial description should reflect the interviewee's view of the world. Of particular interest is the interviewee's use of metaphor. When we talk or write, use of metaphor is unavoidable. The metaphors we choose are powerful in informing the meaning we draw from our experience. As mentioned earlier, there is also a concern with existential issues: how does the interviewee deal with issues of time and existence?

Such themes might seem very abstract and difficult to extract from interview texts. Indeed, the analysis of interviews as a whole can be time consuming and difficult. The important thing is to find themes that can form the structure for the analysis/discussion. These themes may not be apparent straight away. They can come from extensive reflection on the data sets. The audio tape and/or notes and transcript might be listened/read through several times before the structure, tone and themes of the text begin to emerge for the researcher. Particular phrases or words might not strike you as interesting or revealing at first but may do so after more reading and thought.

The researcher should think about the interviewee's 'take' on events, how they arrive at that take, what it reveals about the meaning of their experience. What metaphors does the interviewee use to describe their experience? Do these metaphors re-occur? Are they of a particular kind?

After some reflection, particular themes might emerge that can form the basis for the research analysis. Such themes would act as the organising structure for the findings and subsequent analysis/discussion in the research report. For example, an interview or series of interviews might be characterised by the use of particular kinds of metaphors. The researcher could use these metaphors as a basis for an analysis/discussion which speculates on why these metaphors and not others have been chosen, why they are powerfully expressive for the research participant, what they imply about the phenomenon being studied.

For example, one student researcher conducted a series of phenomenological interviews with entrepreneurs. The study was conducted to provide research data concerning the meaning of becoming and being an entrepreneur, so that insights could be found about the nature of entrepreneurial motivation and success. The analysis focused on the interviewees' biography, their origins and the ways in which life events had informed their entrepreneurial drive. One metaphor that seemed important was the interviewee's use of a 'no big deal' manner in discussing his transition from employee to self-employed entrepreneur. After reading the transcript many times, the researcher realised that the interviewee often played down the difficulty or unusual-ness of what he had accomplished. This seemed striking: having a salaried profession for 30 years and giving up that security for the risks of private business is a significant change, or at least so it seemed to the researcher. It appeared as though the dismissive 'no big deal' playing-card metaphor worked to deflect the realisation of the risk that had been undertaken. Paradoxically, the metaphor revealed exactly what the interviewee was attempting to play down: the risk of and intense motivation required for, entrepreneurship.

The interview approach was idiographic in the sense that the interviewee's entrepreneurial behaviour was considered as part of an evolutionary process tied in with his origins and life experiences. A similar interviewing approach towards a different interviewee resulted in a published paper on the 'social construction of entrepreneurship' (Mumby-Croft and Hackley, 1997).

Doing phenomenological research

Phenomenological research designs, then, normally entail first-hand descriptions and accounts of events from people who directly participate in those events. For example, a study of the effectiveness of in-store merchandising techniques in the clothes sector might generate data sets by interviewing and/or observing shoppers in stores. Interviews could also be conducted in other environments so that shoppers might reflect on their past experiences of in-store merchandising. The phenomenological interview is usually a retrospective account of events or experiences. In retrospect, interviewees can often reconstruct experience and make sense of it in ways that were not available immediately after or during the experience.

Student researchers have conducted phenomenological interviews with other students to generate insights into the experience of undergoing higher education as a mature student. Phenomenological interviewing (or similar approaches such as ethnographic interviewing) can be particularly powerful in chronicling personal change and transformation (Schouten, 1991; McAlexander et al., 2014). It often allows people to reflect on deeply personal issues of motivation and meaning that they have not reflected on before, at least not with the mediating influence of another person. The counselling psychology movement, mentioned above, is premised on the power of the interactional process that occurs when one individual is given the space and time to reflect frankly on their experience in the presence of another non-judgemental person. While the research interview is not designed to foster personal change and transformation it can be a powerful event for both parties, and researchers should remember this. The phenomenological interview is an intimate setting and should be handled sensitively by the researcher.

Shopping experiences as phenomenological research data

Other researchers have explored the experience of shopping as an aspect of consumer behaviour studies. Shopping, reduced to a price and value information processing phenomenon by many consumer behaviour models, is revealed as a rich and powerful experience by a phenomenological perspective. Brown and Reid (1997) had students in Northern Ireland, UK write down their stories of shopping experiences in short essays. Vivid experiences were recounted that revealed something of the complexity and value-laden character of shopping itself. Brown and Reid (1997) used a narrative analysis (discussed later in the book) to focus on storytelling around shopping experiences. People recounted the many meanings of their shopping experience as they appeared to them from a deeply personal perspective. The stories were frequently vivid and compelling, and shopping experiences were woven into complex narratives that encompassed relationships, identity, social positioning and other profoundly personal issues. It was apparent that people go shopping to cheer themselves up or to distract themselves from the cares of everyday life. It was also evident that shopping is an integral part of contemporary culture and forms a landscape within which everyday life takes place.

Another phenomenological study focused on the consumption practices of expectant mothers and how these practices were mediated by considerations of time. Shopping was a part of this study but more important were the insights gained into the complexity of the lives of expectant mothers and the strategies they used to manage time and their consumption behaviour (Carrigan and Szmigin, 2004). For some people, shopping becomes pathological: like drug addicts, they simply cannot stop (Elliott, 1994; Elliott and Gournay, 1996). Interpretive research approaches that focus on subjective experience, like the phenomenological approach, are able to capture just what it is in shopping experiences that many people find so compelling.

Phenomenology-existentialism is perhaps the most influential intellectual tradition in qualitative research, but another tradition also makes a claim to this position – ethnography, discussed in Chapter 7.

Glossary

Emic and etic research In qualitative empirical research studies, the emic approach refers to understanding a group or individual from within, that is, from the perspective of the subject, while etic refers to understanding the subject from the perspective of the researcher.

Existentialism The existentialist literary and philosophical movement focused on the human experience of being and existence. It became linked with the phenomenological perspective in social research because each perspective takes the experiencing, sense-making individual as a starting point.

Humanism A movement in literature and art that has been echoed in social sciences. In social science it draws attention to the agentive, creative experiencing individual and places this model of the person at the centre of research and theorising.

Intentionality In phenomenology, the idea that consciousness is directed onto objects.

Note

1 Available at www.depts.ttu.edu/education/our-people/Faculty/additional_pages/duemer/epsy_6305_class_materials/Hycne-R-H-1985.pdf

Chapter 7

Ethnography, digital ethnography

Autoethnography: practice theory

Chapter outline

Ethnography is one of the most important informing traditions of interpretive research. Anthropologists developed the ethnographic method in their study of indigenous populations, and it has been widely adapted to the investigation of social and cultural phenomena from an emic perspective. This chapter offers an introduction to ethnographic methods, including associated methods including digital ethnography, autoethnography and practice theory.

Chapter objectives

After reading this chapter students will be able to

- understand that the research tradition of ethnography is associated with cultural anthropology
- appreciate ways in which management, marketing and consumer researchers can adapt ethnographic approaches to suit different research questions
- grasp the role of autoethnography in ethnographic and interpretive research
- appreciate some of the ways in which ethnography can be applied to study social practices and digital practices

Introduction to ethnography

Ethnography, the preferred empirical method of cultural anthropologists, is central to the socio-cultural research approach that has characterised much CCT research (Sherry, 1983; McCracken, 1986, 1989; Wallendorf and Arnould, 1988; Arnould and Wallendorf, 1994; Arnould and Thompson, 2005; Schouten, 1991; Schouten[1] and McAlexander, 1995). The emic approach of trying to grasp an insider's viewpoint on group meanings, processes and practices is fundamental to ethnography (as it is to the socio-cultural approaches of CCT). Pink et al. (2016) define ethnography in this way:

> Following Karen O'Reilly, we posit that ethnography is: 'iterative – inductive research (that evolves in design through the study), drawing on a family of methods . . . that acknowledges the role of theory as well as the researcher's own role and that views humans as part object/part subject (2005, p. 3).
>
> (p. 3)

Pink et al. (2016) offer a broad definition (borrowed from O'Reilly, 2005) that emphasises the role of theory in ethnographic interpretation, the multi-method character of ethnographic work, the evolving and iterative proves of ethnographic investigation, and the human-centred approach in which humans can engage in reflexive examination of ourselves. In particular, Pink et al. (2016) argue that ethnography is not a method as such, but, rather, an interpretive process in which a set of values are applied to researching people and culture:

> ethnography is not a very meaningful practice by itself; instead, it is only useful when engaged through a particular disciplinary or inter-disciplinary paradigm and used in relation to other practices and ideas within a research process.
>
> (p. 2)

So, for Pink et al. (2016), ethnography is not necessarily tied to a particular set of rules, it can be applied through, and together with, various alternative theoretical approaches, and we will see examples of this multi-disciplinary approach to ethnography below. Elliott and Jankel-Elliott (2002) describe ethnography as an improvement on the kind of 'armchair' sociology that was based on surveys and second-hand information. It was a way of entering the field to have a first-hand engagement with empirical data sets in naturalistic settings, instead of relying on the search for patterns in archival data sets. A view emerged in sociology that first-hand research might be a better way of understanding alien cultures. In traditional anthropology, a prolonged immersion in a social group became the accepted method (e.g. Malinowski, 1922). At least a year of immersion was recommended so that the researcher could become truly one of the group they were studying. In qualitative sociology and cultural anthropology, shorter field trips, involving observation, participant observation and supplemented by interviews with members of a culture, archival data and other data sources, became regarded as an acceptable approach. One famous school of ethnographic study evolved from Chicago sociologists of the 1930s, who became discontent with 'armchair' sociology and began to study subcultural groups in the USA as if they were studying the indigenous tribes of isolated islands. This became known as 'streetcorner sociology' as it studied the deviant subcultures of America (Downes and Rock, 1982, p. 36; Venkatesh, 2009).

The anthropological turn in marketing research has been seen as a development of *postmodern* (Brown, 1995) and *experiential* (Holbrook and Hirschman, 1982) methods that challenged the ontological and epistemological assumptions and writing conventions of the dominant neopositivistic research reporting model. For Banister et al. (1994) (see Figure 7) ethnographic research is characterised by the use of multiple formal and informal qualitative data sources as the researcher is immersed within the group being studied. These can include conversations, field notes based on thoughts

Figure 7.1 Features of ethnography

Source: Adapted from Banister et al., 1994

and observations (non-participant and also participant observation), documents and interviews. The goal is to gain a holistic, emic understanding from the perspective of the group. For example, Venkatesh (2009), a sociologist, first tried to gain an understanding of a drug dealing gang in a poor part of town by going to them with a questionnaire. He quickly realised that this was not going to generate the insights he sought. He built a relationship with the people he was talking to, developed a degree of mutual trust and rapport, and they allowed him to hang out with them for several years, observing their lifestyle. He became a nominal member of the group (one wonders if he told his university research ethics committee exactly what he was doing). As a participant observer he gained an emic understanding of the socio-cultural dynamics at play and rather than taking a judgemental attitude tried to understand the social situation the members of the group found themselves in. The group leader was in fact a college graduate but most of the group and the community in which they operated were poor and disadvantaged with very constrained life opportunities. Venkatesh (2009) learned that the group was part of an informal and mutually supportive social system that formed spontaneously because of the lack of official mechanisms for social support in this poor and deprived area of the USA.

The study brings to mind one accusation that is sometimes made of ethnographic studies, namely that the researcher is vulnerable to taking the insider perspective so thoroughly that they lose a sense of researcher independence. The immersion in a sub-cultural group by the researcher, as noted earlier is a common ethnographic approach that is used extensively in qualitative studies of consumption (e.g. O'Sullivan, 2016; Hein and O'Donohoe, 2014; Croft, 2013; Schouten, and McAlexander, 1995). However, and this is not suggested that this happened with Venkatesh (2009), the immersive aspect of ethnography can be criticised if the researcher loses their sense of independence as a social scientist and fails to engage sufficiently critically with the subject matter and the values of the group.

Ethnographers, then, seek to understand social and cultural phenomena through the eyes of the group participants, while retaining a sense of scientific detachment, so that they can understand the meanings and dynamics of a social group better than the participants themselves. With its emphasis on qualitative data-gathering techniques and focus on experience and meaning, ethnography is sometimes regarded as a counter-position to traditional social scientific research approaches that focus on facts and causation. Ethnographers seek rich, insightful descriptions of social phenomena as opposed to *nomothetic* generalisations that are founded on large samples and tests of statistical significance. Ethnography and quantitative, causal research share a concern with empirical data, but ethnography seeks to generate interpretive representations that derive from first-hand observation and study. It is, hence, an *applied* research tradition. In applied social research, ethnographic approaches have been used to understand soccer hooliganism, gang violence, drug addiction and other socially marginalised subcultures (Hammersly and Atkinson, 1983).

Victor Turner and liminality

One anthropological concept that has been highly influential in ethnographic social research is Victor Turner's concept of *liminality*. Turner (1967) drew on Van Gennep's (1961) foundational anthropological studies on ritual process. In rituals of transformation, from child to adult, from single to married, or from follower to leader, or in calendrical rites to celebrate the transition from winter to summer, van Gennep (1961) observed three main stages in the ritual process. The pre-liminal stage entails separation from the previous life: the liminal stage refers to the mid-stage of the process when the participant is neither part of their old life and identity, nor yet part of the new one, as social status is suspended and there is the possibility of great change in the midst of the flux. Finally, the post liminal stage occurs when the ritual process is consummated with the participant being confirmed in their new identity and re-integrated in their new status into the social structure. Turner's work (1967, 1969, 1974, 1982) focused on the mid stage of the process, the liminal stage, and extended the theory beyond formal rites of passage (van Gennep, 1961) in pre-economic societies into realms of consumption in advanced economies.

Turner (1986) described the liminal stage as a time of "fructile chaos, a storehouse of possibilities, not a random assemblage but a striving after new forms and structures . . ." (p. 42). Turner's ideas on liminality and ritual process (1967, 1969) have been adapted in many areas of social research to theorise physical and/or psychological spaces, which are characterised by a suspension of normal rules and structures and in which individuals feel a sense of the possibility of change and transformation. Roberts (2015) refers to the "liminoid zones" of urban night life areas in which young people explore alternative identities (often facilitated by alcohol (Hayward and Hobbs, 2007), whilst liminality has been used to theorise gender (Schau and Thompson, 2010), spiritual consumption (Husemann and Eckhardt, 2019), adventure sports (Tumbat and Belk, 2011) cosplay (Seregina and Weijo, 2017) and wine consumption (Smith Maguire, 2010). The engineering of liminal experiences through the design of liminal physical spaces (Pielichaty, 2015; Kozinets et al., 2004) has also been the topic of empirical, qualitative research studies.

From liminal to liminoid experiences

Turner (1982) distinguished between liminal and liminoid experience. With liminoid experience, this fructile chaos can be experienced as a sense of existential liminality that is not bound to a formal and compulsory ritual process, but is voluntary and impermanent. Liminoid experiences are often ludic (oriented to fun and playfulness) (Turner, 1982) and are therefore predicated on the existence of leisure as opposed to work: "One works at the liminal, one plays at the liminoid" (p. 55), thus implying that liminoid experiences are available in advanced economies. Liminoid experience can occur within groups, like sub-cultural movements such as hippies or in sports or celebrity fandom, but liminoid experience can also be manifest in individual consumption of entertainment experiences or commodities: "The liminoid is more like a commodity – indeed, often is a commodity, which one selects and pays for, than the liminal" (Turner, 1982 p. 55). Turner (1982), then, explicitly linked liminoid experience to consumer experience. In effect, consumers in advanced economies can buy liminoid experience in order to experiment and play with identity and personal transformation that is never confirmed by social acceptance into a new order – this experience is engaged in symbolically and can be endlessly perpetuated through consumption experiences.

Varieties of ethnography

Organisational management has long been an area of interest for anthropological researchers since the 1920s (Wright, 1994; Kellogg et al., 2006). Many classic studies of organisational management have, as Wright (1994) shows, used principles derived from ethnography to construct representations of managerial experience to generate insights into the process and practices of organisational management (e.g. Watson, 1994).

As noted, the ethnographer engages in close study of a particular social group in order to understand the cultural norms, values and behaviour of that group, usually over an extended period of time. In organisations, researchers using ethnographic approaches can utilise participant or non-participant observation, alongside interviews, reviews of internal documents and other informal data-gathering approaches. Management and marketing researchers have also adapted ethnographic approaches to use over much shorter periods of time of even a week or a few days. For example, Elliott and Jankel-Elliott (2002) have used ethnography in strategic consumer research for many global brands, while Clarke et al. (1998) studied the culture of the British public house, more commonly known as the pub. Of course, where a researcher decides to do an ethnographic study of a subcultural environment that they regularly occupy anyway, then they arrive at the site of study already immersed in the socio-cultural rituals and understandings of the group. Olsen (2016) is a trained anthropologist who was a partner in an international advertising agency, she made field notes and kept a diary throughout her business career and later, when she became an academic, she wrote up ethnographic accounts of her business experiences. Ritson and Elliott (1999) used ethnographic principles to research the social uses of advertising among UK adolescent advertising audiences using an ethnographic study whereby the first author took a job as a teaching assistant in schools for several periods of months, conducting interviews with the schoolchildren during breaks.

Researchers in management have adapted ethnographic principles to enhance studies of organisational management that are theoretically framed in other ways. For example, Svensson (2007) framed his study of an advertising agency as social phenomenology, although his study also made use of non-participant ethnographic observation because of the extended contact he had with the agency. Kelly et al. (2005) performed a "discourse analysis of ethnographic interviews" (p. 505) thereby adding to the rounded-ness of the discourse analytic interpretation of interview texts through an ethnographic understanding of the research context gained through time spent in the agency as a non-participant observer. Hackley (2000) took a similar approach, also famed as a discourse analysis of interviews with advertising professionals, with interviews that were conducted in the agency itself and interpreted alongside field notes, archival study of internal agency documents and informal data generated from time spent in the agency observing the activities. Hackley (2000) also gained knowledge of the agency in question through informal contact for a year prior to the main data-gathering period.

Video ethnography

Ethnographies have often made use of video as part of, or as the whole of, their data set (Woermann, 2018; Chatzidakas and MacLaran, 2018; Belk et al., 2017; vom Lehn, 2014). Video ethnography follows the same broad aims as all ethnography in the sense of gaining an emic perspective of the sub-cultural group under investigation, but they do this through a close examination of video data sets. Video ethnographies might be conducted as part of a multi-method ethnographic study, or they might be used as a stand-alone method where direct access to the ethnographic site was not possible. In addition, video can be used as a form of participant diary where members of the group under study are asked to film themselves at chosen times or at chosen events.

Video ethnography could be conducted on a social or consumption practice with which the researcher has some familiarity, in order to extend the scope of their study. For example, a researcher studying the social practices of working-class British weddings might use the extensive online resource of wedding video clips as additional material. Hackley and Hackley (2015a) wanted to do an ethnographic study of an East Asian ritual, the Hungry Ghost Festival. There are many hungry ghost festivals in Asia that follow differing Bhuddist traditions and local mythologies. The researchers in this case set up the project by interviewing the festival organiser and some other local people, but then could not get access to the rather inaccessible region in which this particular festival takes place. Instead, they found that quite a lot of videos had been put on online, so they were able to supplement their acquired local knowledge with accounts deriving from the video material they were able to access.

Leading academic conferences in marketing consumer research now have sections for video ethnography and filmed scholarly work, on the basis that video can support robust ethnographic insights and contribute to theory development (Belk et al., 2017). For the student researcher, video might be a problematic medium because most universities probably do not have the flexibility of regulations to permit student researchers to use video as a scholarly medium. However, there would in all likelihood be nothing wrong with student researchers using video as part of their data set.

Digital ethnography

Digital ethnography has become a major subfield of ethnography. Pink et al. (2016) see digital ethnography as an important context for the inherently multidisciplinary field of ethnographic studies since human culture has extended into digital manifestations. They refer to Lupton (2014) who has suggested that digital sociologists tend to engage in four types of practices: using digital tools for data gathering, examining how people use digital media, using digital tools for data analysis and engaging in critical analysis of the implications of digital data. All of these practices can be present alongside each other in digital ethnographic studies, but there will be differences of emphasis. Pink et al. (2016) include within the scope of digital ethnography the investigation of things, experiences, social practices, relationships, events and localities, and social worlds.

As social life becomes increasingly conducted online in various forms, there is a need for ethnography to develop techniques and principles for taking an ethnographic approach to online culture and online communities (Schembri and Latimer, 2016; Arvidsson and Caliandro, 2016). In consumer research, perhaps the best-known brand of digital ethnography is *Netnography* (Kozinets, 2015). Kozinets et al. (2018) explain the basic principle of netnography as follows:

> The basis of netnography is rather simple. It is grounded by the principle that the perspective of an embodied, temporally, historically and culturally situated human being with anthropological training is, for purposes relating to identity, language, ritual, imagery, symbolism, subculture and many other elements that require cultural understanding, a far better analyst of people's contemporary online experience than a disembodied algorithm programmed by statistics and marketing research scientists.
>
> (p. 231)

Kozinets et al. (2018) position netnography as a form of digital ethnography that seeks to reclaim digital and digitised forms of understanding from naïve data science and algorithm-driven formulas and invest it with a human level of insight, seeking "a more experiential and more participative understanding of a shifting social realm" (p. 231) that is, the shifting social realm of the internet and its countless manifestations of social media platforms and communicative technologies. Netnography, like ethnography, is a flexible multimethod approach. It is designed to closely examine online consumer culture focusing on multiple dimensions of computer-mediated social interaction, taking account of the words and language used, and also the particular elements of the platform being used. That is, netnography would consider the characteristics of Instagram, Facebook, Snapchat and so on and how the design of those platforms frames and shapes interaction on the platform. It would also take account of such elements as moderator standards and behaviour, the characteristics of the various communicators making up interactions on the site, the history and evolution of each platform, the types of interaction taking place, the symbols, GIFS, images and videos deployed in the course of interactions, and so on. In effect, netnography shares some characteristics with a discourse analysis (discussed in Chapter 8) in online contexts.

Like ethnography, netnography (or other forms of digital ethnography) attempts to generate insights into the socio-cultural practices and meanings of a community or sub cultural group by immersing the researcher in the community/group and taking account of the social, symbolic and communicative practices of the group in a naturalistic way, in the sense that the researcher engages with the 'natural' ways in which people communicate and express themselves in online contexts, as opposed to setting up experiments or surveys. The process of netnographic 'entrée' occurs when the researcher first enters the site of interest, that is, the online community or group of interest, to orient themselves and immerse themselves in that context in order to absorb the tone, style, platforms and methods of interaction and communication that represent the ways in which participants produce that particular community.

Netnography, like all qualitative approaches, can be combined with others, for example; Capellini and Yen (2016) combined ethnography and netnography while Villegas (2018) combined autoethnography (discussed below) with netnography, calling it auto-netnography (Kozinets and Kedzior, 2009). As we have pointed out earlier, ethnography implies a set of values rather than a method or scope, and ethnographies can be applied in many differing contexts to investigate many different kinds of situation in concert with other paradigmatic approaches. The fields of management, marketing, organisational and consumer research are mainly derivative, they import their theoretical perspectives and methods from the wider human and social sciences. Netnography applies digital ethnography to consumer research topics (although the area of consumer research has of course expanded since almost all human activities have been marketised and rendered consumption activities).

Autoethnography

Autoethnography has made a small but noted contribution to marketing and consumer research. Adopting the principles of ethnography to a sample of one person, autoethnography uses the subjective and reflective perspective of the individual as a source of social research data. Denzin (2014) locates autoethnography in a tradition inspired by C. Wright Mills (1959) and J-P Sartre (1963) because it inspires the sociological imagination and can somehow re-connect the social with the personal. Unlike the phenomenological stance, in autoethnography, experience is not seen as a foundational category, but, rather, experience is performed and constituted through text. In other words, the act of putting words to experience constitutes that very experience. Deetz (1980) notes that, "Speaking speaks not only information but a tradition, a tradition which carries along that which will be recovered as thought. " (p. 13). Autoethnography articulates and constitutes experience from a subjectivist position located in culture, class and race.

Autoethnographic research studies are sometimes written entirely in the first person by the researcher using their own subjective viewpoint as a sample of one (Holbrook, 1995). Alternatively, in narrative autoethnography, the first-person perspective is thrown on to an account of an experience or an event (Olsen, 2003), in contrast to autoethnographies that use the subjectivity of the person in itself as the source of data (e.g. Holbrook, 1995). Autoethnography, like ethnography, makes its points from a non-realist ontological standpoint that stands in opposition to the idea of objectivity and the epistemological assumptions of positivistic/realist scientific reporting (Reed-Danahay, 1997).

Different styles of autoethnographic contribution to published marketing and consumer research include Belk (1996), Brown (1998, 2012a, 2012b), Hackley (2007), Sherry's (1995) teleethnography and Olsen and Gould's (2008) ethnomusicological ethnography, Gould's (1991) introspective-praxis autoethnography and Holbrook's Subjective Personal Introspection (1995), which is discussed below. It is possible to further subdivide autoethnographic styles into many variations. For example, Denzin (2014, p. vii) refers to collaborative autoethnography and collaborative writing (Chang et al., 2013), duoethnography (Norris and Sawyer, 2012), ethnodrama (Saldana, 2011) ethnographic fiction, polyvocal texts and mystories (Richardson, 2000), meta-autoethnography (Ellis, 2009) and sociopoetics (Pelias, 2011). Of these, perhaps only duoethnography (Tiwsakul and Hackley, 2012) has been deployed in marketing, in a study of cross-cultural consumer identity.

Autoethnography foregrounds not only the subjective experience of the writer, but also the writing craft that can draw the reader in to see and understand the emotional texture of what is being expressed. In this sense autoethnography's emphasis on writing reflects Brown's (2005) insistence that writing, as the key representational form of research, is an intrinsic part of constating the meaning of research students and not merely a neutral medium through which researchers communicate their research findings about a 'real' world beyond the text. Indeed, some forms of autoethnography have something in common with creative nonfiction writing (Gutkind, 1996) in that they offer a first-person account of histories, experiences and events. In this regard, autoethnographies have considerable critical potential since they can offer deeply personal accounts that are sometimes written with emotional force, giving voice to the marginalised (Pratt, 1992. For example, racism in British Universities is given deeply personal accounts in one autoethnographic collection (Gabriel and Tate, 2017). Alsop (2002) emphasises the self-reflexivity of autoethnographic writing in a study of the way immigration changes the notions of being home or not home, while Tiwsakul and Hackley (2012) take the same theme of immigration/emigration in a collaborative autoethnography to explore the shifting sense of identity of the immigrant and how that marginalisation is expressed and identity re-ordered through selective consumption. Experience illustrated, autoethnography retains the capacity to generate maximum discomfort and still lacks legitimacy for its perceived scientific shortcomings.

Holbrook's (1995) Subjective Personal Introspection (SPI) approach is probably the most well-known manifestation of autoethnography in marketing research (Shankar, 2000). Introspection strictly entails observing oneself, examining one's own internal responses to stimuli, rather than commenting on the world from the first-person perspective. The latter is referred to as extrospection by Gould (1995, 2018), or sometimes as narrative autoethnography (Olsen, 2003), which consists in first person accounts of experiences and reflections, which bring the personal and biographical into data analysis.

Like all interpretive approaches to research, autoethnography has its critics. Some regard the subjective viewpoint as inherently un-scientific and not worthy of serious consideration as a social research method (Wallendorf and Brucks, 1993; see Gould, 1995). Other criticisms in the field of autoethnography take in the ontology, epistemology, tone of voice and choices of subject matter. Autoethnography, say critics, has no hypotheses and does not have systematic data sets, it celebrates bias as a virtue (Denzin, 2014 p. 70) and it can be a self-indulgent platform for self-indulgent, egoistic writing. There are no glib answers to these criticisms, what constitutes science is an ongoing debate. For the converted, autoethnography liberates the critical voice and mobilises minority viewpoints, hence acting as an important corrective and antidote to prevailing scientific ideologies.

There are also many instances of published studies in marketing that are not labelled as autoethnographies as such, but which use elements of biographical or autobiographical data in their analysis. These might use first-person vignettes and/or direct quotes to use the subjective perspective to illuminate particular topics. Examples include the life history method used by McLeod et al.'s (2009) of advertising creatives' professional lives, in which advertising agency creative professionals described not only their work but their personal life journey to becoming a creative, in which their social class turned out to be an important feature. Other examples include the use of personal subjective vignettes to give reflexive context to a study of top advertising agencies' working practices (Hackley, 2000), or Wohlfeil et al.'s (2019) study of celebrity fandom. In these works, autoethnographic vignettes form a significant part of the data set, along with quotes, field notes and observations. Autoethnography's contribution to academic marketing studies was reflected in a 2012 special issue of the *Journal of Business Research* edited by Stephen Gould with papers including Brown (2012b), Wohlfeil and Whelan (2012), Minowa et al. (2012), Patterson (2012) and Roberts (2012).

Practice theory

We include a brief note on practice theory here because it has been used in tandem with ethnography in a number of published qualitative studies (e.g. Thomas and Epp, 2019; Ghaffari et al., 2019). Ghaffari et al. (2019) followed a number of ethnographic studies of advertising agencies (e.g. Alvesson, 1998; Kelly et al., 2005; Moeran, 1996; Svensson, 2007) in conducting an ethnographic study but supplemented the theoretical framing with a version of the practice theory approach that has become well established in management and organisation studies (Schatzki, 1996, 2002, 2012) and which has been adapted to marketing communications (Ots and Nyilasy, 2017). The ethnographic approach generated the data sets in these studies, through participant and non-participant observation. The data sets included reflexive field notes, recorded observations and interviews. The theoretical perspective of practice theory informed the observations and the data analysis.

Practice theory is a broad school (Skålén and Hackley, 2011) of thought deriving from the work of Pierre Bordieu (1977). The approach attempts to capture the situated-ness of human beings as we work through everyday activities always being constrained by our reliance on symbolic communication and our place in the social structure designated by our social class, ethnicity, gender and citizenship. The idea of a social practice embraces the multi-faceted character of human activity as we do things that often have a ritualistic and performative aspect. Practice theory therefore seeks to capture something of the culturally and socially contextualised character of subjectivity, as called for by Askegaard and Linnet (2011). Human beings operate in the interstices of social structure, exercising agency and trying to shape events, but often constrained by structural and constitutive power. Practice theory approaches attempt to capture the full context of how social relationships and happenings are constituted through this complex dynamic.

For example, Ghaffari et al. (2019) conceived advertising creativity not as a thing or as a process, as many previous studies had done (e.g. Hackley and Kover et al., 1995), but as a set of social practices constituted through the linguistic and symbolic interaction of the various parties, the creatives, the account executives and the client. What emerged as creative output was therefore not simply an idea that was 'owned' by whoever claimed it, but a set of practices through which the creative output was constituted, which Ghaffari et al. (2019) labelled control power, knowledge power and persuasive power. Using direct quotes from the data sets, they described how these practices came about.

Ots and Nyilasy (2017) highlighted five key elements of social practices in the constitution of Integrated Marketing Communications (IMC) plans, listed in Figure 7.2:

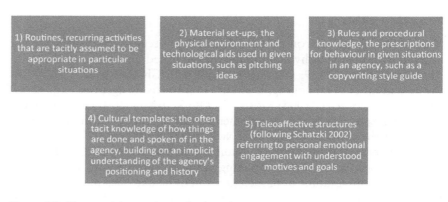

Figure 7.2 Five social practices of advertising creativity

Source: Adapted from Ots and Nyilasy (2017) in Ghaffari et al. (2019)

These five concepts amount to an admittedly simplistic framework for practice theory analyses of ethnographically informed qualitative data sets. The routines roughly echo Bordieu's (1977) notion of habitus, the relatively un-reflexive routines into which organisational workers (and everyone else) falls through the unquestioned acceptance of tacit values and routines. The material set-ups reflect the materiality of social practice, the fact that it is invariably contextualised in a material world full of objects and scenes that can have an effect on how people think and behave. The rule and procedural knowledge are explicit ways of operating that organisational members are expected to know because the organisation insists on them, whilst the cultural templates are the implicit and unspoken rules and values that obtain in any social interaction that people are expected to absorb and enact without being told. Finally, teleoaffective structures refer to the personal emotional engagement actors have with motives and goals. For example, in advertising agencies, creative professionals are highly emotionally involved in the creative ideas that they pitch to clients. These categories act as ways of thinking about and interpreting the ethnographic observations that are made in a study.

'Doing' ethnography

Arnould (1998) suggests that ethnography aims to 'clarify systematically the ways that culture (or sub-culture) simultaneously constructs and is constructed by the behaviours and experiences of members' (p. 86). He suggests that this entails four main principles, illustrated in Figure 7.3:

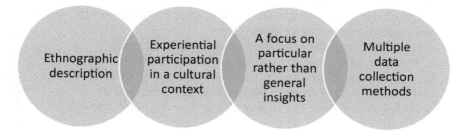

Figure 7.3 Principles of ethnography
Source: Adapted from Arnould, 1998, p. 86

'Doing' ethnography, like doing any interpretive research, entails particular methods of data collection and analysis. But, more importantly, it entails using a set of broad principles that inform the researcher's whole engagement with the subject matter. Interpretive researchers draw on a theoretical perspective: they do not mechanistically apply a 'method'. The ethnographic description is a style of multi-faceted detailing of a social context in which interactions and behaviour take place. The material for such a 'rich' or 'thick' ethnographic description is gathered from the qualitative data sets gained through the researcher's experiential immersion in the social context being studied. The focus is placed on particular insights that obtain in the social and cultural context being studied. These are not generalisable in a positivistic sense but they may resonate with the human experience of the reader of the ethnography much like a work of poetry or literature. Another way of summarising key elements of practical enthnography is listed in Box 7.1 under the categories Assumptions, Methods of Data Gathering and Approach to Data Analysis:

Box 7.1   Key elements of ethnographic research studies

Assumptions
Social and cultural life is created by people through symbolic interaction
    To truly understand a social milieu a researcher must experience it
    Qualitative research data sets are interpreted through a frame of presuppositions: ethnographic interpretation entails an understanding of the local cultural context

Methods of data gathering
    Multiple qualitative methods including observation, interviews, informal conversations and exchanges, field notes, archival records

Approach to data analysis
    Creative interpretation based on researcher knowledge of the social and cultural context in question
    Focus on particular phenomena, not generalised truths
    The researcher creates an imaginative representation of the social life in question in an attempt to convey something of the meanings, motivations and experiential understanding of participants
    Focus on 'repairing' the indexicality of language and gesture

---

The ethnographic research study involves, first, gaining as much 'insider' knowledge as possible about the subject in question. For management researchers, this might involve reading all the available published information about a particular organisation or brand before the primary research is begun. It may mean establishing links with a particular organisation to try to engage members in discussion. A research study into a particular consumption practice or a specific consumption group would begin with a thorough investigation of secondary sources. The research would then progress to a first-hand engagement with the contexts of consumption. For most student researchers in management and marketing, a prolonged period of field research is impractical. Even if access is granted, the time and resources are rarely available to students. But this need not rule out the application of ethnographic principles. Indeed, many management and marketing research studies apply the principles of ethnography to much shorter periods of field work.

Indexicality in ethnographic research

An important ethnographic principle is that of seeking to understand social phenomena in their social and cultural context from the point of view of group participants. This principle can also prove fruitful in interpretive studies that are not necessarily framed as 'ethnography'. The interpretation of, say, a depth interview is always conducted within a frame of presuppositions. The researcher can only understand what an interviewee is talking about to the extent that he or she understands their work, their idiom of expression, and the organisation they work in. The researcher must understand enough about the context of research in order to know just exactly what the interviewee is talking about.

This touches on the issue of *indexicality* of language and gesture. In a famous example, a wink (of an eye) can mean different things depending on the context (Geertz, 1973). A wink can be complicit, seductive, friendly, sexual, patronising, funny, even threatening. Without an understanding of the context, a wink cannot easily be interpreted. Indexicality refers to the contextualised meaning of things people say and do. Our language has a context: if an engineer uses the technical phrases and concepts of engineering in talking about his or her work, then an interviewer who does not have any knowledge of engineering will not fully understand what is being said. In the same way ethnographers feel that interviewers must have firsthand knowledge of the social context of which a research participant is part in order to understand what they are referring to in their interview. Ethnographic principles dictate that we cannot take this understanding for granted. We must go into 'the field' and get to know something of the shared meanings and symbolic social practices in a particular social realm in order to properly understand what people are talking about. Taking account of 'ethnographic context' means interpreting ethnographic research data in the light of a broader understanding of that social context first-hand in the field (also note that indexicality is an important concept in semiotics, discussed in Chapter 8 Grayson and Shulman, 2000).

Particular comments and gestures may carry subtle shades of meaning that are not apparent to an outsider who has no knowledge of the group culture of the interviewee. Language, gesture and social practice have an 'indexical' property in that they refer to a particular social setting for their meaning. The principle of indexicality derives from the *ethnomethodological* sociology of Garfinkel (1967). The researcher carrying out an interpretive analysis of interview transcripts or other primary data cannot 'repair' the indexicality of comments and gestures without this knowledge. Social understanding and the appearance of social competence are far more complex than they may often appear. The ethnographic researcher generates insights into social life by understanding the meaning that language, gestures and other social practices have for participants.

Styles of ethnography

Ethnography makes use of small samples of research participants. Often these samples are chosen simply because they are convenient. The important thing for ethnographers is to generate a 'thick description' of social behaviour, which seeks to understand, and then describe, the complexity of social life (Geertz, 1973). Elliott and Jankel-Elliott (2002) refer to the distinction between 'inductive' ethnography and 'interpretive' ethnography (citing Alvesson and Skoldberg, 2000). The former research style tries to ground findings very securely in a detailed analysis of empirical data. The latter 'interpretive' style of ethnography attempts to render bold or striking creative interpretations of limited data sources. The best ethnography, arguably, falls part way into each camp with detailed and systematic data gathering providing the basis for creative insights that go beyond logical induction into the realm of imaginative representation.

As already discussed, data gathering for formal ethnography tends to mean a long immersion in the social context, but this is curtailed to a few weeks or even a few days in commercial and some academic applications of ethnography. 'Quasi-ethnography', (Elliott and Jankel-Elliott, 2002) makes use of shorter, often opportunistic periods of data gathering. For example, Rust (1993) describes a commercial study in which researchers loitered in supermarkets waiting for families with children to enter. They would then record some information about the family and follow them (discretely, one supposes) around the store. After the family left the researcher would make notes on what they had said and done to generate insights into shopping practices and family interaction. This would take place over just a few days before the researchers had a good sense of the social dynamic of family grocery decision making.

The researcher-as-voyeur position may imply some ethical issues that would need to be addressed on a study-by-study basis. Privacy is important to many people, and personal safety is important for researchers. If a student researcher is thinking of conducting a study like that of Rust (1993), then the explicit permission of the organisation in which the research will be conducted must be obtained. If permission is granted, then great care must be taken in gathering the data. It may be possible to simply 'hang-out' at places of interest. Many famous sociological studies into youth subcultures were conducted by Chicago-based sociologists in the 1960s. As part of their method researchers would make it their business to be where the group of interest would be so they could observe behaviour and listen to talk. In one interview the author conducted with an advertising agency creative professional, the creative (as they are known) said that if he received a brief for tea, he would hang out in supermarkets to watch people buying tea. It was his approach to getting a sense of how the group of interest conducted the social practices of consumption. Armed with this insight, he felt better equipped to communicate with this group about buying tea, or whatever the matter happened to be.

In consumer research applications, researchers have adopted ethnographic principles by, for example, spending time in kindergartens and primary schools to understand how infant children become aware of brands.

In one study, the researcher convened 'focus' groups in which he showed pre-school children brand logos and elicited recognition. In another, the researcher got a job as a school assistant and hung out with the children at break times to interview them about how they talked about advertisements (Ritson and Elliott, 1999). Bassiouni and Hackley's (2016) study entailed the first author spending time helping at a children's after school club in order to understand the role that computer and video games played in children's lives. Commercial researchers seek to understand how children recognise and understand brands for commercial purposes. Academic researchers might have broader terms of reference. Whether the terms of reference for research are commercial and by implication potentially exploitative, or ethically informed and investigative, the ethnographic principle of simply hanging out with group members in the places where they hang out is a powerful one for the generation of insights into group meanings and actions.

Formal and informal ethnographic data

Part of the goal of ethnographic research, then, is to provide a rich description of a social process or phenomena by acquiring a thorough first-hand understanding of that social process or phenomena. This would normally imply multiple methods of data gathering since ethnographic researchers can acquire ideas about a cultural context from many sources. This could include depth interviews, analysis of other textual data such as emails or telephone interviews, historical documents, observation and field notes of researcher reflections and ideas.

Typically, ethnographers combine formal data-gathering methods with informal methods. The formal methods will include the usual qualitative techniques of interview, observation and focus or discussion group. However, our understanding of social contexts is often acquired more intuitively through things we overhear, accidental observations we make, casual phone conversations or off-duty encounters with people who live and/or work in that particular social context. All such sources are potentially useful for the ethnographic researcher.

For example, it is far from unknown for an interviewee to say one thing in a formal interview then to offer a much more candid opinion in the pub afterwards. Indeed, informal social settings, such as staff restaurants, the bar or pub after work or other work-related social gatherings, can be particularly valuable for the ethnographic researcher. It would hardly be appropriate for a student researcher to take an audio-recording device along if they were invited to the bar or pub at lunchtime with work staff. However, the off-duty comments, jokes and ways of talking about work issues and personalities can offer important routes to understanding what happens in more formal work settings.

Researchers have found that the formal research interview held, say, in an office of the host company might yield very different insights to a subsequent interview that is conducted in a less formal setting off-site (Easterby-Smith and Malina, 1999). Such informal settings can 'round out' a researcher's understanding of a topic because the research participant may be more relaxed and less defensive. The author has conducted many interviews with marketing professionals and has had several experiences of people taking him aside to a quiet corner of the office to offer a franker viewpoint than could be offered in a more formal setting. The ethnographic stance gives researchers the license to use this kind of insight actively as research data.

High-quality informal data often emerges if the researcher has established a good rapport with the research participants/interviewees. Indeed, in ethnography as in most qualitative research, the quality of this rapport often dictates the quality of insights generated (Agar, 1996). Easterby-Smith et al. (1991, p. 90) refer to the importance of establishing trust between researcher and participant. The research participant is more likely to be candid and spontaneous if he or she trusts the researcher to use their discretion and not to reveal the sources of any potentially embarrassing quotes or opinions. In many research contexts in which employees or managers are the research participants, they do worry that the researcher might name them as the source if they express a criticism of organisational policy or scepticism towards organisational aims and methods. It is important for the researcher to develop sensitivity for organisational politics and to establish an informal sense of rapport with the research participants.

Field notes and ethnography

Clarke et al. (1998) explored the cultural meanings of the British 'pub' by using a combination of depth interviews and questionnaires administered in pubs. They also drew on semiotic influences to interpret the audio-recorded data. *In-situ* studies such as this allow researchers to utilise rich sources of field data. 'Field notes' are the impressionistic and relatively un-formalised reflections and ideas of the researcher. In a service industry context it is clear that researchers can make great use of such first-hand observation to enrich their understanding. For Spradley (1980) field notes can include comments on such things as the physical space in which interactions take place, descriptions of the people involved, the things they are doing, and the objects that are present, and the timing and sequence of events and the feelings expressed or indicated. Researchers can draw on field notes as they seek interpretations of formal data such as interview transcripts. They can interpret data in the light of their understanding of the social context that is reflected in the field notes.

Revisiting reflexivity in research reporting

A feature of interpretive research that has been mentioned previously in the book is critical reflexivity. Reflexivity is sometimes defined as being aware of being aware, that is, being able to examine one's life as if from an external perspective. In research, reflexivity refers to being able to comment on the way that the research evolved, including being aware of the assumptions brought to it by the researcher, and it is often labelled as critical reflexivity to indicate that one can be critical of the assumptions one brings to one's own research just as one tries to be critical of the assumptions made in other research perspectives.

There are different forms of reflexivity (Johnson and Duberley, 2003) and it is not confined to researchers, for example it is a noted feature of some forms of consumption (Thompson et al., 2018). Reflexivity has two main practical implications for the researcher. One is that the researcher should try to be consciously aware of the values, assumptions and perceptions they bring to the research process. This critical reflexivity is brought into the research report through a self-conscious, and self-critical, writing style. In other research styles it is conventional for the researcher to write and behave as if he or she is detached and independent and that the research report is a neutral channel for conveying the findings. The research report is written to minimise the identification of a thinking, feeling, interpreting individual as author, and any doubt, any dilemmas that the researcher faced, and any digressions that the study took, are erased from the research report text. Interpretive research studies are particularly associated with reflexive writing styles, whilst research in the functionalist paradigm especially realist research based on experiments or survey data, tend to conform to more formal reporting conventions.

Interpretive research studies are often written-up in the 'third person' (although sometimes not (see the section on autoethnography) but nonetheless they should have a reflexive, that is, self-aware, tone and self-conscious style. They can be written in the first person, that is, using the personal pronoun 'I' to represent the author. It can be more difficult to create an impression of rigorous scholarship in this style and student researchers are advised not to use it unless they are very confident about their writing and analytical skills. Even then, it is strongly advised to obtain the opinion of the research supervisor.

Alvesson and Deetz (2000) suggest that, in interpretive research, "people are not considered to be objects . . . but are active sense makers like the researcher" (p. 33). The researcher's part in the interpretive process is, then, openly acknowledged. Researchers seek to use this involvement to deepen their understanding of the research process and they express it in their research reporting through a *reflexive* research reporting style that is open to self-criticism, honest about influences and biases and frank about limitations.

Representation in research writing

Alvesson and Deetz (2000) remind readers that interpretive research reports are *representations* of a slice of social reality. That is, when the researcher writes about a management issue or set of consumption practices, they cannot claim that the research report is the reality of what has happened. It is, self-evidently, an interpretation written down in text. For Brownlie (2001) "interpretive marketing research [is] a highly coded and situated form of representation . . . that works to legitimize and privilege certain kinds of knowledge" (p. 48). But, of course, all research does this – it adopts certain forms of rhetoric and particular writing conventions in order to privilege certain forms of knowledge, or claims about knowledge. Brownlie (2001, p. 50) points out that research does not merely "reproduce a pre-existing world of marketing managers or consumers" but "constructs the research domain" through "scholarly artifice". For example, it is not correct to assume that because ethnographic research seeks a rich and detailed description of a social phenomenon that this in some way produces a representation that is closer to reality. Ethnography is just another representational practice (Van Mannen, 1995; Brownlie, 1997).

'Representation' implies that whatever is written in research represents a viewpoint that is selective and reflects the educational, cultural and political influences on the researcher. It is appropriate, therefore, for the researcher to reflect on the interests that may underlie any particular representation. For Alvesson and Deetz (2000), representation is political in the sense that any representation of reality will concur with some interests and conflict with some others.

For example, much consumer research uses the concepts of consumer 'satisfaction' and 'choice'. However, there are circumstances in which consumption can be a source of dissatisfaction and a restriction of choice. A reflexive piece of interpretive consumer research would acknowledge the conflicting interests that may be invested in the use of particular representational strategies, such as framing consumer experience in terms of constructs like 'choice' and 'satisfaction'. As an example, some interpretive studies of management have painted a picture of organisational management as chaotic and stressful, and managers as unhappy, unfulfilled and stressed (e.g. in parts of Watson, 1994). Other studies celebrate managerial tasks and, by implication, managerial skills and produce a representation of the organisational manager as a folk hero (e.g. in Peters and Waterman, 1982). It does not question the integrity of such studies to discuss what interests may be served by such representations of organisational management.

Particular styles or modes of representation do tend to become accepted and conventional over time. For example, popular marketing management textbooks have developed distinctive rhetorical strategies that have become so familiar that it is difficult to articulate marketing issues through alternative representational strategies (Hackley, 2001, 2003b). This presents a difficulty for researchers. A good researcher will not want to present a picture of the world that relies solely on conventional and perhaps stereotypical ways of representing the world. The challenge to interpretive social researchers is to see the worlds they research through the eyes of the people in them while also retaining a distance from that world, so that what is familiar to participants remains unfamiliar to the researcher.

Chapter 7, then, has discussed another of the most important and influential qualitative research approaches, ethnography. It has outlined the general principles of ethnography and introduced a number of variations, including digital ethnography and autoethnography. In addition, the chapter has outlined practice theory as a theoretical approach sometimes used in tandem with ethnography. Ethnographies and practice theory are often concerned not merely with agnostic description of life experience but with revealing the dynamics of power that impinge on and form experiences of powerlessness and disadvantage.

Chapter 8 introduces another important set of connected intellectual traditions that have been influential in the interpretive analysis of qualitative data sets – literary theory, in which we include semiotics and semiology.

Glossary

Applied research As opposed to theoretical or 'blue skies' research, applied research seeks to solve a specified problem.

Ethnography (see also Chapter 5 glossary) A method of cultural research adapted from anthropology that emphasises the researcher's full participation in the lives of the group being studied.

Experiential To do with apprehended subjective experience.

Indexicality In semiotics and philosophical linguistics, indexicality is the idea that language points to or refers to something, hence repairing indexicality means understanding the context of a piece of speech or talk in order to fully understand its meaning.

Liminality Victor Turner's work on liminal process and rights of passage has been highly influential. Liminality refers to a state of being in-between one position in social structure, and another, during liminal ritual. Turner's work was originally based on rites of passage from adolescent to adult amongst indigenous peoples, but he extended the concept to apply to contemporary society. So, for example, an undergraduate student is neither a child under the care of their family nor an independent member of adult society until they graduate. Liminality indicates a rich potentiality for experimentation and creative change.

Postmodern Often used with the term *post-structural*, postmodernism was an architectural movement that became a term variously used to express an epoch, a style, or a philosophy in literature and social theory.

Post-structural Anthropological studies that reject the structural approach of a fixed reality underlying social life.

Nomothetic Associated with quantitative research designed to produce generalisable truths and relationships.

Netnography A version of applied digital ethnography adapted for consumer research by Kozinets (2015).

Note

1 For an introduction to consumer ethnography from John Schouten, see this video www.youtube.com/watch?v=adkPJhLPb1I

Chapter 8

Literary theory and qualitative research

Chapter outline

Literary theory has been a fruitful source of interpretive theory for qualitative research in marketing and related areas. This chapter outlines some of the key approaches deriving from literary criticism, including reader-response theory, narrative analysis, rhetoric and semiotics/semiology. The focus falls on the communicative dimensions of marketing, management and consumer research, and the ways in which management texts can be written to cue particular effects of interpretation.

Chapter objectives

After reading this chapter students will be able to

- appreciate the contribution of literary theory to social research
- apply some literary concepts to theoretically informed analyses of qualitative data sets such as interviews or other texts
- understand the concepts of symbolism, polysemy and intertextuality for application in research studies

Literary theory, marketing and consumer research

Contemporary marketing practice often hints at its literary character when commentators speak of marketing 'discourse', brand 'storytelling', brand 'narratives' (Russell and Schau (2014), consumer 'engagement' and 'emotional' branding (Brown, 2016b), yet mainstream textbooks and research methods in marketing, management and consumer research seldom offer an exposition of literary methods for research projects. As has been pointed out earlier in the book, a research study is ultimately a piece of literature, a written document, and we have touched on the role of textual analysis in social research. Not only are literary principles important in social research – marketing and management practice are working fields in which communication is central to professional practice. Management and marketing practitioners write emails, reports and presentations, and they use written texts in countless other ways, in addition to the verbal texts of meetings and interviews (Brown, 1999). Much of management is the task of verbal and/or textual persuasion. These are inherently rhetorical tasks (Nilsson, 2019). Marketing has become a popular academic discipline partly through the rhetorical force of the metaphors, tropes and conventions that have come to characterise the field (Hackley, 2003b Brown, 2005). Literary theory can provide useful routes into the understanding of marketing and consumption practices, experiences and processes in both the academic and practice contexts.

Advertising research and literary theory

Literary theory as a research perspective first became noted in academic consumer research around the 1990s (e.g. Stern, 1989, 1990, 1993; Hirschman and Holbrook, 1992; Stern and Schroeder, 1994; Easton and Aráujo, 1997; Brown, 1999, 1999; Brownlie, 1997; Holbrook, 1990; O'Donohoe, 1994, 1997; Sherry and Schouten, 2002). The use of literary methods has continued to flourish in both consumer research and marketing research (e.g. Miles, 2013, 2014; Brown, 2016a, 2016b): Phillips and McQuarrie, 2004, 2008; Hackley et al., 2013). For example, since Stern (1989) introduced the idea of the social text into consumer research, reader response theory (Iser, 1972) has been used to understand how consumers 'read' and respond to advertisements (Scott, 1994a). Reader response theory originated in literary criticism as a counterpoint to formalist literary criticism, but Stern's (1989) perspective allowed researchers to theorise consumers not as passive dupes who unreflexively react to advertising stimuli, but as active readers who interpret and either accept or wholly reject the implied or desired interpretation cued into the message by the brand and its advertising agency. Ritson and Elliott (1999) had pointed out that most academic advertising research lacked ecological validity – that is, it asked individual consumers questions after they'd viewed an advertisement in the controlled and artificial conditions of a viewing booth. In fact, consumers generally view advertisements as part of a social process, and our opinions on the advertising we view are mediated by the opinions of the people with whom we discuss and/or view the ads. The notion of advertisements as texts has been extensively developed in qualitative and conceptual research studies (e.g. Brown et al., 1999). Hackley and Hackley (2018b) have developed this to embrace a paratextual account of contemporary advertising practices both on – and offline.

Stern and Schroeder (1994) point out that research into advertisements has often focused on the 'information' (price, quality, positioning) that is available to be 'processed' by consumers. Such research has neglected the view that consumers draw meaning from advertisements as a whole rather than in distinct parts. We do not look at advertising text, sound and imagery as distinct sources of information. All three wash over us as we are exposed to advertising. Little attention has been paid by information-processing researchers to the ways in which other components of advertising, especially the visual imagery, acts as a source of meaning that can influence the meaning of the other components of an ad. Stern and Schroeder (1994) draw on literary and art criticism to develop an approach to the analysis of visual imagery in advertising.

Polysemy and intertextuality

Student researchers often want to investigate something about advertising, but usually lack the theoretical background to articulate exactly what it is they want to explore. Literary theory approaches such as reader-response allow researchers to analyse how consumers read and interpret advertisements in a way that allows consumers to express their own interpretation of the advertisement, rather than having their responses confined within the parameters of a survey question. In this way, using interviews, researchers can probe into the meanings of, and the discourses around (Cook, 2001) advertisements to generate insights, as opposed to generating cookie-cutter survey responses. Naïve managerial models of advertising affect conceive of an advertisement as a univocal message, the meaning of which is independent of the medium and the receiver (Hackley, 2010). In contrast, literary theories of advertising affect acknowledge that advertisements are texts that are read and interpreted by consumers, hence the meaning of an advertisement is mediated by the interpretation of the receiver. In turn, the receiver will interpret the meaning of an advertisement with reference to their cultural context, the other discourses surrounding the ad including other advertisements, and the medium (Cook, 2001).

Literary concepts such as *polysemy* (Puntoni et al., 2010, 2011) and *intertextuality* O'Donohoe (1997) can be used to theorise, respectively, the potential for advertisements to carry more than one meaning, and the inter-dependence of advertising meaning on other social texts, including the medium on which they are carried, other ads around them, and other discourses around the ad content. For example, many Nike advertising campaigns tap into current cultural priorities, news events and currently newsworthy individuals. This gives their campaigns emotional resonance evoked by the consumer's knowledge of the cultural context. Intertextuality invests advertisements with cultural meaning by reference to other social texts from the worlds of news, sport, celebrity news and entertainment. Polysemic advertising can draw the consumer in to the game of interpretation, as the creative execution intrigues the consumer/reader who wants to finish the story (Puntoni et al., 2010). The literary concept of polysemy can show us that advertisements without a clear message are not necessarily poorly designed ads but, in contrast, can be the most creatively ingenious ads of all, since they invest the ad with strategic ambiguity (Puntoni et al., 2011) that inscribes meaning into the brand.

Advertising, brands and ideology

Another literary idea used in the analysis of advertisements is ideology (Eagleton, 2007). At least, Eagleton (2007) has treated ideology not just as a concept of political science but as a communicative phenomenon that can be understood through the literary lens. Elliott and Ritson (1997) postulated that advertising collectively carries considerable persuasive force as what they termed a superideology promoting the consumer lifestyle. Other researchers adopted versions of the ideological perspective to analyse particular advertisements for their ideological character (e.g. Wernick, 1991; Williamson, 1978; Barthes, 2000). Conceiving of advertisements as ideological in character hints at the rhetorical dimensions of all advertising and marketing – that is, it is all designed to be persuasive, and the study of rhetoric is the study of persuasion, in linguistic forms or in other forms, including visual or aural rhetoric (Scott, 1990, 1994b; McQuarrie and Mick, 1992, 1996). Consumer ideologies sometimes tap into myth to mobilise and articulate brand meanings for consumers (Luedicke et al., 2009).

Of course, ideology is a term more commonly associated with political forms of persuasion, and Zhao and Belk (2008) analysed the ideological effect of advertising in reversing the strong antipathies in China that existed toward market values before the Chinese government embraced markets, including advertising. Although the ideological effect of advertising is not overtly political it does have a connection with political attitudes to market capitalism. In addition, in the contemporary environment political advertising has become more like commercial advertising, whilst commercial advertising has taken on more of the techniques of ideological propaganda, so it is sometimes hard to see the distinction between the political and ideological rhetorics of persuasion in mediated communication, and their commercial counterparts (Cronin, 2018; Davis, 2013). Indeed, some analyses would hold that commercial advertising is inherently political in the sense that it reproduces values and norms that mask narrow interests and seek to exploit power differences between corporations and consumers (Elliott and Ritson, 1997).

Holt (2002) and Holt and Cameron (2010) looked at ideology not from a critical perspective but from a managerial perspective. Holt's (2004) cultural branding approach conceives of brands as ideological vehicles in the sense that they need to tap into prevailing sub-cultural values and trends and identify with those. By so doing, successful brands resolve ideological dilemmas, as the iconic advertising image the Marlboro Man tapped into myths of American masculinity and resolved the tension between traditional masculinity and the modern world. Clearly, the resolution is merely symbolic, achieved through brand consumption. The cultural branding perspective focuses on brands as socio-cultural phenomena and not as bundles of attributes and associations that reside in the consumer's cognitive apparatus, hence it stands in direct opposition to the more cognitively nuanced theories of branding that tend to be more popular in the managerial marketing and branding literature.

Advertising ideology can be understood not as an unintended consequence of commercial activity but as a fundamental part of its operation (Elliott and Ritson, 1997; Holt and Cameron, 2010). Brands and advertising 'work' as ideological forces that normalise brand consumption practices (like smoking cigarettes, driving cars that will go at 150mph, buying food in plastic packaging, eating breakfast 'cereals', wearing fur, eating bacon and eggs) and universalise the values of consumption. Note that there is not necessarily a moral judgement in the above – advertising operates ideologically, but this does not mean that what is promoted is necessarily bad or wrong. It is simply the way (or one way of understanding) how marketing 'works'. Consumers are fully enabled to exercise choice and to resist the blandishments of consumer ideology, such as where sub-cultural consumption practices emerge that subvert brand ideologies (Schouten and Alexander, 1995). However, these resistant readings of consumer culture are sometimes quickly co-opted back into the service of corporate marketing (Thompson and Coskuner-Balli, 2007), for example, through cultural branding strategies (Holt, 2002).

Rhetoric in organisational and academic practice

Rhetoric, the art of persuasion, is typically regarded as a literary art, although as we point out above, other forms of representation such as visual art and music can also be seen to have a rhetorical character. Brown et al. (2018) have commented upon the rhetorical character of marketing research and practice and the need for more detailed rhetorical analyses of marketing practices. Brown (2005) has also noted the rhetoric styles of noted marketing academics and 'gurus', while Hackley (2003b, c) drew attention to the rhetorical tropes by which mainstream marketing text books produce a sense that they are a-theoretical and focused on practice (as if they were practical marketing activities in themselves rather than books about practice). Marketing, as the science of persuasion, seems a prime candidate for rhetorical analysis, yet the topic of rhetoric has been neglected in research in the field, notwithstanding a special issue of the *Journal of Marketing Management* (Miles and Nilsson, 2018).

The word 'rhetoric' is often used in a pejorative sense to mean insubstantial or empty. Tonks (2002), writing of marketing rhetoric in consumer contexts, dates this pejorative usage of the term back to Plato who criticised the Sophists' teaching of rhetoric for being 'mere cooking' associated with 'trickery, deceit, immorality and superficiality' (Kennedy, 1963, p. 15, in Tonks, 2002, p. 807). Aristotle took a rather more benign view and the study of rhetoric became a key part of the school curriculum right through to medieval times. Rhetoric, in fact, became regarded as the overarching intellectual discipline, unifying the sciences because of its integrative 'epistemic' (Tonks, 2002, p. 810) character. It was studied as part of the school and university curriculum throughout the medieval era and, in the UK, up to the 1800s.

The interest in rhetoric has returned in many studies that consider it not only as a part of literary analysis, but more fundamentally as an organising principle for thought and argument. There is no necessary implication that to use rhetoric is deceitful or cunning. It is, simply, the means by which humans argue and persuade. Language and, hence, thought itself, are rhetorically organised to produce certain (rhetorical) effects. For some psychological theorists, rhetoric is more than simply a literary craft of persuasion. It is an important organising principle of human psychology (Billig, 1987, 1991). In a sweeping sense we can be seen to depend on particular kinds of accounts of events and experiences to make sense of the world. We have explanations for our behaviours that seem, to us, to justify them. We understand our beliefs and actions in terms of accounts we construct of our lived experience.

The rhetoric of absence

The literary study of rhetoric, then, focuses on the persuasive character of particular forms of written language. It is important to note that rhetoric is not simply about what is written, or indeed, what is said. It is also about what is excluded. Expressing a view or idea in a persuasive or plausible way distracts attention from other possible ways of expressing that idea. Alternative forms of expression with quite different implications might seem equally plausible. Forms of expression tend to privilege certain ways of seeing the world and accounting for events while, by default, silencing alternatives. Social psychological researchers Edwards and Potter (1992) note that a major feature of rhetorical analysis is 'the demonstration of how, in order to understand the nature and function of any version of events, we need to consider whatever real or potential alternative versions it may be designed to counter' (p. 28, citing Billig, 1988, 1989).

In accounting for events, mental states or actions we are, in effect, arguing a point of view to others, and also to ourselves. As we construct particular accounts (of events, actions or experiences) we make sense of them: we fill in the account with implied motivations and explanations. Other accounts or explanations then become rhetorically less forceful or persuasive: they become 'alternative' rather than accepted 'common sense'. In this way the rhetorical use of language is highly significant in not only describing, but also in constitutively forming our psychological states.

Particular writing or speaking strategies invite the question: what potential threat or criticism was this way of putting things designed to counter? If I come home and my son opens the door and says 'it wasn't me, Dad' I immediately wonder what he's done wrong. What potential accusation or criticism is his denial intended to counter? If a marketing text proclaims that 'This book is focused on practical marketing management', a focus on rhetoric might prompt questions like 'why write that? In what way is marketing management not practical? What does the text accomplish by saying this?' Rhetorical strategies seek to exclude possible alternative accounts or claims (such as the claim that marketing management text books fail to adequately explain marketing practice). Marketing is a textual genre in the sense that marketing ideas, research and thought are produced, sustained, perpetuated and defended through writing. These words and phrases then become the instruments of managers and others in organisational settings.

Rhetorical analysis is inherently a critical method since it seeks to reveal the mechanisms by which consensus and agreement are produced. The study of rhetoric is therefore bound up with the issue of power. The power of particular rhetorical devices and strategies to persuade can be seen to have a historical basis in particular social structures and institutions. 'It's only rhetoric' is sometimes a comment levelled at political or commercial claims and discourse that suggests that rhetoric is trivial and reflects a mendacious, half-truth approach to accounts and claims. In social research, rhetoric is far more than this. The study of rhetoric is the study of how meaning and persuasion are mobilised through language and social practice.

For example, Brown (1999) drew on literary analysis to compare the rhetorical styles of two leading marketing writers and consultants, Professors Theodore Levitt and Morris Holbrook. Such critical rhetorical analysis is not always well received by business academics who feel that a focus on rhetoric demeans their work. They write as if they are offering solutions that can be applied in the practical worlds of business. Many do not wish attention to be drawn to the rhetorical skills that enable them to write persuasively. The study of rhetoric is based on the truism that all knowledge is mediated: we cannot convey experience except through language and writing. Many business consultants have won influence and credibility through the ability to write and speak as if they are offering homespun wisdom deriving from direct experience of organisational management. This ability itself is a mark of high-order rhetorical skill, as Brown (1999) points out. Other researchers have critiqued the rhetoric of management buzz-words and fads as Case (1999) did with business process re-engineering (Hammer and Champy, 1993), while Hackley (2003b) and Furusten (1999) have critiqued the rhetoric of popular management text books (such as Peters and

Waterman, 1982, and Kotler, 1967). McCloskey (1983) drew attention to the rhetorical character of economics, a discipline that still succeeds in selling itself as a science.

Student researchers considering a rhetorical analysis for their project or dissertation could do worse than to take a look at Nilsson (2015), which is a PhD thesis that is available open access.[1] Nilsson (2015) undertook a close study of classical philosophical studies of rhetoric and applied those principles to an analysis of the sales conversations of business professionals in B2B contexts in order to understand how expert professionals deployed rhetorical strategies in order to be persuasive (see also Nilsson, 2019). As we have noted earlier, it is also possible to conduct studies of visual and aural rhetoric to understand the persuasiveness of marketing and other corporate communications (Scott, 1990, 1994b; Schroeder, 2002; Schroeder and Borgerson, 2015).

Narrative analysis

Narrative analysis is another literary influence that has been drawn on in interpretive marketing, management and consumer research. A 'narrative' is a linguistic account of an event or events that is organised into a sequence or structure so it can be understood and connected. Some literary studies of narrative have focused on the structures of narrative and how these come to be imbued with meaning. Other approaches have emphasised the interpretation of narrative by focusing on the reading strategies that people employ

---

Box 8.1　Key concepts of narrative analysis

Narrative – a verbal or written account of something that has story-like elements

Social construction of reality – the ontological assumption is that social reality is not fixed and independent of the narrative but, rather, is constituted through narratives

First person perspective – in empirical narrative research, personal stories can be useful material

Researcher description – the researcher will describe the story, its content, context and other key features

Accounts – (of experiences, events)

Context – the surrounding context that informs the account

Story structure – beginning, middle, end, dramatis personae, events, content

Function – what function the story serves, e.g. identity positioning, entertainment, instruction

in order to draw meanings from narrative accounts. Narrative analysis in qualitative research often focuses on personal accounts, stories of events or experiences related from the first person perspective, and in that sense has something in common with autoethnography (discussed in Chapter 7) as it does with discourse analysis (discussed in Chapter 10).

Narrative analysis in qualitative research is often conducted to analyse the personal stories and accounts of individuals, but it can also refer to textual narratives. For example, academic research into management fields can be seen in terms of 'narrative projects' since it consists of literary texts that construct narratives, or stories, about, for example, marketing (Stern et al., 1998; Shankar et al., 2001). In most popular marketing management books, the text is organised persuasively to give marketing a sense of narrative. There is a familiar story of the evolution of marketing as a constantly improving technique (Brown, 1995; Brown et al., 1996; Kerin, 1996; Keith, 1960). Marketing management theory is given origins (normally placed in the late 1950s in the USA), there is a time of struggle (the 'production' and 'sales' eras of business orientation) and it achieves great popular success in the modern era. Marketing has its pantheon of management guru-heroes and there are the trials and tribulations of misunderstanding and mistakes along the way (Hackley, 2001). The historical accuracy of these claims is not important: the textual organisation of marketing management texts gives the discipline a striking and persuasive narrative character. But literary theory also gives us a critical antidote to modernist progressiveness. Lyotard (1984, p. xxiv) writes that 'I define postmodern as incredulity towards metanarratives'. For Lyotard the narrative form is a highly significant cultural artefact that frames the way we think. He seems to position postmodernism as an antidote in that it seeks to recover these narrative forms and, by questioning their unstated assumptions and exposing their rhetorical techniques, undermine their effect.

Narrative studies in marketing and consumption

Marketing texts, then, do tend to be characterised by certain very distinctive narrative conventions (see Kotler, 1967, and any subsequent editions, discussed in Hackley, 2003b) that are notably absent in other disciplines of university study. However, there has also been much critical scholarship in marketing that has challenged these narrative conventions, such as in Brown and Patterson (2000) and many other examples (e.g. Drummond, 2018; Sherry and Schouten, 2002; Brown, 2006; Holbrook, 1990). Literary tracts of all kinds have a narrative character, they have a story arc, and a beginning, a middle and an end. And, to some extent, so do brands (Russell and Schau, 2014; van Laer, 2014). Narrative analysis focuses on how the narrative is structured, what purposes the story might serve, what is the content of the story, and how it is performed.

Referring again to textual narratives, we are used to scientific research being presented as if it stands outside narrative because it is represented as if it were a discourse separated from storytelling by its objectivity and rigor. Science is supposed to be about facts, not about stories. Yet (even) scientific research tracts can also be seen to have narrative characteristics (Latour and Woolgar, 1979; McCloskey, 1983). Scientific research and development, for example, can be seen as an enterprise that invents narratives to interpret compounds and substances in terms of new 'uses' for need satisfaction. The effects of the drug that became marketed as Viagra, for example, were known for a long time as an unacceptable side-effect, before somebody connected the drug to the narrative of male sexual performance enhancement and made it into a huge marketing success (Letiche, 2002).

We are acculturated into narrative forms from the stories we read and hear from infancy. We learn narrative structures and expect the accounts we read and hear as adults to conform to these narrative characteristics that we have learned. Our preconceptions about which narrative forms are appropriate in given contexts frame our interpretations. However, brand communication often disrupts narrative convention. For example, hero myth stories have been subverted and disrupted by contemporary social media since individuals today can launch themselves into celebrity status without the infrastructure of intermediaries and without observing the traditional narrative of heroic struggle and triumph (Hackley and Hackley, 2015b: Mills et al., 2015). Many brand communications today depart from the traditional media create formats and consist in fragmented inter-texts and vignettes that have little in common with narrative conventions or poetics but generate meanings through polysemic intertexts (Hackley, 2018; Hackley and Hackley, 2018b). What is occurring when consumers respond emotionally to brand paratexts, arguably, is not so much narrative transportation (van Laer et al., 2014), but a form of intertextual semiosis (see below).

However, whilst the idea that brands tell 'stories' needs to be reconfigured for the social media age, it still makes sense to use versions of narrative analysis to understand how consumers receive and interpret brand communications of differing types. Human beings seem to have a need for narrative (van Laer et al., 2018) Narrative analysis is a well-established qualitative research approach (e.g. Brown and Reid (1997) Shankar and Goulding (2001) Stern et al. (1998), and Grayson (1997). Olsen (2003) used narrative analysis in an ethnographic study, while van Laer et al. (2019) used a form of narrative analysis to understand how online consumer reviews generate consumer engagement. Shankar and Goulding (2001, p. 1) adapt a table of narrative characteristics from Gergen and Gergen (1988). These authors suggest that narratives have some important characteristics that make them compelling. Narratives can have a point, in the sense that they develop a moral or theme that is valued. Narratives have selected events that are ordered and causally linked to lead up to and support the main point of the story. They might have components of drama, such as protagonists, divergence or disruption, and resolution. Finally, narratives have signs that they are narratives, such as a middle, beginning and an end. Understanding narrative structures helps us to understand their poetics, that is, the ways in which narrative structures tap into the human need for narrative to generate emotional engagement.

Semiotics/semiology: origins and scope

Many students wish to explore the visual imagery of branding and advertising in their research projects. To do so it is useful to know something of the vocabulary of semiotics. Semiotics has gone a little out of fashion now as a method in academic consumer and marketing research studies, but its key concepts still retain great explanatory power (Danesi, 2004,[2] 2016) and semiotics is still invoked as part of the methodological approach in qualitative studies in some recent studies (e.g. Humphreys, 2010; Roux and Belk, 2018). Semiotics is, broadly, the study of signs and their meaning in communication. A sign in this sense is something that can stand for something else. 'Semiotics' or 'semiology' is etymologically derived from the Greek *sema*. It can be traced back to the ancient Greek medical techniques of Hippocrates and Galen who inferred medical conditions from the symptoms reported or presented by patients.

The word semiology is usually associated with the study of linguistic signs. The tradition of semiology deriving from European linguistics is associated with Ferdinand de Saussure (1974). The North American tradition (known as semiotics) reflects work by philosopher C.S. Peirce (1953–66, 1986). Scholars have borrowed indiscriminately from each tradition so the distinction between the two is blurred in many research studies. This chapter will emphasise the concepts and terminology of the North American tradition. In 'semiotics' the focus of study is on any signs whatever in regard to their capacity for communicating and generating meaning. That is, the focus can be on visual, aural, word-signs, written or non-written signs. 'Semiosis' is the process of extracting messages and significance from signs, and thereby generating meaning. In human semiosis, the central problem is to understand how signs come to have meaning. Some traditions of semiotic analysis attempt to reveal the codes through which humans draw meaning from signs in particular cultural contexts. However, such codes need not be stable or enduring: they may not pre-exist the relation of sign and *interpretant*. The meaning of signs, according to Peirce (1986), is arbitrary. In principle, anything could stand for anything else. It is the cultural context that frames the interpretation of signs and imbues particular signs with localised meanings.

Danesi (1993) explains how the colour red can have many different meanings, depending on the cultural context for semiosis. A red traffic light, a blushing cheek, a red armband can all communicate different messages. Red faces in Western cartoons often signify anger, while in China red is a lucky colour. An open window, footprints in the snow, a bloodied knife are classic signifiers in detective stories (Hackley, 1999, p. 137). The Marlboro man, a classic marketing sign, stands for 'American culture, independence and self-reliance, but may also stand for rebellion, chauvinism, fatalism, ill-health or the genocide of Native American Indians, depending on the communication context and the particular interpreter' (Mick, 1997, p. 251). National flags are such powerful signs that some are revered in one country and regarded with contempt in another. The variation in cultural contexts means that people can bring quite differing interpretive strategies to the same signs.

Semiotic studies have been developed in a wide range of human fields. For Mick (1997) semiotics is 'one of the richest sources of principles, concepts and tools for studying communication and meaning' (p. 260). There have been studies of the semiotics of cinema (Metz, 1974), communication (Fiske, 1982; Fry and Fry, 1986), theatre and drama (Elam, 1988) and language (Barthes, 1968; Eco, 1976, 1984), not forgetting the semiotics of emojis (Danesi, 2016). For some semioticians, semiotic study can form a superordinate human science of communication (Sebeok, 1991), ranging from the communication of single cells to the communicative codes of entire cultures. *Semiosis* in marketing and consumption occurs through language (both spoken and printed) and other visual and aural signs. Marketing communications and brands can be seen as a system of 'strings of signs' (Sebeok, 1991, p. 146) that communicate values through brand imagery, packaging design, prices, advertisements and a plethora of other signs.

While marketing as a whole has, in the past, been a fertile site for semiotic analysis (e.g. see Umiker-Sebeok, 1987; Umiker-Sebeok et al., 1988; Larsen et al., 1991; *International Journal of Research in Marketing*, special issue 1988, vol. 4, nos. 3 and 4) two particular marketing fields have proved especially interesting for semioticians. These are advertising and consumer research. Researchers such as Williamson (1978), Tanaka (1994) and Bertrand (1988) have explored the semiotics of advertising in depth. Sherry and Camargo (1987) developed a semiotic analysis of the use of English language words in Japanese advertising. Consumer research has also proved important in stimulating semiotic analysis (Holbrook and Hirschman, 1993; Holbrook and Grayson, 1986; Mick, 1986, 1997; Mick and Buhl, 1992) although, as we note above, more recent studies tend to invoke semiotics terminology or semiotics as a part of their analysis (e.g. Kozinets, 2019) since it has been absorbed into the basic vocabulary of interpretive research.

The symbolic character of human communication is seen as a 'central and differentiating aspect of the species' (Mick, 1986, p. 196) and nowhere is this more evident than in the worlds of marketed consumption. The world of consumption is replete with signs, as Mick (1997) notes: 'Examples of signs in the consumer world are everywhere a person wished to look, listen, smell, feel or taste: brand names and logos, lyrics, melodies and tempos in music; deodorants and perfumes; wool sweaters and silk pillows; pizza and whiskey...' (p. 251). The semiotic arena of marketing reflects and constitutes the wider cultural setting for semiosis. Anthropological researchers such as Leach (1976), Belk et al. (1988) and Wernick (1991) emphasise the revealing nature of consumption and promotional and marketing culture. They show that marketing appropriates values and signs from non-marketing culture and attaches them to marketed entities to serve corporate aims. Your ownership of branded goods can signify much about you, such as your social status, the groups to which you claim membership and your aspirations and fantasies about yourself (Belk, 1988; Roux and Belk, 2018; Thompson et al., 2018).

Box 8.2   Features of semiotic analysis

Themes
Semiotics is the study of signs and their meaning
Focus on semiosis as meaning-making in a given cultural context
Humans are interpreting creatures: the universe is suffused with signs. Semiotics is an inter – and cross-disciplinary field
Important concepts include the sign, icon, index and symbol

Assumptions
The symbolic interpretation of signs is a defining characteristic of human understanding
The relation of sign and signifier is arbitrary: in principle, anything can stand for anything else. It is the cultural context of communication that frames semiotic interpretation

Methods of data gathering
Semiotic studies have often used judgement samples of advertisements or other visual data such as brand logos
The ways in which consumers interpret particular signs could be investigated through focus groups or other qualitative data-gathering techniques

Approach to data analysis
Focus on revealing the semiotic codes that cue particular interpretive strategies in a given context
Any kind of sign can in principle be subject to semiotic analysis such as marketing brand logos, packaging, advertising, the spaces of consumption such as shopping malls, other media texts such as movies, radio jingles, etc.

Themes and concepts of semiotics

There may be many ways in which signs signify (sixty-six for Peirce, according to Mick, 1997, p. 253; also see discussion in Leach, 1976, p. 10). Three particular forms of semiosis are often used as the basis for analysis. These three forms of semiotic relation are not mutually exclusive: they do overlap but nonetheless can be useful organising categories for researchers. That is, a sign can act as an index, a symbol and an icon (see Box 8.2). As an index, the sign points to something: as a symbol, it stands for something, and as an icon, it is identified with something. So, for example, a religious icon such as a status of a holy figure is treated by adherents as if it is holiness manifest in the object: an example of an index could be a silhouette image of a man on a bathroom door, and an example of a symbol could be a Nike Swoosh that stands for the sportswear brand Nike.

Semiosis 'takes place on a boundary of cultural, historical and sociological analysis' (Hackley, 1999, p. 141). This cultural dimension has been neglected in some studies that over-emphasised the individual, private aspect of interpretation and the putatively fixed relation of sign to signifier. As Wernick (1991) has pointed out, many studies of advertising 'eclipsed attention both to the historicity of promotional texts and to their contextual dimension' (p. 25). In other words, our interpretation of signs is culturally mediated. We must learn the cultural codes that predetermine particular modes of interpretation. These cultural codes may be culturally specific and they may change over time, so this is not the same as saying that there can be only one culturally correct interpretation of a sign, since signs and interpretants are necessarily embedded in a given (and highly specific) cultural context.

Dyadic and triadic semiotic relations

The context of interpretation is important because of the differing cultural codes that may be drawn on for interpretive cues in differing cultural contexts. Seen in this light, meaning is something that authors attempt to control or influence, but texts are subject to unpredictable interpretations. Consequently, imposing authorial meaning on the interpretation of a text is a delicate balance and a complex achievement. Advertising agencies that understand this know that they must take great care to isolate the right groups of consumers and to understand them as an 'interpretive community'. Agencies must also create ads that attempt to impose particular meanings in powerfully suggestive but subtle ways by drawing on the semiotic codes that are used within a given interpretive community.

The process of interpretation can be seen as a dyadic or triadic relation. For Peirce, semiosis has a *triadic* character since it depends on a relation between the sign, the object and the interpretant (i.e. the interpretation). This contrasts with du Saussure's ideas about semiosis as a *dyadic* relation between the sign and the signified. As Mick (1986) suggests, the interpretant refers to the interpretation placed on the sign and not to the entity (such as a person) doing the interpreting. The interpretant (interpretation) will vary depending on the cultural context. It will also be influenced by the extent to which its meaning in a particular context is dependent on previous interpretations of the same object.

A dyadic model of semiotic interpretation (Figure 8.1) the sign, and the signified. So, for example, the sign might be an image on a bathroom door, and the signified might be a bathroom designated for males. The sign in this case would be operating as an index (much like a road sign signifying a sharp bend ahead or a speed limit). The sign could also operate as a symbol, as in the aforementioned example of a brand image that consumers have become acculturated into interpreting as the brand. This interpretation of course is culturally and historically specific. The Nazi symbol of the swastika existed for perhaps thousands of years as an East Asian symbol of peace and religious piety before Adolf Hitler appropriated it, and for many people today it can only signify the Nazi party. Finally, an iconic sign, such as a religious symbol, signifies the religion or piacular aspects of it.

The variability of interpretive possibilities is perhaps easier to conceptualise using Pierce's triadic model of semiotic interpretation. For example, some years ago, the Skoda motor car brand first entered the UK market,

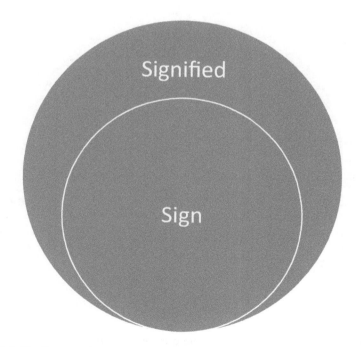

Figure 8.1 Du Saussure's dyadic model of semiotic interpretation

it was portrayed in UK advertising as a cheap alternative to mainstream brands. However, negative reports about the car's reliability and engineering quality resulted in media stories and jokes in the UK that poked fun at the brand. The Skoda brand and its associated signs (the word-sign Skoda and the brand badge on the cars) were interpreted in terms of a communicative code that denigrated the brand. However, a reorganisation of the brand, re-engineering of the car and a re-launch with new advertising changed this code in the UK. The Skoda brand signs are now interpreted much more positively because of favourable quality reports in motor trade magazines and generally positive media coverage. The advertising campaign intertextually (and humorously) referred to Skoda's old negative image so that people bought into the new interpretation of Skoda. The relation between the object (Skoda motor cars), its various signs (the word-sign 'Skoda', the brand badge, the advertising) and the interpretant (the interpretive reaction the sign elicited) changed as a result of a change in cultural understanding. For people to understand the new meaning of Skoda from the new advertising, they had to understand the references the ads made to the old meaning of Skoda. The interpretation of the Skoda band signs changed as a result of consumers' exposure to contradictory signs in the media.

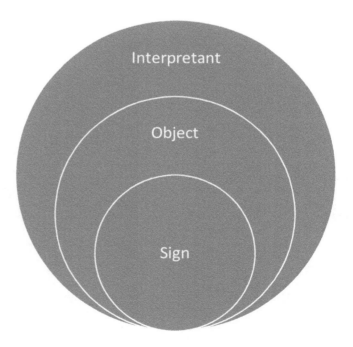

Figure 8.2 Pierce's triadic model of semiotic interpretation

Doing semiotics

As evidenced by the published work cited above, semiotics can be a useful approach in empirical research studies that seek insights into the arbitrary and culturally mediated character of human understanding in communication. It is particularly so when the research data set includes pictures or other kinds of visual image, such as advertising images. However, many other contexts of consumption could be useful areas for semiotic research, as long as the aim of the study is to uncover meanings and their relation to signs.

Practical semiotics entails the deconstruction of meaning in given contexts. In semiotics as with all interpretive research the obvious, everyday and taken for granted must be made strange and unfamiliar. The object of the researcher is to understand the complexity and arbitrariness of taken-for-granted modes of meaning-making. To do this, researchers have to try to understand the world view of particular groups while also standing outside those groups. This is precisely because much of our everyday understanding is unreflexive. We are not aware of the assumptions and cultural knowledge that are built into our common-sense, subjective understanding. The task

---

Box 8.3   An approach to semiotic deconstruction

Questions to ask:	What does X signify to me?
	Why does X signify this to me?
	What might X signify for others?
	Why might X signify this for others?
Possible sources of X:	
Objects (visual semiosis)	For example, clothes, hairstyles, make-up styles, the ways objects are used by people, use in press ads of printed copy, typeface, use of logo/pictorial symbolic image, the spatial inter-relationships of objects
Gesture (bodily semiosis)	For example, body types, facial types, expressive gestures, facial expressions, posture, gaze, juxtaposition of bodies, juxtaposition of bodies with products
Speech (verbal semiosis)	For example, use of idiomatic expressions, regional or national accent or dialect, use of metaphor/metonymy, tone and volume of speech, pace of delivery, use of voiceover, use of humour, emphasis on particular words/ phonemes

of the social researcher is to go beyond the taken for-granted to speculate on its implications. As a starting-point for semiotic analysis of advertising, the check-list in Box 8.3 is offered, adapted from Hackley (1999), p. 145. This is an informal framework for beginning to think like a semiotician – if students and researchers wish to conduct more advanced studies they might like to refer to the frameworks in one of the cited works in this chapter, for example the semiotic square is used as a framework for analysis in several studies (e.g. Kozinets, 2008; Humphreys, 2010; Williams Bradford and Sherry, 2015).

This check-list is designed to help student researchers to deepen their semiotic analysis of visual material such as advertising. Many first-time researchers find that beginning the process of deconstruction of an advertisement is difficult. Until one acquires the habit of deconstruction, meanings can appear to have a 'given' and 'common-sense' character. Box 8.3 focuses on specific aspects of an advertisement. If the student researcher can begin to understand the complexity of apparently simple advertisements as 'strings of signs', then he or she has taken a step towards deconstructing the way in which an advertisement seeks to tap into particular cultural codes of communication in order to frame and privilege particular interpretations over others. The way in which advertising semiosis occurs can be spontaneous and unreflexive: we take for granted the meanings that we read into symbols. Without careful reflection it is easy to overlook the mechanics of semiosis.

Semiotics, and literary theory more generally, offer social researchers ways of understanding marketing and consumer culture that generate very different types of insight to the ones generated by quantitative and positivistic research studies. Literary concepts are well suited to qualitative research studies and student researchers are urged to look into some of the published studies cited in this short introduction to this rich area of research.

Glossary

Narrative   The organisation of writing or language to portray accounts of events in a way, which seems sequential and connected.

Polysemy   A message or entity is said to be polysemic if it displays not one but many possible meanings.

Dyadic   Relation with two dimensions, as when one interviewer interviews one interviewee (a dyadic interview).

Icon   A sign that is similar in some ways to its referent, in the way that a photograph bears a resemblance to the image it portrays, or an onomatopoeic word resembles a sound, such as in 'plop' or 'roar'.

Index   A form of semiosis in which a sign points to or indicates something else, such as where the word 'TAXI' lights up on the top of a yellow car.

Interpretant   The entity (usually human) that interprets the sign. The word 'interpretant' is also used to refer to the interpretation.

Semiology   The study of linguistic signs and their relation to concepts.

Semiosis   The process of semiotic interpretation.

Semiotics   The study of signs and their interpretation.

Sign   For C.S. Peirce, a sign is anything that can stand for something else.

Structuralist   The term is often used in social research to imply a realist ontology. That is, explanations for social phenomena can reveal universal structures of meaning that underlie social processes.

Symbol   A form of semiosis in which something acts as a symbol of something else, such as when a clenched fist symbolises aggression.

Triadic   A relation with three dimensions, e.g. in Peirce's model of semiosis with sign, object and interpretant.

Notes

1 http://lnu.diva-portal.org/smash/record.jsf?pid=diva2%3A1095759&dswid=-402

2 https://pdfs.semanticscholar.org/8b8a/3b9a47eb948866b75c03727493c3eac9970a.pdf

Chapter 9

Critical research

Power, ethnicity, gender

Chapter outline

Research in the interpretive research paradigm is sometimes accused of lacking a critical edge. In this chapter we review the idea of critical research in the light of traditions of critical management studies and critical marketing. The chapter discusses the meanings of criticality in research and examines how critical perspectives on power, gender and ethnicity can be incorporated into qualitative research projects.

Chapter objectives

After reading this chapter students will be able to

- explain some of the key aims and values of critical social research
- understand distinctions between the colloquial usage of the word 'critical' and the more specific usages associated in research
- critically discuss issues of power in social research in relation to ethnicity and gender

The aims of 'critical' research

The idea of 'critical' intellectual work has been introduced earlier in the book. In this chapter we examine the notion of the critical in a different sense to simply meaning intellectually and critically engaged. As we noted earlier in the book, in many management texts the word 'critical' is used as a synonym for 'important', as in 'marketing is a critical business function'. In educational contexts, 'critical' intellectual work refers to a deep engagement with the subject matter, an uncompromising examination of the assumptions of any given point of view or theory, and an independent stance that acknowledges that versions of the truth in social science may serve particular interests more than others. In this sense all research writing should have a critical dimension since it should rigorously evaluate the intellectual and moral grounds for claims. Intellectual work that is critical in this sense engages with the explicit and implicit assumptions of any given research perspective.

In social research, 'critical' can have a much more specific meaning focusing on structural and constitutive power (introduced earlier in the book) and its implications for individuals and groups. Critical research in this sense engages with the inequalities and inequities of class, ethnicity and gender. The theoretical stance, though, from which critical studies engage with their subject matter can differ. For many researchers, 'critical' research implies a particular theoretical stance that is informed by Marxist theorists such as Horkheimer and Adorno (1944) and the 'Frankfurt school' of writers and developed by writers such as Althusser (1971). Critical historical sociology (e.g. Foucault, 1977) has also been an important influence. In marketing, management and consumer research, critical research traditions have been invoked with two broad aims. One has been to contribute to an intellectually viable management education agenda that moves away from 'how to' consulting prescriptions and develops the wider critical intellectual awareness of managers, students and researchers.

A second, connected aim has been to promote a more fundamental and far-reaching reappraisal of the aims, methods and ideologies of both management education and organisational practice (e.g. Tadajewski et al., 2019, 2014; Ellis et al., 2011; Tadajewski and Maclaran, 2009; Maclaran et al., 2007; Hackley, 2009a, b). From a managerial perspective, critical theorists point out that much management theory is inherently *ideological* in character and this tends to place limits on the intellectual scope of representations of theory in the field. One argument is that one cannot faithfully evaluate the use or truth of a theory or model unless one asks whose interests are served by this particular form of representation. From a broader ethical standpoint, critical theorists seek to critically reappraise the ways in which practice and representation impose narrow values and reproduce narrow interests. Critical research questions the moral conduct of organisational marketing and management and attempts to put forward alternative agenda from the point of view of less powerful parties, i.e. consumers, citizens and employees. For example, Henderson et al. (2016) examine the extent to which inequalities and inequities are reproduced through consumption, while Foster Davis (2018) explores race in the 'whiteness' of the marketing research canon. There are academic initiatives that examine racism in academia and academic research (e.g. 'Race in the Marketplace',[1] in the USA, and Gabriel and Tate, 2017, in the UK) that have emerged as part of wider attention being given to racism in society (e.g. Eddo-Lodge, 2018; Akala, 2019). Critical gender studies have also begun to appear in marketing and consumer research literature (e.g. Martin et al., 2006; Bettany et al., 2010; Enck and Morrissey,

2015; Thompson and Ustunier, 2015), including some major edited works (Dobscha, 2019). Such work reappraises how assumptions about race and gender are often institutionalised in the values and priorities of academia and research, and these works seek to reveal the inherent inequalities and inequities of power that result. A central aim of critical research is to pick apart the assumptions and values underlying world views, so that prevailing power relations are not uncritically reproduced by and for researchers and the users of research, but, rather, are revealed and held up to critical examination.

Critical perspectives in management research are by no means new, but there has been a renewed awareness and scope of the role race, class and gender play in constituting power relations through academic research, writing and teaching. Older work that began the critical perspective in management areas includes Hirschman and Stern's (1994) work on women as commodities in prostitution, while Alvesson and Deetz (2000), Alvesson and Willmott (1992) and Murray and Ozanne (1991) (see also Murray et al., 1994) were amongst those who established the critical (as opposed to the managerial) perspective in management and consumer research respectively. Alvesson and Deetz (2000) draw attention to the common ground between interpretive and critical research and suggest that critical perspectives can often usefully be conjoined with interpretive approaches, such as ethnography and discourse analysis. They cite critical ethnography (Thomas, 1993) as a useful approach and offer examples of work that have combined ethnographic principles with varied data-gathering approaches such as direct observation and interviewing to powerful effect as with Kunda (1992). Critical research, like interpretive research, tends to focus on the particular rather than the general. It is situational in that its main concern is to conduct micro-sociological studies of power in a given organisational or other context, but which also connect to wider discourses and ideologies of structural power. In the discussion and analysis of such studies it may sometimes be possible to go beyond the particular social context to trace the historical and cultural origins of a particular form of social relations or interactional practices, such as where local asymmetries of power result from a history of class relations.

Marketing, it is generally accepted, has a less well-developed critical tradition than some other management fields. Arguably this may be because the marketing management point of view is widely accepted and propagated as an ideology heavily informed by consulting and other financial interests. In addition, the case method and its un-critical managerial aims have become heavily identified with marketing research and education. In other words, the marketing 'philosophy' and attendant concepts are often put forward as unquestionable organisational and managerial virtues the sole aim of which is to support managerial and organisational goals (e.g. Brownlie et al., 1999; Hackley, 2001, 2003b, c, 2009a).

The critical research 'stance'

Language and power in critical research

Critical research, broadly conceived, can be characterised by a number of priorities and precepts. In this introduction one particularly important precept deserves special mention. This is the position that language is assumed to be *constitutive* in the sense that it constructs, or constitutes, its objects. That is, language does not merely refer to entities and concepts like 'marketing' or 'management': it actively constructs them. This 'linguistic turn' in (critical and interpretive) research (O'Shaughnessy and Holbrook, 2015; Alvesson and Kärreman, 2000) is reflected in a concern with language, texts, discourse and narrative in research approaches. Because of this concern with language and representation, interpretive approaches to social research in management fields fit particularly well with critical analyses.

Critical research in marketing and management does not focus solely on the managerial problems of how to do marketing/management more effectively. Rather, it focuses on the ways in which language is used to construct marketing/management phenomena. Large, global commercial organisations, in whose name much academic business research is conducted, are powerful entities. An important part of their power lies in the ability to define what is normal, taken-for-granted, and of value, through their communications and influence. It is this power that is placed under scrutiny in critical research. This does not necessarily mean that critical research is anti-capitalist or anti-organisations, although much critical social research is indeed critical of neo-liberal aspects of capitalism (e.g. Felix and Fuat Firat, 2019; Zwick, 2018; Khare and Varman, 2017; Varman et al., 2011; Tadajewski et al., 2014; Schöps et al., 2019). Critical research acknowledges a political reality, that is, the interests of large commercial organisations, reflected in the values of university research, may not always coincide with those of citizens, consumers or employees.

Critical research practices

Critical research is not a method but an intellectual approach to social studies. The intellectual criticality that is the benchmark of excellent academic work is taken to its next logical step when not only does the researcher examine the deep assumptions that underlie taken-for-granted values and priorities, but also examines the social and cultural conditions that led to those deep assumptions becoming taken-for-granted. The critical researcher does not settle for easy, conventional or superficial explanations but 'unpacks' concepts and develops a reflexive dialogue with the reader. This is accomplished by using the research data (whether primary or secondary) as material to develop lines of discussion, argument and investigation that do not simply accept the apparent order of things but question it in order to reveal obscured relations of power and control. Box 9.1 below is necessarily over-simplified but attempts to capture some of the major concepts and practices of critical qualitative research studies.

Qualitative data sets are often the basis for critical empirical research studies. However, the critical stance applies to the interpretive strategies and representational practices that the researcher brings to their objects of study, regardless

---

Box 9.1   Some key features of critical research

Themes
Power; discourse and language; ideology; emancipation; class; gender; race; history

Assumptions
Social constructionist or critical realist ontologies
Language actively constitutes its objects, it does not merely refer to them
Social relations are infused with power: social structures and institutions exercise deep influence over the ways in which people talk, think and feel
Agency is strictly constrained by social structures and institutions
Indeed, a sense of agency may be illusory if people have simply internalised values and norms that reflect asymmetrical relations of power
This sense of agency may unwittingly serve narrow interests rather than self-interest, for example in some management initiatives to 'empower' workers that in fact do the opposite
'Normality' and 'common sense' are taken-for-granted as are the values of things that are produced in social life under the influence of social structures and institutions that have a historical basis
Critical perspectives are thought to have moral force as they might generate practical change and individual liberation

Methods of data gathering
Qualitative, naturalistic, ethnographic, phenomenological, observational

Approach to data analysis
Interpretive approaches (such as critical discourse analysis) are used to draw categories, metaphors and other themes from data. These are used to develop lines of discussion that seek to generate insights into the ways in which interests and values are reproduced in 'normal' and 'everyday' interactional practices, as in Critical Discourse Analysis

---

of whether the study includes quantitative or qualitative data sets, or both. The critical perspective informs research design but can also be applied in the literature reviewing and analysis/discussion aspects of any research study.

Social critique, discourse and power

Researchers familiar with the work of the Frankfurt school of political/economic theorists understand critical research as a more radical approach than one that demonstrates (only) intellectual values. For those researching in the Frankfurt school tradition it is capitalism itself in its many forms that is the object of critique. Capitalist *discourses* are considered to be repressive in the sense that they exclude and rule out ways of talking, thinking and being that may be more fulfilling of human potential. Discourses of marketing (that is, ways of talking and writing about marketing) are said to reproduce structures of control and domination, especially the domination of corporations and allied political and governmental institutions over the social and psychological life of citizens. Critical social research, then, has a role in revealing, through critique, how these structures of domination are reproduced in everyday working and consumer life. By so doing, critical research aims to create discursive space for resistance, thereby making possible a form of *emancipation* (Murray and Ozanne, 1991). Critical perspectives aim to promote a reflexive awareness of how language and discourse construct particular relations, subjectivities and ways of being and working.

Much managerial research is decidedly non-critical in the sense that it seeks to provide organisational managers with solutions to business and policy problems based on the blanket assumption that what is good for organisations, managers and shareholders is necessarily good for individual citizens, social groups and societies. It reproduces a social order assuming it to be a natural, unquestionable thing. The authority of managers, the social benefits of organisational marketing and the desirability of ever greater levels of consumption are assumed as given.

Marketing discourse, for example, stands accused of excluding or playing down consideration of other interests such as environmental concerns, gender and race inequities, the ability of citizens to resist the power of corporations, and the legality and fairness of organisational policies and practices (Skålen et al., 2008; Maclaran et al., 2007). Critical research seeks to overturn the apparently 'natural' or 'given' order of things to explore how these have become taken for granted. The aim is to achieve a greater integrity in research by openly revealing the interests bound up with particular ways of knowing and describing. The assumption is that all representations of knowledge are political in the sense that they serve some interests more closely than others.

Ideology and critical research

Ideology is a central concept in critical social research and cultural studies (Eagleton, 2007), including critical marketing (Marion, 2006; Hackley, 2009b; Patterson and Elliott, 2002; Elliott and Ritson, 1997; Tadajewski, 2014). Althusser (1971) broadened the Marxist notion of ideology as a system of *structural power* by drawing attention to its *constitutive power* to form *subjectivities*. He suggested that social institutions such as schools, religions, the law and the media perpetuate values, practices and interests that serve the state in ways which become so taken for granted that they form our very subjective system of values and presuppositions, and hence inform our thought and behaviour in subtle and penetrating ways. Edgar and Sedgwick (1999) suggest that the word 'ideology' derived from French educational philosophy that associated ideas with some underlying cause in biological, social or material conditions. Napoleon ridiculed the *idéologues* and ideology became a pejorative term. For Marx, ideology referred to the ideas of the economic ruling class that invariably became the accepted way of seeing the world.

In later social theory, ideology becomes a more subtle notion that manifests in the micro-practices of everyday life and is continually reconstructed and renegotiated through social practice and interaction. Ideology does not refer to a delusion or untruth, as it did for Marx. In contemporary social research ideology cannot be counterposed to an absolute truth of which it is a distortion. Ideological beliefs are simply part of the socially constructed world of ideas that reflect differing perspectives. Hirschman (1993) adopts Eagleton's (2007)[2] definition of ideology in her investigation of the influence of masculine ideology in consumer research. Ideology refers to the ways in which a 'world-view or value-and-belief system of a particular class or group of people' (Hirschman, 1993, p. 538) is reproduced through certain kinds of representational strategy, particular writing tropes, metaphors and styles being a primary form of ideological representation in marketing (Hackley, 2003c).

The notion of ideology is sometimes used in marketing, management and consumer research to refer broadly to sets of ideas and implied relations that have become taken for granted. Since ideas are always political in the sense that they emerge from particular sets of historical circumstances, they may serve interests that are not immediately apparent. The use of the term ideology in social research does not necessarily have pejorative implications even though it is often used in a highly critical context. Alvesson and Deetz (2000) note that academics in management studies are often viewed as ideologists (p. 84) in that 'they serve dominant groups through socialization in business schools, support managers with ideas and vocabularies for cultural – ideological control at the workplace level, and provide an aura of science to support the introduction and use of managerial domination techniques'.

While Alvesson and Deetz (2000) do not intend this as a compliment, many management academics suggest that they are entirely satisfied with the role of ideologist in university business schools, promoting pro-business values as a good in and of itself. Prominent researchers in marketing who claim no critical agenda readily concede that marketing is ideological in character (e.g. Brownlie et al., 2013; Deshpandhe, 1999; Gronhaug, 2000).

Ideology critique in organisational management

In critical organisational research, ideology critique focuses on 'worker's self – understanding of experience' (Alvesson and Deetz, 2000, p. 83, citing Gramsci, 1971; Burawoy, 1979). Workers, a category into which most of us fall one way or another whether we are a CEO, an intern or a managerial trainee, articulate the experience of being a worker in ways which reflect the ideological norms we have assimilated. In business schools and through our reading of popular texts we may have absorbed ideas as if they are taken for granted. These ideas inform our preconceptions and values which, in turn, underlie our values and behaviour as workers. An important thing to note regarding the comment on 'self-understanding' is that it is the subjectivity of workers that is formed by ideology. That is, as workers we deeply internalise particular values because we accept the assumption that they are consistent with our own interests. In this sense, ideology critique attempts to dig deep into our 'self-understanding' as workers to see where our internalised values came from and to recover the implications these have for our subjective sense of identity and personal realisation.

As an example, it has been suggested that marketing management students are used to assimilating sets of ideas that are presented in many introductory texts as unquestionable and ethically neutral. Marketing students and managers often feel that the marketing curriculum produced through popular texts consists of ethically neutral problem-solving techniques and practical concepts (Hackley, 2009b). These techniques and concepts are presented as if they are in the interests of all: marketing activity creates wealth for society, promotes opportunity and growth for individuals and corporations, and confers expertise and privilege on the managers (and academics) who learn and espouse them.

However, these ideas can be seen in an entirely different light. For some critical commentators, managerial-(ist) social research tends to be loaded with un-stated presuppositions and lacks intellectual rigor. Such work tends to reproduce, rather than challenge and expose, narrow interests and relations of power that serve certain consulting and corporate interests at the expense of other groups. Marketing management concepts are derived from particular historical conditions. They emerged during a huge rise in wealth in Western Europe and North America after the Second World War. They were popularised by a growing group of management 'gurus' with origins in business consulting. Many of these gurus then took their ideas into the academic world as business schools became established in universities. Through publishing and the huge growth in interest in marketing studies (Hackley, 2009b) these ideas became widely accepted as authoritative and taken for granted. Marketing management assumed the characteristics of an ideology that is perpetuated through the use of particular rhetorical strategies (Hackley, 2003; and see also Meamber and Venkatesh, 1995; Firat, 1985; Firat and Venkatesh, 1995a; Furusten, 1999).

Whether or not marketing management ideas are managerially useful, socially beneficial or intellectually sustainable is not the main issue here. The suggestion that they are ideological in character has implications for how they are judged as intellectual products. It also has implications for how we understand the ways in which people draw on marketing and management discourses to account for and justify events and practices in the contexts of work, management and consumption and social policy. Of course, how they are judged as intellectual products may well, in turn, have implications for how people view their managerial usefulness and social value.

Constructing managerial authority in organisations

Critical research normally assumes a social constructionist ontology. That is, it assumes that social life is constructed in interaction through language and social practice. Interaction and social practice are, in turn, framed by the context given by social structures and institutions (Askegaard and Linnet, 2011). Our power to act freely and in our own interest in local interactions is constrained by social realities of economics, social class, gender, ethnicity, education and other social structures and institutions. The social constructionist ontology implies that there is an important distinction between two kinds of power. On the one hand there is *structural power*: structural power derives from a particular arrangement of social institutions and allows certain individuals to demand co-operation from others. Structural power is wielded by those who have legal authority, such as legally sanctioned officials like police, customs and immigration agents and so on, those that have organisationally sanctioned power such as managers who have authority to fire or sanction junior staff, or those with authority invested in them by custom and practice, such as teachers or, in some cultures, parents. Constitutive power, on the other hand, is a more subtle concept, since it alludes to the ways in which power is manifest in and through language in interaction in ways that are not necessarily obvious or explicit.

To offer an example, a manager might have structural power over an employee because they can impose sanctions for non-compliance on that employee, such as pay deductions, the denial of promotion opportunities or disciplinary action. However, it might be the case that the employee is better educated than the manager and is a member of the social class of more senior managers even though they do not hold that rank in the organisation. In such circumstances it may be difficult for the manager to negotiate their authority against the background of class superiority that frames interaction with the subordinate. In the UK, as in other countries, some people who have been educated in elite institutions can convey this confidence through their speech and manner, and some people who have a less prestigious and/or wealthy background can sometimes feel intimidated by such displays of social status. One could also assume that BAME (Black and Ethnic Minority) managers who are promoted to their positions may sometimes find that white subordinates undermine their authority, or that national citizens undermine the authority of promoted non-nationals, and so on. Even legal structural power can be undermined by the social institutions of race, ethnicity and class.

Managerial authority is sometimes regarded as a given, a taken-for-granted aspect of organisational life. Books such as *In Search of Excellence* (Peters and Waterman, 1982) have shown management in a powerful light as the class of worker that can make or break an organisation through their skills of analysis, leadership and problem-solving. Other academic studies have shown management in a different light, as a group of people trying to cope with enormous organisational pressures in difficult circumstances (Watson, 1994); still other studies have shown how the idea of managerial power is itself highly questionable (Munro, 1997). Some studies have suggested that managerial power within some organisations can be seen as a discursive effect produced not by explicit sanctions and rewards but by expropriating certain forms of language and imposing certain values on employees (Hackley, 2000). At the centre of managerial marketing is the marketing mix, the idea that marketing managers hold the key to organisational success through their judicious use of the four Ps of Product, Price, Place (distribution channels) and Promotion (Kotler, 1967). This ideology of marketing management retains considerable influence in marketing education, yet, the marketing manager is seldom if ever in control of these variables in real organisations, notwithstanding the highly simplistic framing of the marketing task that the mix implies (Brownlie and Saren, 1992). The marketing manager is given a heroic status in managerial marketing texts (Hackley, 2003b) that does not square with organisational reality.

Constitutive power, then, refers to the ways in which power is manifest in particular ways of talking and acting that have historical, social and cultural origins. A particular manager might, say, wear a dark lounge suit to work and exhort the workforce to be more 'customer-facing'. The lounge suit carries with it overtones of authority because of its class-based history. In many countries the suit (still) signifies membership of a non-manual class of workers that has access to education and wealth. A manager might feel that he or she would be taken less seriously if he or she wore casual clothing to work (although this convention is increasingly challenged today). Language is another important rhetorical aspect in constructing managerial authority. Invoking management buzz-phrases such as 'customer-facing' or 'customer-focused' has become a particularly powerful resource for managers to extract compliance from workers in organisations. The jargon of managers is important in producing managerial authority since it can imply that managers have technical knowledge and, therefore, hold power over subordinates. Much management jargon also implies that individual action is part of a collective enterprise that cannot be questioned. If a call-centre worker is disciplined for not being sufficiently 'customer-sensitive', it can be very difficult for them to defend such charges because the notion of being 'customer-sensitive' is so widely accepted as an unquestioned virtue in itself. Managers have the power to define exactly what terms like this mean in terms of behaviours in the organisational context.

Gender studies and feminism in research

Research into gender studies and feminism has a well-established record of publications in consumer research going back many years (e.g. Stern, 1993; Hirschman, 1993; Hirschman and Stern, 1994; Catterall et al., 2001). For example, the extent to which marketing images mediate the construction of gender has been one recurring topic of gender research (Patterson and Elliott, 2002; Schroeder and Borgerson, 2015; Borgerson and Schroeder, 2018), as have feminist perspectives on management (Martin, 2004) and marketing, reflected, for example, in several major research collections (e.g. Dobscha, 2019; Catterall et al., 2000; Maclaran, 2012, 2015; Hearn and Hein, 2015).

A major concern of such research is the way that social identity formation and relations of gender are informed by marketed images (Schroeder and Borgerson, 2015; Borgerson and Schroeder, 2018) and values. Marketing is a pervasive influence in developed economies. Do the values and norms implicit in marketing activity reproduce particular relations of power and domination? For example, do magazine images reproduce male dominance as a norm? (Patterson and Elliott, 2002). Much consumption is visual, in the sense that we 'consume' marketed images on a vast scale in advertising, packaging, movies and other media replete with marketing imagery, yet the practices of visual consumption are still under-theorised and the visual remains relatively under-recognised in research (Schroeder, 2002). However, visual imagery offers a fruitful source of material for research. For example, some student researchers have found that, by analysing the visual imagery and/or editorial content in popular magazines over a period of time, they have been able to develop critical analyses of gender representations in such magazines. This might entail a focus on the portrayal of gender relations, or a focus solely on the construction of ideologies of masculinity or femininity in media representations.

Interpretive analysis of gender representation has to engage at some level with the issue of power when the researcher asks why certain forms of representation are popular or prevalent and others are not. For example, Alvesson (1998) studied the ways in which gender relations were produced through the discourse of an advertising agency. Workplaces are important sites in the play of gender relations. Issues of equal opportunities and the 'glass ceiling' phenomenon of male-dominated promotion procedures can be investigated through such gender-based research perspectives.

Researchers could employ a phenomenological approach in seeking to understand the experience of gender, race or class in the workplace, as Gabriel and Tate (2017) did with BAME academics' experience of race in universities. Such autoethnographic accounts of the lived experience of being a member of a minority in white and male dominated institutions generate powerful testimony and give voice to minority views that are often crowded out of mainstream academic discourse. Continuing with racial imbalance but in a very different context, notoriously, the UK and US prison populations have a disproportionately high representation of black and ethnical minority prisoners. In the UK, 13 per cent of the general population identify as non-white, but 27 per cent of the prison population do so (Sturge, 2019). In the USA the disparity is even more striking. Black inmates alone make up almost 40 per cent of the 2 million prison population even though only 13 per cent of the general US population identifies as black.[3] The reasons for these disparities are complex, but can we be sure that marketing does not contribute to the perpetuation of negative racial stereotypes through the images it uses and the values it reinforces? This kind of topic clearly falls within the scope of a critical marketing research project.

Some professions, especially caring professions such as primary school teaching and hospital nursing, are predominantly female occupations, even though most senior medical positions and head teacher positions tend to be occupied by males. Other professions, such as stock broking or civil engineering, are predominantly male. It cannot be denied that progress has been made in race and gender equality in many countries in many fields of employment. Yet, there remains much to be done. Again, it falls to the researcher to ask what is the role of universities, academics and organisational management in perpetuating, or addressing and challenging, negative stereotypes that limit the life chances of individuals? Gender-based studies can elucidate these and many related issues in marketing and management.

The postmodernist critique of marketing 1990–2007

Postmodernist themes (Harvey, 1989) (often linked, or conflated with, poststructuralism) have been singularly influential in developing the critical interpretive stance in marketing and consumer research (Thompson, 2002;

Holt, 1997; Thompson and Tambyah, 1999) and, arguably, remain relevant although perhaps now of mainly historical interest. Firat and Venkatesh (1995a, 1995b), Firat et al. (1995), Featherstone (1991) and Brown (1994, 1995) have each set out themes of postmodernism in consumer research and in marketing respectively. Postmodernism in marketing and consumer research became a label for a set of precepts and positions which, collectively, challenge modernist notions of progress, unity and coherence. Postmodern influences have been important in art, architecture and literature (for a 'genealogy' of post-modernism see Firat and Venkatesh, 1995a, p. 241). Epistemologically, postmodernism indicates a reaction against modernist notions of epistemological unity, objective truth and linear historical progress. Prominent in postmodernist themes is a sense of the fragmentation of meaning into multiple contested meanings (or *'polysemy'*) and a break in the reliance on 'grand narratives' or organising themes that, in previous historical eras, were thought to have ordered social structure and, hence, private thought (Lyotard, 1984). Postmodernist writing often emphasises a 'de-centring' of knowledge so that what might once have been unified, absolute, progressive and consensual is now fragmented, relative, temporally indeterminate and contested. Postmodern writing stands for experimental narrative forms, challenging prose styles and (purportedly) new ideas. It tends to be irreverent and sceptical, questioning norms and challenging convention.

Much postmodern writing remarks on the curious character of marketing institutions such as 'shopping centres, department stores, advertising campaigns, package designs, new product development and the entire consumption experience' (Brown, 1995, p. 8). Indeed, marketing has been identified as the quintessential site of postmodernism (Firat and Venkatesh, 1995a, b). Postmodernist reflections on marketing point to the simulated character of vaunted consumption experiences as in the 'hyperreality' of Disneyland. It indicates the pastiche of differing styles and genres in advertising text and visuals, brand names and product design. For example, 'Retro' design in furniture, popular music and motor cars combines modern styles with classic designs to produce a new effect that rehabilitates the old. The culturally trivial nature of popular marketing phenomena and the privileging of style over substance is also addressed by post-modernist writing that refers, for example, to 'reality' TV shows and 'designer' clothes labels. Postmodern critique in marketing includes Brown et al. (1999) using postmodernism and literary theory to critique gender bias in advertising (also see Stern, 1993), while Üstüner and Holt (2007) referred to postmodern consumer acculturation in their study of poor migrant women living in a Turkish squatter camp. There are few topics that cannot fall within the scope of a critical marketing and consumer research treatment.

In postmodernist writing, the text is a major focus of attention and the media is a major source of texts. Postmodernist writing is often highly critical of conventional practice and beliefs and uses irony to undermine 'grand narratives' of belief and practice. Marketing, a 'narrative project' as noted above, has become part of the media complex with its big-selling text books, web-based resources and video-star management consulting gurus. Not only have marketing phenomena provided a showground for the literary talents of postmodern commentators: marketing writing has itself attracted the critical attention of postmodernists. As noted above, popular marketing writing's relentless progressivism (the drive to universalise marketing orientation) and essentialism (the 'core' concepts of marketing) make it particularly vulnerable to postmodernist critique. Some of the most pungent criticism comes from Brown (1995): 'I don't think marketing has all, or even many, of the answers: I don't think the marketing concept can be applied to everything under the sun . . . and I suspect that . . . marketing theory seems resolutely stuck in a modernist time-warp' (p. 181). The certainties of marketing management texts never seem to change while postmodernism 'reminds us of the reflexive or circular nature of social knowledge, where the very existence of a concept influences and alters the phenomena to which it pertains' (Brown, 1995, p. 178). In mainstream marketing writing, the text refers to a 'real' world of marketing practice that lies beyond the text. Postmodernist and poststructuralist writers indicate that marketing as object is constructed through and by the text. Marketing reality is, therefore, not merely referred to by marketing texts. It is constituted through texts.

Postmodernism and student research projects

While the postmodern tendency in marketing writing is avowedly critical of the verities of mainstream marketing management, it also points to the novel insights and intellectual vigour that can derive from postmodernist perspectives. Nevertheless, from the student researcher's perspective, a postmodern empirical research project is probably a risky undertaking, at least in most university business schools. Empirical postmodern marketing research might be quite implausible, or at least highly problematic (Brown, 1995, p. 172) so the student researcher interested in postmodernism is largely confined to a conceptual project that engages in a postmodern critique of a branch of theory or practice. Postmodernist themes lend themselves aptly to critique of marketing culture and practices, especially writing and other text-based practices. Some of the most penetrating, critical and witty scholarship in the marketing field has been produced under the postmodern brand.

Students considering wading into the swirling waters of postmodernism for their student project would be well advised to discuss this carefully with their supervisor. They should be advised that mention of postmodernism can provoke heated (and heatedly negative) responses from some business school academics. For many academics, postmodernism is a byword for obscurantism, literary self-indulgence, aimlessness and inaction.

Postmodernism loftily critiques everything without having a position itself on anything. Even those student researchers who gain approval for such a project should not congratulate themselves too quickly. They have a difficult task ahead of them. It could also be a rewarding one to the diligent and open-minded student researcher who is prepared to read a large number of difficult books and articles. The researcher could begin by reading some of the texts cited here (especially Brown, 1995). Student researchers can go from there to make their own observations on marketing culture, texts and practices. They can do this from their vantage point as consumers of products and services and aspirants to the status of marketers, and also as consumers of marketing itself.

Mainstream managerial marketing is an example of commodified knowledge that is produced (by management consultants), distributed (by academics, publishers and trainers) and consumed (by all the above plus citizens and students). A critique of one's own experience of consuming marketing education would make a distinctively postmodern research project, although much of the critical marketing work cited in this chapter has now moved beyond using postmodernism as a label. To the extent that postmodernism is, or rather, was, hugely important in inspiring major movements in marketing and consumer research that remain influential, it deserves at least some recognition if only, as mentioned earlier, as a historical note in the development of critical perspectives in the field.

Having looked at some of the major critical research perspectives in marketing, management and consumer research, Chapter 10 turns to one of the major analytical approaches in doing critical research – discourse analysis, also known as critical discourse analysis.

Glossary

Constitutive Language is said to constitute its objects rather than merely refer to them. Language actively constructs the meaning of terms and concepts. In the context of power, constitutive power refers to power that is reproduced in and through particular discourses. Language and discourse are said to actively constitute relations of power and not simply to reflect them. Constitutive power is intrinsic to social interaction.

Conversation analysis Associated with ethnomethodology, conversation analysis takes a minute and detailed interest in the way that everyday interactions are ordered, produced and controlled. It has been widely used in positivistic research to document particular interactions. Topics of study have included the role of pauses in conversations and the negotiation of turn-taking and conversational topics in telephone conversations.

Discourse In common usage, a dialogue between speakers. In interpretive social research 'discourse' means 'that which can be described'; it is a broad term that refers to sets of conventions for talking or thinking about a given object or idea.

Emancipation The critical research stance is that discourses can be repressive. In its moderate form 'emancipation' refers to the critical research aim of promoting reflexive awareness about the ways in which ideologies are formed and reproduced.

Ethnomethodology Refers to an approach to the sociology of everyday life promoted by Harold Garfinkel (1967). It focuses on how participants jointly produce a sense of everyday normality in social life and places great importance on the agency and social competence of individuals. Less emphasis is placed on the influence of social structures and institutions over local interactions and practices.

Managerialist Managerialist research reflects and supports the apparent aims, given assumptions and taken-for-granted priorities and values of organisational managers. It is usually positioned as an attempt to address or solve a managerial 'problem'.

Performative This refers to the distinction between language use as a referring device to indicate objects and concepts and as a social positioning device through which we signal particular motives or claim status. In other words, we *perform* social accomplishments through language and other social practices.

Structural power The power to coerce and gain compliance through the implicit or actual threat of tangible or intangible sanctions. Structural power is extrinsic to social interaction since it reflects power relations that pre-exist a particular interaction.

Subjectivities Subjectivity refers to unreflexive personal consciousness. This subjectivity may appear to be private and unique but can be shown to be socially derived in important respects. We may absorb certain historical, linguistic and cultural practices and ideas so that they intimately form our values and assumptions. We may take these values and assumptions as taken for granted and forget that, in fact, they were learned.

Notes

1 www.rimnetwork.net/aboutus/
2 From Eagleton's 1991 work, an earlier edition of his 2007 work cited in this book
3 www.worldatlas.com/articles/incarceration-rates-by-race-ethnicity-and-gender-in-the-u-s.html

Chapter 10

Discourse analysis

Chapter outline

Discourse analysis is one of the most influential analytical approaches of critical and qualitative research. In this chapter we offer a brief, fairly practical introduction to doing discourse analysis in empirical research. The chapter outlines some of the theoretical principles of discourse analysis, especially the analytical emphasis on structure, function, action-orientation and variation in texts. The chapter concludes with some comments on the commonalities of interpretive approaches to qualitative research.

Chapter objectives

After reading this chapter students will be able to,

- outline the main theoretical influences in discourse analysis
- list the key assumptions in discourse analysis
- conduct a discourse analysis of text as part of an empirical study

Discourse, language and interaction

Discourse analysis focuses on the ways in which we construct our sense of social reality through language in interaction. Language is a major feature of discourse, but the term 'discourse' can refer to other interactional and representational practices in addition to language. 'Discourse' is referred to as 'a system of statements that construct an object' (Parker, 1992, p. 5). 'Discourse' is also described as anything that can be described, and hence can be represented as text; it therefore refers to both speech and writing (Stubbs, 1983). It is regarded by some authors as a broader concept still, referring to all genres in which someone 'organizes language to an audience' (Benveniste, 1971, p. 208). In its non-technical sense discourse refers simply to conversation.

Discourse has become an important concept in marketing and consumer research (Thompson and Haytko, 1997; Thompson and Hirschman, 1995), particularly in analyses of constitutive power (Thompson, 2004). We draw on discourses or ways of speaking and writing about certain things, to articulate our experience and account for our actions and beliefs. These discourses, or ways of speaking and writing about certain things, become conventional, that is, taken-for-granted after a time. Foucault (1977) drew attention to the ideological character of discourses, meaning that particular discourses emerged under historical conditions and reflect relations of power that are then reproduced constitutively when the discourse becomes normalised and taken-for-granted.

The use of the term discourse in interpretive and critical social research implies that it is considered to be a central concept in understanding social, and also psychological, organisation. Discourses are ways of organising, describing and talking about certain events or things. They can be drawn upon by individuals to make sense of the world and to account for actions or events. We might also draw on certain discourses or 'ways of talking about' things to produce a sense of normality. We might adapt discourses to form our own strategies of social positioning and identity formation in local contexts. Studies of discourse focus on language as a major feature of constitutive social interaction.

The scope of discourse analytic research

The possible subjects of discourse analysis are as varied as the theoretical influences. The ways in which marketing managers construct their professional identity and work experiences through discourse have been studied by Ardley and Quinn (2014), Ellis and Hopkinson, 2010). Humphreys (2010) conducted a discourse analytic study of newspaper coverage of gambling and tracked its putative influence on the legitimacy of gambling. Moufahim et al. (2007) and Lim and Moufahim (2011) have studied the discourse of populist politics, while Ybema et al. (2009) used discourse analysis to explore how organisational identities are worked up using discursive strategies, as have Ellis et al. (2012). Ritson and Elliott (1999) combined discourse analysis with ethnography to study the ways in which school age adolescents produced a sense of identity within their group through their discourses about advertisements. As with most of the qualitative methods in this book, discourse analysis lends itself well to multi-method studies in combination with other intellectual traditions, including ethnography, critical theory and phenomenology/existentialism. As a method of textual analysis, discourse analysis is essentially a thematic analysis of texts that is informed and guided by specific theoretical principles.

Discourse theory is operationalised in qualitative research through discourse analysis. Discourse analysis has been a significant development in organisational sociology (Fairclough, 1985, 2010) and management research (Rod and Ellis, 2014; Ellis and Hopkinson, 2010; Alvesson et al., 2008; Morgan, 1992; Burawoy, 1979) as well as in marketing and consumer research (Elliott, 1996; Roux and Belk, 2018; Moufahim et al., 2007; Lim and Moufahim, 2011; van Laer and Izberk-Bilgin, 2019). The techniques of discourse analysis may differ, but the notion of 'discourse' and the associated focus on the role of language and social practice in constructing social reality has become widely employed in critical marketing and management studies (e.g. Morgan, 1992). Critical discourse analysis is seen as part of the poststructuralist movement in its focus on language and discourse as a site of contest and negotiation. Unlike postmodernism, poststructuralism can provide powerful techniques for empirical research through deconstruction (Stern, 1993) critical ethnography and critical discourse analysis (Elliott and Ritson, 1997). Hackley et al. (2011) used discourse analysis in a study of young people's alcohol consumption practices, with reference to the influence of marketing and the public policy implications.

Discourse, then, refers broadly to the ways in which certain relations and phenomena are constituted through the ways in which they are represented in text and talk. Critical analyses of the discourses of marketing have been conducted applying differing intellectual traditions. For example, Skålén et al. (2008) conducted a critical discourse analytic study adapting Foucauldian influences, and Mautner (2016) has conducted extensive discourse analytic studies of marketing and consumption phenomena from a linguistics disciplinary perspective. Cook (2001) also used linguistics as a point of departure for a study of the discourse of advertisements. Hackley (2000) studied the discourse of advertising work in ad agencies using a version of discourse analysis adapted from qualitative social psychology (Potter and Wetherell, 1987; critical perspective in Burman and Parker, 1993; see van Dijk, 1984, 1985). Potter and Wetherell's (1987) social psychological version of discourse analysis is informed to varying degrees by other research traditions including *ethnomethodology*, semiotics and *conversation analysis*. Svensson (2007) and Alvesson (1998) also studied the discourses of advertising work, but from a more critically informed perspective.

Critical Discourse Analysis (CDA)

Foucauldian influences have been important in framing the use of the concept of discourse in management and organisation studies. Fairclough's (2010, 2014) critical discourse analysis (CDA) is probably the most influential version of discourse in organisational research, drawing on Foucauldian influences. For Foucault (1977), discourses embrace all the presuppositions, historically derived rules and institutions and social practices that make certain forms of representation possible (Mills, 1997). In this poststructuralist sense, discourses are the preconditions for everyday knowledge. The task of the critical researcher is to critically interrogate and unravel social phenomena so that the preconditions for their production become apparent. In other words, the task is to see how particular ways of seeing the world become accepted and 'normal'. Outside management research, a focus on discourse has been used in ideology critique to explore, for example, how a particular scholarly discipline ('oriental studies') consolidated certain ways of understanding and thinking about colonialism (Said, 1978). Foucault (1977) famously explored the ways in which certain social groups acquired and sustained their own power over others by defining the terms of normality. 'Discursive closure' (Deetz, 1992) occurs where a given and accepted way of expressing things excludes or closes off alternatives. In this way particular discourses can be powerful in perpetuating particular ways of seeing the world. The idea of discourse, then, in ideology critique, becomes closely linked to ideology (Gramsci, 1971) in that discourses act as vehicles for the reproduction of and perpetuation of, ideological norms.

Discourse is an important feature of the organisation of individual psychology because of the link between structural power in society and its constitutive manifestations in individual subjectivity. In other words, the ideological force of particular discourses leads us to internalise them unreflexively. Through our language and interactional practices, we may feel that we are asserting our individual sense of agency and realising our own 'personality' when in fact we are drawing on historically derived discourses that reproduce the power of other groups and sustain our own relative powerlessness (Edwards and Potter, 1992). Discourse analysis seeks to recover this sense of the history of certain forms of discourse as well as revealing the detailed process of how social life is produced in local contexts.

Doing discourse analysis: structure, function and variation in social texts

A social text such as a transcript of a depth interview or a set of written documents can be analysed for these three characteristics: structure, function and variation (see Figure 10.1). With regard to *structure*, the text is likely to display features that seem to recur. A person talking may use particular strategies of accounting for events and actions, particular metaphors, tropes of speech, grammatical techniques or tone of voice that become evident on reading and re-reading the text. The same may be true of any kind of text: there are likely to be structural regularities of some kind, whether these are stylistic, thematic or grammatical. Very often such structural characteristics are not evident on first listening or reading but become so after the text has been reflected upon and re-read over a period of time.

Once a text has been analysed for structural regularities the researcher needs to reflect upon what rhetorical purpose they may serve, that is, what is their *function*. This is also sometimes called 'action-orientation' and refers

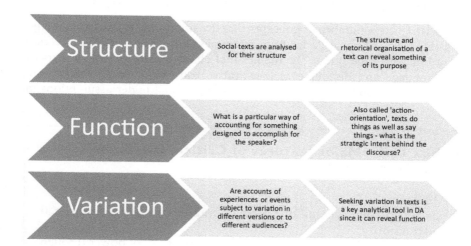

Figure 10.1 Structure, function and variation in discourse analysis of social texts

to the performativity of words and text, the fact that representation is characterised by strategic motive as well as content. The idea of function in discourse reflects a tradition of linguistic philosophy that took as axiomatic the idea that words do not merely refer to concepts or things, they *do* things as well (Austin, 1962). Language has a *performative* role in this sense. As ethnomethodological researchers seek to show, speakers seek to accomplish certain social effects by their speech. If I am lecturing a class, I want to engage their interest by referring to theories and practices in my field. However, I also have to accomplish a professional role, that of lecturer. To this end I have to try to sound plausible as an academic researcher and lecturer. Performative speech-acts can also take tactical forms, such as when you ask someone a question not as a genuine query but as a social gambit at a party.

In discourse analysis, as in rhetorical analysis, what is said is important not only in itself but with regard to what it leaves unsaid (Antaki, 1994). That is, one kind of expression tends to omit or gloss over other, alternative expressions. For example, in a piece of the author's research (Hackley, 2000), one advertising agency's account team professionals tended to account for actions and decisions in terms of a corporate way of doing things. It was 'the way we do things here'. This way of accounting for particular actions and decisions was, among other structural regularities, called upon frequently by junior account team staff during depth interviews and referred to an implicit code about the agency's values and methods that new employees were expected to assimilate intuitively without being explicitly told what it is. By doing so successfully, new employees would demonstrate that they were the 'right' kind of people who would fit well with the culture of the agency.

Key themes and assumptions in discourse analysis

Box 10.1 lists a number of concepts that are important in discourse analysis (DA). It lists these under four categories, but these categories overlap and leak into each other. The themes that characterise DA include a focus on language and discourse as constitutive features of social interaction. This implies a social constructionist ontology (listed under assumptions in

---

Box 10.1   Major features of Critical Discourse Analysis (CDA)

Themes
Focus on language and discourse as constitutive features of social interaction
Focus on ideology and the reproduction of relations of power through everyday talk and social practice
Performativity of language and social practice
Interaction

Assumptions
Social constructionist ontology; but the possibility of agency is heavily circumscribed by social structures and institutions
Discourses as broad categories of speech, writing and representation carry ideological influences and preserve particular forms of understanding
We perform acts of social positioning and identity formation through our language and other interactional practices

Methods of data gathering
Qualitative, any methods that can generate descriptive text: depth interviews, ethnography, digital capture of talk and interaction, focus/discussion groups, analysis of published texts, e.g. media stories

Approach to data analysis
Seeking structure, function and variation in social texts: evidence of structure regarding recurring themes, tropes of speech, metaphors, evidence of variation in accounts; analysis of the rhetorical function of these positions (also called action-orientation) and accounts in terms of the maintenance of particular meanings that have implications for social positioning and identity formation
Emphasis on revealing 'interpretive repertoires' or discourses that account for and justify particular ideas, actions or procedures
Ethnographic context is considered in order to repair indexicality
Consideration of materiality

Figure 10.1) but, importantly, it does not exclude a sense of the ways in which social structure and institutions circumscribe agency. In other words, social reality is worked up through text and talk in interaction, but this all occurs within social structures and institutions from which emanate ideologies and norms that may be internalised by speakers, and which may inform the speaker's sense of subjectivity.

Social constructionism is sometimes criticised by social theorists because they feel that it underplays social structure and materiality, the inescapable fact that we are embodied beings in a material world. In DA, the analysis of social texts embraces the context when it asks about the motives and interests behind variation in accounts and links these to aspects of materiality and/or ideology. DA also entails asking whose interests are served by certain discourses, in other words, what is the strategic intent behind social texts and how does in manifest?

Interaction is another key concept in DA. The assumption is that human psychology is inherently relational. We do not come into the world as blank sheets of paper, and we do not originate our thoughts and ideas – we get them from others, from social interaction. We may organise and experience them in ways that are unique to us, but we are not islands, our very subjectivities connect to other humans. So, all discourse is seen in the light of interaction – all discourse is a rhetorical counterpoint to alternative possible ways of arranging those particular thoughts, words and/or ideas. Rhetorically, all communication is intended for an imaginary or actual receiver.

DA focuses on text as the point of analysis, but it is important for the researcher to gain a sense of the ethnographic context that frames the text. Simply reading transcripts of interviews and focus groups will not allow the researcher to repair indexicality, that is, to understand deeply the meaning of every word, story, reference, pause, intonation and gesture. For example, the author conducted a study of London advertising agency creative processes using DA, but he also got to know the agencies well by communicating with them over a long period of time, visiting them and spending extended time in them, watching them at work and conducting interviews in the agencies' premises.[1] DA is not just about the text, it entails interpreting the text in the light of what goes on in the whole context of the text. To this end, researchers who are fortunate enough to gain access to organisational settings in which to conduct research interviews, should always take account of any informal data sources and make field notes of their impressions and thoughts. In another example from research in which the author was involved, a major study into young people and alcohol in the UK, the study used discourse analysis as its primary method but also made use of ethnographic data.[2] In addition, the research assistants who conducted the interviews and focus groups also carried out the transcription and took part in the data analysis meetings. In this way, the project authors sought to repair the indexicality of the transcripts through a fuller understanding of the context.

The 'interpretive repertoire'

In discourse analysis, researchers will sort and code the content of a text into themes, called 'discourses' or, following Potter and Wetherell's (1987) approach *interpretive repertoires*. This expression is used by Potter and Wetherell (1987) to mean a particular device or technique of accounting for and justifying particular actions or ideas. The way these authors use the term 'interpretive repertoire' usually refers to one specific linguistic device, or arrangement of tropes and other expressive vehicles that seem to recur in the data set, while the term 'discourse' is more often used in poststructuralist research to refer to a collection of such devices that, together, reflect and reproduce a particular view of the world and justify certain positions or actions.

The interpretive repertoires (or discourses, if the researcher prefers) are the units that structure the research report. The researcher will sort the various texts into interpretive repertoires that are essentially the key findings of the research. Each will be described in the research report, with examples from the transcribe data 'sets, and with analytical discussion with regard to the function these repertoires serve and to any variation in usage that could underpin the intended function.

Variation in accounts

Function in social texts can often be revealed through the *variation* in accounts that people offer. Structural irregularities in social texts might be found as the text accounts for certain events or actions, perhaps for different purposes or to different audiences, or where the data set was generated in different contexts. The researcher can then use variations in accounts to speculate on the function such accounts might serve, perhaps in terms of social positioning and the maintenance of a professional identity. The performative dimension of language is key in this respect. The things that interviewees say can be seen as devices designed to accomplish certain social tasks, such as the social task of appearing a competent professional in a given organisation. This does not imply that interviewees were not competent professionals. It simply acknowledges the self-evident truth that, in our various social roles, we must accomplish certain effects in order to be perceived as plausible and credible, and socially competent.

The analysis of discourse, then, takes as its starting-point the assumption that humans construct social life through language and social practice within a cultural setting replete with prevailing ideologies that derive from social structures and institutions. We are seen as autonomous individuals possessed of human agency, but we act within social structures, which sharply constrain our freedom and power to act in our own interests, and even sometimes constrain our ability to see where our own interests lie.

The analysis of language and other practices of social interaction is central to critical research because language is said to be constitutive of social life, that is, language does not only refer to social reality: it actively constructs it.

Variation in accounting practices does not necessarily imply that the speaker is disingenuous or lacking reflexive insight (although of course both are possibilities). The repertoires and discourse we draw upon to articulate our experiences and to account for our actions and beliefs are targeted both at others and at ourselves, in the sense that we seek to maintain a particular world view that seems coherent and consistent. However, we tend to be far less consistent than we like to think. In our talk and interaction, we are constantly in a notional dialogue with an imaginary interlocutor. In this sense, the psychological organisation of our subjectivity is rhetorical, and dialogic (Billig, 1987, 1988; see also Antaki and Condor, 2014; Antaki, 1994). In our talk and social practices, we construct subject positions that are designed to counter possible alternative versions, as we try to represent ourselves in a way that seems coherent and consistent with the identity and values we wish to project. In so doing, try to accommodate or anticipate and counter the preconceptions of others, and our own wishes about our status and aims, in the positions we take and the things we say. This accommodation depends on our understanding of the social context of the interaction. We constantly interpret words as signs to understand what is meant (to construct meaning) in specific social contexts. The analysis of social texts can reveal this process of construction through structure, function and variation in accounts.

Discourse analysis and critical qualitative research

Discourse analysis was left to the end of the book because it exemplifies two key issues for qualitative data analysis. First, it emphasises the *performativity* of words and social practices when it seeks function or action-orientation in social texts. Qualitative data sets should not be analysed merely for their content – to do so implies that qualitative data sets can be used in the same way as quantitative data sets are used for positivistic, realist research. For theoretically informed qualitative research that reaches a threshold of critical analysis, there has to also be a critical appraisal of why that content is as it is. In other words, what is the strategic purpose of a piece of communication?

For example, does a media story carry an implicit political agenda? Does an interview passage defend the speaker against a possible attack on their sense of identity? Does an advertisement promote implicit values or ideologies? This perspective on the strategic intent behind communication opens up channels of critical analysis that remain obscured if the focus falls merely on the content as it appears. For example, ways of expressing and articulating certain objects or ideas become habitual and un-reflexive, but might embody and reproduce relations of power and domination. In such instances, referring to the strategic intent of the communication does not necessarily imply any intended deceit, or even self-deceit, from the speaker or the source of the communication, but, rather, it alludes to the ideologies that are carried within discourses.

Another way of stating this is to look for sub-text. What is the story behind the story? How did the story get there, why is it placed where it is placed, and why is it expressed in the way it is expressed and not in other ways? What other, alternative version is it designed to counter?

Another, more commonplace, feature of qualitative research exemplified by discourse analysis is the fact that qualitative data sets are coded and sorted for themes, that is, the structure and content of the data set is examined to find recurring patterns. These patterns are resolved through coding and sorting into the themes that will structure the research report. This is a similar process in empirical studies that employ thematic analysis, grounded theory, ethnography or practice theory. In discourse analysis, the process is guided by the specific, theoretically-grounded, concepts of structure, function and variation. Structure and function we have noted above, variation alludes to the social constructed character of memories and emotions. When we offer accounts of experiences or events, we are relying on our memory to reconstruct those events or experiences, and we construct them in a way that seems to present them, and us, in a way we deem acceptable. We may be far less consistent in our world views than we like to think, and discourse analysis researchers are sensitive to variations in accounting practices, that is, subtle differences in the ways in which we might represent the same thing in differing contexts, to different audiences, or for different purposes. These variations in accounting practices reveal the motives and strategies, and sometimes the ideological influences, behind discourses.

Discourse analysis (DA), then, is a powerful qualitative method of data analysis that embraces a wide but coherently related range of theoretical influences. These influences draw on some important critical and interpretive intellectual traditions to link DA with other critical and interpretive streams of research.

We will now end the book with some comments about the commonality of qualitative research approaches.

Concluding comments

The commonalities of theoretically informed qualitative research

The book has tried to encompass the most influential and commonly used intellectual traditions for theoretically informed qualitative research in management and related areas, but there are others that may be equally useful.

To take just a few examples, there are studies in cultural studies (e.g. Du Gay et al., 1997), ethnomethodology and conversation analysis (Garfinkel, 1967; Heritage, 1984) sociology (e.g. Ritzer, 2000) and communication, journalism and media studies (McStay, 2010; Bakir and McStay, 2018) that cover important topics that also fall within the scope of management, marketing and consumer research. Of course, the book has also cited many examples of work that are located in one discipline but reaches out across others, such as Schroeder's (2002) analysis of visual consumption in marketing by drawing on the discipline of art history, and the extensive use of ethnographic methods in studying cultures and sub-cultures of consumption (Schouten and McAlexander, 1995; Belk et al., 1989; Sherry et al., 2013). We have also made use of theoretical and methodological influences from a range of disciplines, including qualitative psychology and literary theory.

One of the aims of the book is to promote not only plurality of research methods in business and management education, but also to promote interdisciplinarity. There is a tendency for subject areas taught in universities to become rather inward-looking. One of the great benefits of an appreciation of qualitative research methods is that it can help to highlight the commonalities and linkages between different methods and fields of social research. Qualitative methods, broadly, share many features – all are, after all, trying to make sense of 'messy' data sets, therefore all are, more or less, inductive (or abductive) methods that seek patterns, regularities, irregularities and structures in data sets. There is a vocabulary for qualitative research theory that may at times seem daunting and esoteric (although they should hold little fear if you can handle words like 'daunting' and 'esoteric') but, at the same time, qualitative research is an approach that can help us to access the most everyday and ordinary aspects of social life to reveal how, in fact, social life is a complex and multi-faceted construction. This complexity can be appreciated when qualitative social researchers stand back from the taken-for-granted understanding of everyday interactions to make the familiar, strange (De Yong et al., 2013; Agar, 1996), that is, to view the emic understanding of social phenomena from the etic standpoint.

There are many philosophical similarities between interpretive traditions. Semiotics, for example, can be seen as a 'phenomenological doctrine of consciousness' (Zeman, 1977, quoted in Mick, 1986, p. 199). In the sense that semiosis reflects apprehended reality, this may well be a notable area of commonality with phenomenological research. However, for C.S. Peirce, semiosis reflects the reality not of experience but of the world of signs. Furthermore, the particular interpretation placed on any given sign depends on a socially agreed code for many semioticians. Phenomenology, in contrast, seldom emphasises social agreement but, rather, focuses on private, apprehended experience. Ethnography has much in common with some strands of critical discourse analysis, especially in the form of critical ethnography (Forester, 1992). However, traditionally, ethnography would seek to recreate the conditions of localised social life without necessarily offering a political critique of those conditions.

For all the many commonalities between qualitative social research methods, it is by no means a unified field and the differences in nuance between methods and intellectual traditions are important. As Chapter 5 emphasises, the theoretical framing of qualitative research projects is key to the overall coherence and quality of the project. The philosophical choices of research perspective are of crucial importance since they frame the questions that can be asked and presuppose the kinds of answers that can be offered.

The book has sought to encourage student researchers to reflect on their own and other's presuppositions about social research in marketing, management and consumer studies in order to make the conduct of research projects a creative and intellectually rewarding experience. The book is written from a conviction that the student research project can and should be such an experience and that it can also constitute a highly positive aspect of the student's academic and personal intellectual development.

As Rorty (1982) has remarked, choices between theories cannot be made solely on the basis of what theory is most efficient or correct. The choice should reflect questions such as 'What would it be like to believe that? What would happen if we did? What would I be committing myself to?' (p. 163). This book hopes to encourage students to investigate their own assumptions and to see where they lead in terms of research perspectives, methods and findings. In this regard, the book is conceived as a point of reference for the creative intellectual endeavours of student researchers, and it is hoped, a point of departure for many more such studies.

Glossary

Function   In discourse analysis refers to the function of speech-acts with regard to the social positioning they are intended to achieve.

Interpretive repertoire   A linguistic device, which accounts for and/or justifies a particular view of the world or specific acts.

Performativity   In this book, deriving from Austin's (1962) work on the ways in which words *do* things for the speaker as well as *say* things, in the sense that utterances may indicate desired or intended identity positioning, distancing from other subject positions, or other strategic intent. Performativity has been subsequently developed in complex renderings in poststructuralism, gender studies and anthropology.

Structure   In the discourse analysis of social texts researchers seek structural regularities with regard to tropes of speech, metaphors or ways of accounting for actions, ideas or decisions.

Variability   In social texts the accounts given to justify actions or ideas may vary in different circumstances. This variation may be revealing with regard to the rhetorical function that it served in that version of events.

Notes

1 PhD thesis https://ethos.bl.uk/OrderDetails.do?uin=uk.bl.ethos.247100
2 Project report here www.researchgate.net/publication/264083129_ESRC_Alcohol_ and_Young_People_project_report_2008 and some of the project papers are cited elsewhere in the text e.g. Hackley et al. (2015), Griffin et al. (2009)

References

Agar, M. (1996) *The Professional Stranger*, London, Academic Press.

Akala (2019) *Natives: Race and Class in the Ruins of Empire*, London, Two Roads.

Alexander, J.C. and Smith, P. (2001) 'The strong program in cultural sociology: Elements of a structural hermeneutics', in J. Turner (ed.) *The Handbook of Sociological Theory*, New York, NY, Kluwer, pp. 135–150.

Alsop, C.K. (2002) 'Home and away: Self-reflexive auto-/ethnography', *Forum Qualitative Sozialforschung/Forum: Qualitative Social Research*, vol. 3, no. 3, Art. 10. http://nbn-resolving.de/urn:nbn:de:0114-fqs0203105.

Althusser, L. (1971) *Lenin and Philosophy and Other Essays*, London, New Left Books.

Alvesson, M. (1998) 'Gender relations and identity at work: A case study of masculinities and femininities in an advertising agency', *Human Relations*, vol. 51, no. 8, pp. 969–1005.

Alvesson, M. and Deetz, S. (2000) *Doing Critical Management Research*, London, Sage.

Alvesson, M., Hardy, C. and Harley, B. (2008) 'Reflecting on reflexivity: Reflexive textual practices in organization and management theory', *Journal of Management Studies*, vol. 45, no. 3, pp. 480–501.

Alvesson, M. and Kärreman, D. (2000) 'Taking the linguistic turn in organizational research', *Journal of Applied Behavioral Science*, vol. 36, no. 2, pp. 136–158.

Alvesson, M. and Skoldberg, K. (2000) *Reflexive Methodology*, London, Sage.

Alvesson, M. and Willmott, H. (eds.) (1992) *Critical Management Studies*, London, Sage.

Antaki, C. (1994) *Explaining and Arguing: The Social Organisation of Accounts*, London, Sage.

Antaki, C. and Condor, S. (2014) *Rhetoric, Ideology and Social Psychology: Essays in Honour of Michael Billig* (Explorations in Social Psychology), London, Routledge.

Ardley, B. (2009) *A Phenomenological Perspective on the Work of the Marketing Manager: An Analysis of the Process of Strategic Planning in Organisations*, Riga, Latvia, LAP Lambert Academic Publishing.

Ardley, B. (2011) 'Marketing theory and critical phenomenology: Exploring the human side of management practice', *Marketing Intelligence & Planning*, vol. 29, pp. 628–642. DOI: 10.1108/02634501111178668.

Ardley, B. and Quinn, L. (2014) 'Practitioner accounts and knowledge production: An analysis of three marketing discourses', *Marketing Theory*, vol. 14, no. 1, pp. 97–114.

Arndt, J. (1985) 'On making marketing science more scientific: Role of orientations, paradigms, metaphors, and puzzle solving', *Journal of Marketing*, vol. 49, no. 3, Summer, pp. 11–23.

Arnould, E.J. (1998) 'Daring consumer-oriented ethnography', in B.B. Stern (ed.) *Representing Consumers: Voices, Views and Visions*, London, Routledge, pp. 85–126.

Arnould, E.J. and Thompson, C.J. (2005) 'Consumer culture theory (CCT) 20 years of research', *Journal of Consumer Research*, vol. 31, no. 4, March, pp. 868–882. https://doi.org/10.1086/426626.

Arnould, E.J. and Wallendorf, M. (1994) 'Market-orientated ethnography: Interpretation building and marketing strategy formulation', *Journal of Marketing Research*, vol. XXXI, November, pp. 484–504.

Arvidsson, A. and Caliandro, A. (2016) 'Brand public', *Journal of Consumer Research*, vol. 42, no. 5, February, pp. 727–748. https://doi.org/10.1093/jcr/ucv053.

Askegaard, S. and Linnet, J.T. (2011) 'Towards and epistemology of consumer culture theory: Phenomenology and the context of context', *Marketing Theory*, vol. 11, no. 4, pp. 381–404.

Austin, J. (1962) *How to Do Things with Words*, London, Oxford University Press.

Ayer, A.J. (1936) *Language, Truth and Logic*, London, Penguin Books.

Baker, M. and Saren, M. (eds) (2000) *Marketing Theory: A Student Text*, Third Edition, Sage, London.

Bakir, V. and McStay, A. (2018) 'Fake news and the economy of emotions: Problems, causes, solutions', *Digital Journalism*, vol. 6, no. 2, pp. 154–175. https://doi.org/10.1080/21670811.2017.1345645.

Banister, P., Burman, E., Parker, I., Taylor, M. and Tindall, C. (1994) *Qualitative Methods in Psychology: A Research Guide*, London, Sage.

Bardhi, F. and Eckhardt, G. (2017) 'Liquid Consumption', *Journal of Consumer Research*, vol. 44, no. 3, October 2017, pp. 582–597. https://doi.org/10.1093/jcr/ucx050.

Barthes, R. (1968) *Elements of Semiology*, trans. A. Lavers, New York, NY, Hill and Wang.

Barthes, R. (1977) *Image – Music – Text*, London, Fontana.

Barthes, R. (2000) *Mythologies*, London, Vintage.

Bassiouni, D. and Hackley, C. (2016) 'Video games and young children's evolving sense of identity: A qualitative study', *Young Consumers*, vol. 17, no. 2, pp. 127–142. www.emeraldinsight.com/doi/abs/10.1108/YC-08-2015-00551

Beckman, S. and Elliott, R. (eds.) (2001) *Interpretive Consumer Research: Paradigms, Methodologies and Applications*, Copenhagen, Copenhagen Business School Press, Handelshøjskolens Forlag.

Belk, R.W. (1988) 'Possessions and the extended self', *Journal of Consumer Research*, vol. 15, no. 2, pp. 139–168.

Belk, R.W. (ed.) (1991) *Highways and Byways: Naturalistic Research from the Consumer Behaviour Odyssey*, Provo, UT, Association for Consumer Research.

Belk, R.W. (1996) 'On aura, illusion, escape, and hope in apocalyptic consumption: The apotheosis of Las Vegas', in S. Brown, D. Carson, and J. Bell (eds.) *Marketing*

Apocalypse: Eschatology, Escapology and the Illusion of the End, London, Routledge, pp. 87–107.

Belk, R.W. (ed.) (2006) *Handbook of Qualitative Research Methods in Marketing*, New York, NY, Edward Elgar.

Belk, R.W. (2017) 'Qualitative research in advertising', *Journal of Advertising*, vol. 46, no. 1, pp. 36–47.

Belk, R.W., Caldwell, M., Devinney, T.M., Eckhardt, G.M., Henry, P., Kozinets, P. and Plakoyiannaki, E. (2017) 'Envisioning consumers: How videography can contribute to marketing knowledge', *Journal of Marketing Management*, vol. 34, no. 5–6, pp. 432–458. DOI: 10.1080/0267257X.2017.1377754.

Belk, R.W., Fischer, E. and Kozinets, R.V. (eds.) (2012) *Qualitative Consumer and Marketing Research*, London, Sage.

Belk, R.W., Sherry, J.F. and Wallendorf, M. (1988) 'A naturalistic inquiry into buyer and seller behaviour at a swap meet', *Journal of Consumer Research*, vol. 14, March, pp. 449–470.

Belk, R.W., Wallendorf, M. and Sherry, J. (1989) 'The sacred and profane in consumer behaviour: Theodicy on the odyssey', *Journal of Consumer Research*, vol. 16, June, pp. 1–38.

Benhabib, S. (1992) *Situating the Self: Gender, Community, and Postmodernism in Contemporary Ethics*, New York, NY, Routledge.

Benveniste, E. (1971) *Problems in General Linguistics*, Miami, FL, University of Florida Press.

Berger, P.L. and Luckman, T. (1966) *The Social Construction of Reality*, London, Penguin.

Bertrand, D. (1988) 'The creation of complicity: A semiotic analysis of an advertising campaign for Black and White Whiskey', *International Journal of Research in Marketing*, vol. 4, no. 4, pp. 273–289.

Bettany, S., Dobscha, S., O'Malley, L. and Prothero, A. (2010) 'Moving beyond binary opposition: Exploring the tapestry of gender in consumer research and marketing', *Marketing Theory*, vol. 1, no. 10, pp. 3–28.

Billig, M. (1987) *Arguing and Thinking: A Rhetorical Approach to Social Psychology*, Cambridge, Cambridge University Press.

Billig, M. (1988) 'Rhetorical and historical aspects of attitudes: The case of the British monarchy', *Philosophical Psychology*, vol. 1, pp. 84–104.

Billig, M. (1989) 'Psychology, rhetoric and cognition', *History of the Human Sciences*, vol. 2, pp. 289–307.

Billig, M. (1991) *Ideology and Opinions*, London, Sage.

Bordieu, P. (1977) *Outline of a Theory of Practice*, Cambridge Studies of Social and Cultural Anthropology, Cambridge, Cambridge University Press.

Borgerson, J.L. and Schroeder, J.E. (2018) 'Making skin visible: How consumer culture imagery commodifies identity', *Body and Society*, vol. 24, no. 1–2, pp. 103–136.

Braun, V. and Clarke, V. (2006) 'Using thematic analysis in psychology', *Qualitative Research in Psychology*, vol. 3, pp. 77–101.

Brown, S. (1994) 'Marketing as multiplex: Screening postmodernism', *European Journal of Marketing*, vol. 28, no. 8/9, pp. 27–51.

Brown, S. (1995) *Postmodern Marketing*, London, International Thompson Business Press.

Brown, S. (1996) 'Art or science? Fifty years of marketing debate', *Journal of Marketing Management*, vol. 12, no. 4, pp. 243–267. DOI: 10.1080/026725 7X.1996.9964413.

Brown, S. (1998) 'What's love got to do with it: Sex, shopping, and subjective personal introspection', in S. Brown, A.M. Doherty, and B. Clarke (eds.) *Romancing the Market*, New York, NY, Routledge, pp. 137–171.

Brown, S. (1999) 'Marketing and literature: The anxiety of academic influence', *Journal of Marketing*, vol. 63, pp. 1–15. DOI: 10.2307/1251997.

Brown, S. (2005) *Writing Marketing*, London, Sage.

Brown, S. (2006) *The Marketing Code*, London, Cyan Books and Marshall Cavendish.

Brown, S. (2012a) 'Wake up and smell the coffin: An introspective obituary', *Journal of Business Research*, vol. 65, no. 4, pp. 461–466.

Brown, S. (2012b) 'I have seen the future and it sucks: Reactionary reflections on reading, writing and research', *European Business Review*, vol. 24, no. 1, pp. 5–19.

Brown, S. (2016a) 'Bow to stern: Can literary theory plumb an unfathomable brand?' *Marketing Theory*, vol. 15, no. 4, pp. 445–464. DOI: 10.1177/1470593115572670.

Brown, S. (2016b) *Brands and Branding*, London, Sage.

Brown, S., Doherty, A.M. and Clarke, B. (eds.) (1988) *Romancing the Market*, London, Routledge.

Brown, S., Hackley, C., Hunt, S.D., Marsh, C., O'Shaughnessy, J., Phillips, B.J., Tonks, D., Miles, C. and Nilsson, T. (2018) 'Marketing (As) rhetoric: Paradigms, provocations, and perspectives', *Journal of Marketing Management*, pp. 1336–1378. https://doi.org/10.1080/0267257X.2018.1548799.

Brown, S., Maclaran, P. and Stevens, L. (1996) 'Marcadia postponed: Marketing, utopia and the millennium', *Journal of Marketing Management*, vol. 12, pp. 671–683.

Brown, S. and Patterson, A. (eds.) (2000) *Imagining Marketing: Art, Aesthetics and the Avante-Garde*, London, Routledge.

Brown, S. and Reid, R. (1997) 'Shoppers on the verge of a nervous breakdown: Chronicle, composition and confabulation in consumer research', Chapter 4 in S. Brown and D. Turley (eds.) *Consumer Research: Postcards from the Edge*, London, Routledge, pp. 79–149.

Brown, S., Stevens, L. and Maclaran, P. (1999) 'I can't believe it's not Bakhtin! Literary theory, postmodern advertising, and the gender agenda', *Journal of Advertising*, vol. 28, no. 1, pp. 11–24. DOI: 10.1080/00913367.1999.10673573.

Brown, S., Stevens, L. and Maclaran, P. (2017) 'Epic aspects of retail encounters: The Iliad of Hollister', *Journal of Retailing*, vol. 94, no. 1, pp. 58–72. DOI: 10.1016/j. jretai.2017.09.006.

Brownlie, D. (1997) 'Beyond ethnography', *European Journal of Marketing*, vol. 31, no. 3/4, pp. 264–284. https://doi.org/10.1108/03090569710162362.

Brownlie, D. (2001) 'Interpretation as composition: Debating modes of representation in marketing research', in R.H. Elliott and S. Beckmann (eds.) *Interpretive Consumer Research: Paradigms, Methodologies and Applications*, Copenhagen, Copenhagen Business School Press, pp. 47–86.

Brownlie, D., Hewer, P. and Tadajewski, M. (eds.) (2013) *Expanding Disciplinary Space: On the Potential of Critical Marketing*, London, Routledge.

Brownlie, D. and Saren, M. (1992) 'The four Ps of the marketing concept: Prescriptive, polemical, permanent and problematical', *The European Journal of Marketing*, vol. 26, no. 4, pp. 34–47.

Brownlie, D., Saren, M., Wensley, R. and Whittington, R. (eds.) (1999) *Rethinking Marketing: Towards Critical Marketing Accountings*, London, Sage.

Bryman, A. (2012) *Social Research Methods*, Oxford, Oxford University Press.

Burawoy, M. (1979) *Manufacturing Consent*, Chicago, IL, Chicago University Press.

Burman, E. and Parker, I. (eds.) (1993) *Discourse Analytic Research*, London, Routledge.

Burrell, G. and Morgan, G. (1979) *Sociological Paradigms and Organisational Analysis*, London, Heinemann.

Capellini, B. and Yen, D.A. (2016) 'A space of one's own: spatial and identity liminality in an online community of mothers', *Journal of Marketing Management*, vol. 32, no. 13–14, pp. 1260–1283. https://doi.org/10.1080/0267257X.2016.1156725.

Carrigan, M. and Szmigin, I. (2004) 'Time, uncertainty and the expectancy experience: An interpretive exploration of consumption and impending motherhood', *Journal of Marketing Management*, vol. 20, no. 7–8, pp. 771–798. DOI: 10.1362/0267257041838755.

Carson, D., Gilmore, A., Perry, C. and Gronhaug, K. (2001) *Qualitative Marketing Research*, London, Sage.

Case, P. (1999) 'Remember re-engineering? The rhetorical appeal of a managerial salvation device', *Journal of Management Studies*, vol. 36, no. 4, pp. 419–442.

Catterall, M. and Maclaran, P. (1997) 'Focus group data and qualitative analysis programs: Coding the moving picture as well as the snapshots', *Sociological Research Online*, vol. 2, no. 1, pp. 1–9. https://doi.org/10.5153/sro.67.

Catterall, M., Maclaran, P. and Stevens, L. (2000) *Marketing and Feminism: Current Issues and Research*, London, Routledge.

Catterall, M., Maclaran, P. and Stephens, L. (2001) *Marketing and Feminism: Current Issues and Research*, London, Routledge.

Chandler, D. (2002) *Semiotics for Beginners*. www.aber.ac.uk/media/Docu-ments/S4B/window.html.

Chang, H., Ngunjiri, F.W. and Hernandez, K.A.C. (2013) *Collaborative Autoethnography*, Walnut Creek, CA, Left Coast Press.

Chatzidakis, A. and Maclaran, P. (2018) 'On critical collaborative videographies', *Journal of Marketing Management*, vol. 34, no. 5–6, pp. 509–517. DOI: 10.1080/0267257X.2018.1477820.

Chowdhury, M.F. (2015) 'Coding, sorting and sifting of qualitative data analysis: Debates and discussion', *Quality and Quantity*, vol. 49, no. 3, pp. 1135–1143. https://doi.org/10.1007/s11135-014-0039-2.

Clarke, I., Kell, I., Schmidt, R. and Vignall, C. (1998) 'Thinking the thought they do: Symbolism and meaning in the consumer experience of the British Pub', *Qualitative Market Research: An International Journal*, vol. 13, pp. 132–144.

Contardo, I. and Wensley, R. (1999) 'The Harvard business school story: Avoiding knowledge by being relevant', paper presented at the conference *Re-organizing Knowledge, Transforming Institutions, Knowing, Knowledge and the University in the XXI Century*, Amherst, September.

Cook, G. (2001) *The Discourse of Advertising*, London, Routledge.

Cova, B. and Elliott, R. (2008) 'Everything you always wanted to know about interpretive consumer research but were afraid to ask', *Qualitative Market Research*, vol. 11, no. 2, pp. 121–129. https://doi.org/10.1108/13522750810864396.

Croft, R. (2013) 'Blessed are the geeks: An ethnographic study of consumer networks in social media, 2006–2012', *Journal of Marketing Management*, vol. 29, no. 5–6, pp. 545–561. DOI: 10.1080/0267257X.2013.787113.

Cronin, A. (2018) *Public Relations Capitalism: Promotional Culture, Publics and Commercial Democracy*, London, Palgrave Macmillan.

Danesi, M. (1993) *Messages and Meanings: An Introduction to Semiotics*, Toronto, Canadian Scholar's Press Inc.

Danesi, M. (2004) *Messages, Signs and Meanings, a Basic Textbook in Semiotics and Communication* (3rd edition), Toronto, Canadian Scholars Press.

Danesi, M. (2016) *The Semiotics of Emoji: The Rise of Visual Language in the Age of the Internet* (Bloomsbury Advances in Semiotics), London, Bloomsbury Academic.

Davis, A. (2013) *Promotional Culture: The Rise and Spread of Advertising, Public Relations, Marketing and Branding*, Cambridge, Polity Press.

De Yong, M., Kamsteeg, F. and Ybema, S. (2013) 'Ethnographic strategies for making the familiar strange: Struggling with "distance" and "immersion" among Moroccan-Dutch students', *Journal of Business Anthropology*, vol. 2, no. 2, pp. 168–186. https://rauli.cbs.dk/index.php/jba/article/viewFile/4157/4577.

Deetz, S. (1980) *Hermeneutics, Textuality, and Communication Research*, Seattle, WA, Summer Institute on Communication Theory. http://files.eric.ed.gov/fulltext/ED197419.pdf. Accessed 25 May 2014.

Deetz, S. (1992) *Democracy in an Age of Corporate Colonization: Developments in Communication and the Politics of Everyday Life*, Albany, NY, State University of New York Press.

Deleuze, G. and Guattari, F. (1987) *A Thousand Plateaus*, Minneapolis, University of Minnesota Press.

Denzin, N.K. (2014) *Interpretive Autoethnography* (2nd edition), Thousand Oaks, CA, Sage.

Deshpandhe, R. (1999) 'Forseeing marketing', *Journal of Marketing*, vol. 63, pp. 164–167.

Dobscha, S. (ed.) (2016) *Death in a Consumer Culture*, London, Routledge.

Dobscha, S. (2019) *Handbook of Research on Gender and Marketing*, Cheltenham, Edward Elgar.

Downes, D. and Rock, P. (1982) *Understanding Deviance*, Oxford, Clarendon Press.

Drummond, K. (2018) *The Road to Wicked: The Marketing and Consumption of Oz, From Frank L. Baum to Broadway*, London, Palgrave Macmillan.

Du Gay, P., Hall, S., Janes, L., Mackay, H. and Negus, K. (1997) *Doing Cultural Studies: The Story of the Sony Walkman*, London, Sage.

Eagleton, T. (2007) *Ideology*, London, Verso.

Easterby-Smith, M. and Malina, D. (1999) 'Cross-cultural collaborative research: Toward reflexivity', *Academy of Management Journal*, vol. 42, no. 1, pp. 76–86.

Easterby-Smith, M., Thorpe, R., Jackson, P.R. and Jasperson, L. (2018) *Management and Business Research* (6th edition), London, Sage.

Easterby-Smith, M., Thorpe, R. and Lowe, A. (1991) *Management Research: An Introduction* (2nd edition, 2002), London, Sage.

Easton, G. and Aráujo, L. (1997) 'Management research and literary criticism', *British Journal of Management*, vol. 8, pp. 99–106.

Eco, U. (1976) *A Theory of Semiotics*, Bloomington, Indiana University Press.

Eco, U. (1984) *Semiotics and Philosophy of Language*, London, Palgrave Macmillan.

Eddo-Lodge, R. (2018) *Why I'm No Longer Talking to White People About Race*, London, Bloomsbury.

Edgar, A. and Sedgwick, P. (1999) *Key Concepts in Cultural Theory*, London, Routledge.

Edwards, D. and Potter, J. (1992) *Discursive Psychology*, London, Sage.

Elam, K. (1988) *The Semiotics of Theatre and Drama*, London, Routledge.

Elliott, R. (1994) 'Addictive consumption: Function and fragmentation in post-modernity', *Journal of Consumer Policy*, vol. 17, no. 2, pp. 157–179.

Elliott, R. (1996) 'Discourse analysis: Exploring action, function and conflict on social texts', *Marketing Intelligence and Planning*, vol. 14, no. 6, pp. 65–69.

Elliott, R. (1998) 'A model of emotion-driven choice', *Journal of Marketing Management*, vol. 14, no. 1–3, pp. 95–108. DOI: 10.1362/026725798784959408.

Elliott, R. and Gournay, K. (1996) 'Revenge, existential choice and addictive consumption', *Psychology and Marketing*, vol. 3, no. 8, pp. 753–768.

Elliott, R. and Jankel-Elliott, N. (2002) 'Using ethnography in strategic consumer research', *Qualitative Market Research: An International Journal*, vol. 6, no. 4, pp. 215–223. https://doi.org/10.1108/13522750310495300.

Elliott, R. and Ritson, M. (1995) 'Practicing existential consumption: The lived meaning of sexuality in advertising', in F.R. Kardes and M. Sujan (eds.) *NA – Advances in Consumer Research*, volume 22, Provo, UT, Association for Consumer Research, pp. 740–745. http://acrwebsite.org/volumes/7849/volumes/v22/NA-22.

Elliott, R. and Ritson, M. (1997) 'Post-structuralism and the dialectics of advertising: Discourse, ideology, resistance', Chapter 6 in S. Brown and D. Turley (eds.) *Consumer Research: Postcards from the Edge*, Routledge, London, pp. 190–248.

Elliott, R. and Wattanasuwan, K. (1998) 'Brands as symbolic resources for the construction of identity', *International Journal of Advertising*, vol. 17, no. 2, pp. 131–144. DOI: 10.1080/02650487.1998.11104712.

Ellis, C. (2009) *Revision: Autoethnographic Reflections on Life and Work*, Walnut Creek, CA, Left Coast Press.

Ellis, N., Fitchett, J., Higgins, M., Jack, G., Lim, M., Saren, M. and Tadajewski, M. (2011) *Marketing: A Critical Textbook*, London, Sage.

Ellis, N. and Hopkinson, G. (2010) 'The construction of managerial knowledge in business networks: Managers' theories about communication', *Industrial Marketing Management*, vol. 39, no. 3, pp. 413–424. https://doi.org/10.1016/j.indmarman.2007.08.011.

Ellis, N., Rod, M., Beal, T. and Lindsay, V. (2012) 'Constructing identities in Indian networks: Discourses of marketing management in inter-organizational relationships', *Industrial Marketing Management*, vol. 41, no. 3, pp. 401–412.

Enck, S.M. and Morrissey, M.E. (2015) 'If orange is the new Black, I must be color blind: Comic framings of post-racism in the prison-industrial complex', *Critical Studies in Media Communication*, vol. 32, no. 5, pp. 303–317.

Engel, J.F., Blackwell, R.D. and Miniard, P.W. (1990) *Consumer Behaviour* (6th edition), London, Dryden Press.

Fairclough, N. (1985) 'Temporality in human action: An alternative to historicism and positivism', *American Psychologist*, vol. 40, November, pp. 1179–1188.

Fairclough, N. (2010) *Critical Discourse Analysis: The Critical Study of Language*, London, Routledge.

Fairclough, N. (2014) *Language and Power* (3rd edition), London, Routledge,

Featherstone, M. (1991) *Consumer Culture and Postmodernism*, London, Sage.

Felix, R. and Fuat Fırat, A. (2019) 'Brands that "sell their soul": Offshoring, brand liquefication and the excluded consumer', *Journal of Marketing Management*, vol. 35, no. 11–12, pp. 1080–1099. DOI: 10.1080/0267257X.2019.1604562.

Firat, A. (1985) 'Ideology versus science in marketing changing the course of marketing, alternative paradigms for widening marketing theory', *Research in Marketing*, Suppl 2, pp. 135–146.

Firat, A., Dholakia, N. and Venkatesh, A. (1995) 'Marketing in a postmodern world', *European Journal of Marketing*, vol. 29, no. 1, pp. 40–56.

Firat, A. and Venkatesh, A. (1995a) 'Liberatory postmodernism and the re- enchantment of consumption', *Journal of Consumer Research*, vol. 22, no. 3, pp. 239–267.

Firat, A. and Venkatesh, A. (1995b) 'Postmodern perspectives on consumption', in R. Belk, N. Dholakia, and A. Venkatesh (eds.) *Consumption and Marketing, Macro Dimensions*, Cincinnati, South- Western College Publishing, pp. 234–265.

Fiske, J.C. (1982) *Introduction to Communication Studies*, London, Methuen.

Forester, J. (1992) 'Critical ethnography: On fieldwork in a Habermasian way', Chapter 3 in M. Alvesson and H. Willmott (eds.) *Critical Management Studies*, London, Sage, pp. 46–64.

Foster Davis, J. (2018) 'Selling whiteness? – A critical review of the literature on marketing and racism', *Journal of Marketing Management*, vol. 34, no. 1–2, pp. 134–177. DOI: 10.1080/0267257X.2017.1395902.

Foucault, M. (1977) *Discipline and Punish: The Birth of the Prison*, trans. A. Sheridan, New York, NY, Pantheon.

Foxall, G. (1995) 'Science and interpretation in consumer research: A radical behaviourist perspective', *European Journal of Marketing*, vol. 29, no. 9, pp. 3–99.

Fromm, E. (1941) *Escape from Freedom*, New York, NY, Ishi Press International (2011 reprint).

Fry, D. and Fry, V.L. (1986) 'A semiotic model for the study of mass communication', in M. McLaughlin (ed.) *Communication Yearbook 9*, Beverly Hills, Sage, pp. 443–461.

Furusten, S. (1999) *Popular Management Books: How They Are Made and What They Mean for Organisations*, London, Routledge.

Gabriel, D. and Tate, S.A. (eds.) (2017) *Inside the Ivory Tower: Narratives of Women of Color Surviving and Thriving in British Academia*, London, UCL Institute of Education Press.

Gabriel, Y. (2017) 'Case studies as narratives: Reflections prompted by the case of victor, the wild child of Aveyron', *Journal of Management Inquiry*, vol. 28, no. 4, pp. 403–408. https://doi.org/10.1177/1056492617715522.

Gabriel, Y. and Lang, T. (2015) *The Unmanageable Consumer* (3rd edition), London, Sage.

Garfinkel, H. (1967) *Studies in Ethnomethodology*, Englewood Cliffs, NJ, Prentice-Hall.

Geertz, C. (1973) *The Interpretation of Cultures*, London, Fontana Press.

Gergen, K. and Gergen, M. (1988) 'Narrative and the self as relationship', *Advances in Experimental Social Psychology*, vol. 21, pp. 17–56.

Gerring, J. (2006) 'Single-outcome studies: A methodological primer', *International Sociology*, vol. 21, no. 5, pp. 707–734.

Ghaffari, M., Hackley, C. and Lee, Z. (2019) 'Control, knowledge, and persuasive power in advertising creativity: An ethnographic practice theory approach', *Journal of Advertising*, vol. 48, no. 2, pp. 242–249. DOI: 10.1080/00913367.2019.1598310.

Gioia, D.A., Corley, K.G. and Hamilton, A.L. (2013) 'Seeking qualitative rigor in inductive research: Notes on the Gioia methodology', *Organizational Research Methods*, vol. 16, no. 1, pp. 15–31.

Glaser, B.G. and Strauss, A.L. (1967) *The Discovery of Grounded Theory*, Oxon, Routledge.

Goldman, W. (1996) *Adventures in the Screen Trade- A Personal View of Hollywood* (2nd edition, first published 1983), New York, NY, Abacus.

Gould, S.J. (1991) 'The self-manipulation of my pervasive, perceived vital energy through product use: An introspective-praxis perspective', *Journal of Consumer Research*, vol. 18, no. 2, pp. 194–207.

Gould, S.J. (1995) 'Researcher introspection as a method in consumer research: Applications, issues and implications', *Journal of Consumer Research*, vol. 21, no. 4, pp. 719–722.

Gould, S.J. (2008) 'An introspective genealogy of my introspective genealogy', *Marketing Theory*, vol. 8, no. 4, pp. 407–424.

Goulding, C. (2005) 'Grounded theory, ethnography and phenomenology', *European Journal of Marketing*, vol. 39, no. 3/4, pp. 294–308. https://doi.org/10.1108/03090560510581782.

Goulding, C., Shankar, A. and Canniford, R. (2013) 'Learning to be tribal: Facilitating the formation of consumer tribes', *European Journal of Marketing*, vol. 47, no. 5/6, pp. 813–832. https://doi.org/10.1108/03090561311306886.

Goulding, C., Shankar, A., Elliott, R. and Canniford, R. (2009) 'The marketplace management of illicit pleasure', *Journal of Consumer Research*, vol. 35, no. 5, pp. 759–771

Gramsci, A. (1971) *Selections from the Prison Notebooks*, New York, NY, International Publisher.

Grayson, K. (1997) 'Narrative theory and consumer research: Theoretical and methodological perspectives', *Advances in Consumer Research*, vol. 24, pp. 67–70.

Grayson, K. and Shulman, D. (2000) 'Indexicality and the verification function of irreplaceable possessions: A semiotic analysis', *Journal of Consumer Research*, vol. 27, no. 1, June, pp. 17–30. https://doi.org/10.1086/314306.

Griffin, C., Bengry-Howell, A., Hackley, C., Mistral, W. and Szmigin, I. (2009) ' "Every time I do it I absolutely annihilate myself": Loss of (self)-consciousness and loss of memory in young people's drinking narratives', *Sociology*, vol. 43, no. 3, pp. 457–477.

Griffiths, J. and Follows, T. (2018) *98% Pure Potato- the Origin of Advertising Account Planning as Told to us by Its Pioneers*, London, Unbound.

Gronhaug, K. (2000) 'The sociological basis of marketing', in M.J. Baker (ed.) *Marketing Theory: A Student Text*, London, Thompson Business Press.

Gruber, T., Szmigin, I., Reppel, A. and Voss, R. (2008) 'Designing and conducting online interviews to investigate interesting consumer phenomena', *Qualitative Market Research*, vol. 11, no. 3, p. 256–274. https://doi.org/10.1108/13522750810879002.

Gummeson, E. (2000) *Qualitative Methods in Management Research*, London, Sage.

Gurswitch, A. (1974) *Phenomenology and Theory of Science*, Evanston, Northwestern University Press.

Gutkind, L. (1996) *The Art of Creative Nonfiction*, New York, NY, John Wiley & Sons.

Habermas, J. (1970) 'Knowledge and interest', in D. Emmett and A. Macintyre (eds.) *Sociological Theory and Philosophical Analysis*, London, Palgrave Macmillan.

Hackett, P.M.W. (ed.) (2016) *Qualitative Research Methods in Consumer Psychology*, New York, NY and London, Routledge, pp. 105–117 ISBN 978-1-138-02349-9.

Hackley, C. (1998a) 'Mission statements as corporate communications: The consequences of social constructionism', *Corporate Communications: An International Journal*, vol. 3, no. 3, pp. 92–98.

Hackley, C. (1998b) 'Management learning and normative marketing theory: Learning from the life-world', *Management Learning* (Q1), vol. 29, no. 1, pp. 91–105.

Hackley, C. (1999) 'The communications process and the semiotic boundary', Chapter 9 in P. Kitchen (ed.) *Marketing Communications: Principles and Practice*, London, International Thomson Business Press, pp. 135–155.

Hackley, C. (2000) 'Silent running: Tacit, discursive and psychological aspects of management in a top UK advertising agency', *British Journal of Management*, vol. 11, no. 3, pp. 239–254.

Hackley, C. (2001) *Marketing and Social Construction: Exploring the Rhetorics of Marketed Consumption*, London, Routledge.

Hackley, C. (2002) 'The Panoptic role of advertising agencies in the production of consumer culture', *Consumption, Markets and Culture*, vol. 5, no. 3, September, pp. 211–229.

Hackley, C. (2003a) 'Account planning: Current agency perspectives on an advertising enigma', *Journal of Advertising Research* (Q2/1), vol. 43, no. 2, pp. 235–246.

Hackley, C. (2003b) 'We are all customers now: Rhetorical strategy and ideological control in marketing management texts', *Journal of Management Studies*, vol. 40, no. 5, pp. 1325–1352.

Hackley, C. (2003c) 'Divergent representational practices in advertising and consumer research: Some thoughts on integration', *Qualitative Market Research: An International Journal* special issue on representation in consumer research, vol. 6, no. 3, pp. 175–184.

Hackley, C. (2007) 'Auto-ethnographic consumer research and creative non-fiction: Exploring connections and contrasts from a literary perspective', *Qualitative Market Research: An International Journal*, vol. 10, no. 1, pp. 98–108.

Hackley, C. (2009a) *Marketing- A Critical Introduction*, London, Sage.

Hackley, C. (2009b) 'Parallel universes and disciplinary space: The bifurcation of managerialism and social science in marketing studies', *Journal of Marketing Management*, vol. 2, no. 7–8, pp. 643–659.

Hackley, C. (2010) 'Theorizing advertising: Managerial, scientific and cultural approaches', Chapter 6 in P. Maclaran, M. Saren, B.B. Stern, and M. Tadajewski (eds.) *The Sage Handbook of Marketing Theory*, London, Sage, pp. 89–107 ISBN 9781847875051.

Hackley, C. (2016) 'Autoethnography in consumer research', Chapter 8 in P.M.W. Hackett (ed.) *Qualitative Research Methods in Consumer Psychology*, New York, NY and London, Routledge, pp. 105–117 ISBN 978-1-138-02349-9.

Hackley, C. (2018) 'Advertising, marketing and PR: Deepening mutuality amidst a convergent media landscape', Chapter 4 in J. Hardy, I. MacRury, and H. Powell (eds.) *The Advertising Handbook (Media Practice)* (3rd edition), London, Routledge, pp. 58–74 ISBN-13: 978-1138678835; ISBN-10: 113867883X.

Hackley, C. (2019) 'Advertising practice and critical marketing', in M. Tadajewski, M. Higgins, J. Denegri-Knott, and R. Varman (eds.) Chapter 11 in *The Routledge Companion to Critical Marketing Studies*, London, Routledge, pp. 185–195 ISBN 9781138641402.

Hackley, C., Bengry-Howell, A., Griffin, C., Mistral, W. and Szmigin, I. (2011) 'Young peoples' binge drinking constituted as a deficit of individual self-control in UK government alcohol policy', Chapter 15 in C.N. Candlin and J. Crichton (eds.) *Discourses of Deficit*, Hampshire, Palgrave, Macmillan, Palgrave Studies in Professional and Organizational Discourse, pp. 293–310.

Hackley, C., Bengry-Howell, A., Griffin, C., Mistral, W., Szmigin, I. and Hackley, R.A. (2013) 'Young adults and "binge" drinking: A Bakhtinian analysis', *Journal of Marketing Management*, vol. 29, no. 7–8, pp. 933–949.

Hackley, C., Bengry-Howell, A., Griffin, C., Szmigin, I., Mistral, W. and Hackley, R.A. (2015) 'Transgressive drinking practices and the subversion of proscriptive alcohol policy messages', *Journal of Business Research*, vol. 68, no. 10, pp. 2125–2131. https://doi.org/10.1016/j.jbusres.2015.03.011.

Hackley, C. and Hackley, R.A. (2015a) 'How the hungry ghost mythology reconciles materialism and spirituality in Thai death ritual', *Qualitative Market Research: An International Journal* (Q2), vol. 8, no. 2, pp. 427–421.

Hackley, C. and Hackley, R.A. (2015b) 'Marketing and the cultural production of celebrity in the convergent media Era', *Journal of Marketing Management*, vol. 31, no. 5/6, pp. 461–477. www.tandfonline.com/doi/full/10.1080/02672 57X.2014.1000940. Accessed 15 January 2015.

Hackley, C. and Hackley, R.A. (2018a) *Advertising and Promotion* (4th edition), London, Sage.

Hackley, C. and Hackley, R.A. (2018b) 'Advertising at the threshold: Paratextual promotion in the era of media convergence', *Marketing Theory*, vol. 19, no. 2, pp. 195–215. https://doi.org/10.1177/1470593118787581.

Hackley, C. and Kover, A. (2007) 'The trouble with creatives: Negotiating creative identity in advertising agencies', *International Journal of Advertising*, vol. 26, no. 1, pp. 63–78.

Hackley, C., Tiwsakul, A. and Preuss, L. (2008) 'An ethical evaluation of product placement-a deceptive practice?' *Business Ethics- A European Review*, vol. 17, no. 2, pp. 109–120.

Hammer, M. and Champy, J. (1993) *Re-engineering the Corporation: A Manifesto for Business Revolution*, London, Nicholas Brealey.

Hammersly, M. and Atkinson, P. (1983) *Ethnography: Principles and Practice*, London, Routledge.

Harvey, D. (1989) *The Condition of Postmodernity: An Enquiry into the Origins of Cultural Change*, Oxford, Blackwell.

Hayward, K. and Hobbs, D. (2007) 'Beyond the binge: Market-led liminalization and the spectacle of binge drinking', *The British Journal of Sociology*, vol. 58, no. 3, pp. 437–456.

Hearn, J. and Hein, W. (2015) 'Reframing gender and feminist knowledge construction in marketing and consumer research: Missing feminisms and the case of men and masculinities', *Journal of Marketing Management*, vol. 31, no. 15–16, pp. 1626–1651. DOI: 10.1080/0267257X.2015.1068835.

Heidegger, M. (1962) *Being and Time*, Oxford, Basil Blackwell.

Hein, W. and O'Donohoe, S. (2014) 'Practising gender: The role of banter in young men's improvisations of masculine consumer identities', *Journal of Marketing Management*, vol. 30, no. 13–14, pp. 1293–1319. DOI: 10.1080/0267257X.2013.852608.

Henderson, G.R., Hakstian, A.M. and Williams, J.D. (2016) *Consumer Equality: Race and the American Marketplace* (Racism in American Institutions), Santa Barbara, CA, Praeger.

Heritage, J. (1984) *Garfinkel and Ethnomethodology*, Cambridge, Polity Press.

Hirschman, E.C. (1986) 'Humanistic inquiry in marketing research, philosophy, method and criteria', *Journal of Marketing Research*, vol. 23, pp. 237–249.

Hirschman, E.C. (ed.) (1989) *Interpretive Consumer Research*, Provo, UT, Association for Consumer Research.

Hirschman, E.C. (1990) 'Secular immortality and the American ideology of affluence', *Journal of Consumer Research*, vol. 17, June, pp. 344–359.

Hirschman, E.C. (1993) 'Ideology in consumer research, 1980 and 1990: A Marxist and feminist critique', *Journal of Consumer Research*, vol. 19, no. 4, pp. 537–555.

Hirschman, E. C. and Holbrook, M.B. (1992) *Postmodern Consumer Research: The Study of Consumption as Text*, Sage, London.

Hirschman, E.C. and Stern, B.B. (1994) 'Women as commodities: Prostitution as depicted in the Blue Angel, Pretty Baby, and Pretty Woman', in C.T. Allen and D.R. John (eds.) *NA – Advances in Consumer Research*, volume 21, Provo, UT: Association for Consumer Research, pp. 576–581. www.acrwebsite.org/volumes/5985/volumes/v21/NA-21.

Holbrook, M.B. (1990) 'The role of lyricism in research on consumer emotions: Skylark, have you anything to say to me?', *Advances in Consumer Research*, vol. 17, pp. 1–18.

Holbrook, M.B. (1995) *Consumer Research: Introspective Essays on the Study of Consumption*, London, Sage.

Holbrook, M.B. (2018) 'A subjective personal introspection essay on the evolution of business schools, the fate of marketing education, and aspirations toward a great society', *Australasian Marketing Journal*, vol. 26, no. 2, pp. 70–78.

Holbrook, M.B. and Grayson, M.W. (1986) 'The semiology of cinematic consumption: Symbolic consumer behaviour in *Out of Africa*', *Journal of Consumer Research*, vol. 13, pp. 374–381.

Holbrook, M.B. and Hirschman, E.C. (1982) 'The experiential aspects of consumption: Consumer feelings, fantasies and fun', *Journal of Consumer Research*, vol. 9, pp. 132–140.

Holbrook, M.B. and Hirschman, E.C. (1993) *The Semiotics of Consumption: Interpreting Symbolic Consumer Behaviour in Popular Culture and Works of Art*, New York, NY, Mouton de Gruyter.

Holbrook, M.B. and O'Shaughnessy, J. (1988) 'On the scientific status of consumer research and the need for an interpretive approach to studying consumer behaviour', *Journal of Consumer Research*, vol. 15, pp. 398–403.

Holt, D.B. (1997) 'Poststructuralist lifestyle analysis: Conceptualizing the social patterning of consumption in postmodernity', *Journal of Consumer Research*, vol. 23, no. 4, March, pp. 326–350. https://doi.org/10.1086/209487.

Holt, D.B. (2002) 'Why do brands cause trouble? A dialectical theory of consumer culture and branding', *Journal of Consumer Research*, vol. 29, no. 1, pp. 70–90. https://doi.org/10.1086/339922.

Holt, D.B. (2004) *How Brands Become Icons- the Principles of Cultural Branding*, Cambridge, MA, Harvard University Press.

Holt, D.B. and Cameron, D. (2010) *Cultural Branding: Using Innovative Ideologies to Build Breakthrough Brands*, Oxford, Oxford University Press.

Horkheimer, M. and Adorno, T.W. (1944) *The Dialectic of Enlightenment*, New York, NY, Continuum.

Hudson, L.A. and Ozanne, J. (1988) 'Alternative ways of seeking knowledge in consumer research', *Journal of Consumer Research*, vol. 14, no. 4, pp. 508–521. DOI: 10.1086/209132.

Humphreys, A. (2010) 'Semiotic structure and the legitimation of consumption practices: The case of casino gambling', *Journal of Consumer Research*, vol. 37, no. 3, October, pp. 490–510. https://doi.org/10.1086/652464.

Humphreys, A. and Wang, R.J.H. (2018) 'Automated text analysis for consumer research', *Journal of Consumer Research*, vol. 44, no. 6, April, pp. 1274–1306. https://doi.org/10.1093/jcr/ucx104.

Hunt, S.D. (2003) *Controversy in Marketing Theory: For Reason, Realism, Truth, and Objectivity*, Armonk, NY, M.E. Sharpe, Inc.

Husemann, K. and Eckhardt, G.M. (2018) 'Consumer deceleration', *Journal of Consumer Research*, vol. 45, no. 6, pp. 1142–1163. https://doi.org/10.1093/jcr/ucy047.

Husserl, E. (1931) *Ideas*, London, Allen & Unwin.

Husserl, E. (1970) *Logical Investigations*, London, Routledge and Kegan Paul (first published 1900).

Hycner, R.H. (1985) 'Some guidelines for the phenomenological analysis of interview data', *Human Studies*, no. 8, pp. 279–303. www.depts.ttu.edu/education/our-people/Faculty/additional_pages/duemer/epsy_6305_class_materials/Hycne-R-H-1985.pdf.

Iser, W. (1972) 'The reading process: A phenomenological approach', *New Literary History*, vol. 3, no. 2, pp. 279–299.

Jankowicz, A.D. (1991) *Business Research Projects for Students*, London, Chapman and Hall.

Jarzabkowski, P., Bednarek, R. and Lê, J.K. (2014) 'Producing persuasive findings: Demystifying ethnographic text work in strategy and organization research', *Strategic Organization*, vol. 12, no. 4, pp. 274–287.

Johnson, P. and Duberley, J. (2003) 'Reflexivity in management research', *Journal of Management Studies*, vol, 40, no. 5, pp. 1279–1303. http://doi.org/10.1111/1467-6486.00380.

Keith, R.J. (1960) 'The marketing revolution', *Journal of Marketing*, vol. 24, January, pp. 35–38.

Kellogg, K., Orlikowski, W.J. and Yates, J. (2006) 'Life in the trading zone: Structuring coordination across boundaries in post-bureaucratic organizations', *Organization Science*, vol. 17, no. 1, pp. 22–44.

Kelly, G.A., Lawlor, K. and O'Donohoe, S. (2005) 'Encoding advertisements: The creative perspective', *Journal of Marketing Management*, vol. 21, no. 5–6, pp. 505–528. DOI: 10.1362/0267257054307390.

Kennedy, G. (1963) *The Art of Persuasion in Greece*, London, Routledge and Kegan Paul.

Kerin, R.A. (1996) 'In pursuit of an ideal: The editorial and literary history of the *Journal of Marketing*', *Journal of Marketing*, vol. 60, no. 1, pp. 1–13.

Khare, A. and Varman, R. (2017) 'Subalterns, empowerment and the failed imagination of markets', *Journal of Marketing Management*, vol. 33, no. 17–18, pp. 1593–1602. DOI: 10.1080/0267257X.2017.1403138.

Knights, D. and Willmott, H. (2017) *Introducing Organizational Behaviour and Management* (3rd edition), London, Cengage Learning.

Knorr Cetina, K.D. and Mulkay, M. (eds.) (1983) *Science Observed: Perspectives on the Social Study of Science*, London, Sage.

Kotler, P. (1967) *Marketing Management: Analysis, Planning and Control*, Upper Saddle River, Prentice-Hall.

Kover, A.J., Goldberg, S.M. and James, W.L. (1995) 'Creativity vs effectiveness? An integrating classification for advertising', *Journal of Advertising Research*, vol. 35, no. 6, pp. 29–41.

Kozinets, R.V. (2008) 'Technology/ideology: How ideological fields influence consumers' technology narratives', *Journal of Consumer Research*, vol. 34, no. 6, April, pp. 865–881. https://doi.org/10.1086/523289.

Kozinets, R.V. (2015) *Netnography- Redefined* (2nd edition), London, Sage.

Kozinets, R.V. (2019) 'Consuming technocultures: An extended *JCR* curation', *Journal of Consumer Research*, ucz034. https://doi.org/10.1093/jcr/ucz034.

Kozinets, R.V. and Kedzior, R. (2009) 'I, avatar: Auto-netnographic research in virtual worlds', in M. Solomon and N. Wood (eds.) *Virtual Social Identity and Consumer Behavior*, Armonk, NY, M.E. Sharpe, pp. 3–19.

Kozinets, R.V., Scaraboto, D. and Parmentier, M-A. (2018) 'Evolving netnography: How brand auto-netnography, a netnographic sensibility, and more-than-human netnography can transform your research', *Journal of Marketing Management*, vol. 34, no. 3–4, pp. 231–242. DOI: 10.1080/0267257X.2018.1446488.

Kozinets, R.V., Sherry Jr, J.F., Storm, D., Duhachek, A., Nuttavuthisit, K. and DeBerry-Spence, B. (2004) 'Ludic agency and retail spectacle', *Journal of Consumer Research*, vol. 31, no. 3, pp. 658–672.

Kuhn, T. (1970) *The Structure of Scientific Revolutions*, Chicago, University of Chicago Press.

Kunda, G. (1992) *Engineering Culture: Control and Commitment in a High-Tech Corporation*, Philadelphia, PA, Temple University Press.

Kvale, S. (1983) 'The qualitative research interview: A phenomenological and a hermeneutical mode of understanding', *Journal of Phenomenological Psychology*, vol. 14, no. 2, pp. 171–196.

Larsen, G. and Patterson, M. (2018) 'Consumer identity projects', in O. Kravets, P. Maclaran, S. Miles, and A. Venkatesh (eds.) *Sage Handbook of Consumer Culture*, London, Sage, pp. 194–213.

Larsen, H.H., Mick, D.G. and Alsted, C. (1991) *Marketing and Semiotics: Selected Papers from the Copenhagen Symposium*, Copenhagen, Handelshøjskolens Forlag.

Labroo, A.A. and Patrick, V.M. (2008) 'Psychological distancing: Why happiness helps you see the big picture', *Journal of Consumer Research*, vol. 35, no. 5, pp. 800–809.

Latour, B. and Woolgar, S. (1979) *Laboratory Life*, London, Sage.

Leach, E. (1976) *Culture and Communication: The Logic by Which Symbols Are Connected – an Introduction to the Use of Structuralist Analysis in Social Anthropology*, Cambridge, Cambridge University Press.

Letiche, H. (2002) 'Viagra(ization) or Technoromanticism', *Consumption, Markets and Culture*, vol. 5, no. 3, pp. 247–260.

Levitt, T. (1965) 'Exploit the product life cycle', *Harvard Business Review*, November. https://hbr.org/1965/11/exploit-the-product-life-cycle.

Levy, S.J. (2006) 'History of qualitative research methods in marketing', in *Handbook of Qualitative Research Methods in Marketing*, Edward Elgar Publishing, pp. 3–18. https://doi.org/10.4337/9781847204127.00006; http://criticalmanagement.uniud.it/fileadmin/user_upload/Levy_in_Belk_2006.pdf.

Lim, M. and Moufahim, M. (2011) 'Co-production and co-consumption: Perspectives on immigration through a discourse analysis of voters' blogs in the 2010 general election', *Journal of Marketing Management*, vol. 27, no. 7–8, pp. 656–674. DOI: 10.1080/0267257X.2011.593539.

Loo, B.K. and Hackley, C. (2013) 'Internationalisation strategy of iconic Malaysian high fashion brands', *Qualitative Market Research: An International Journal* (Q2), vol. 16, no. 4, pp. 406–420.

Luedicke, K., Thompson, C.J. and Giesler, M. (2009) 'Consumer identity work as moral protagonism: How myth and ideology animate a brand-mediated moral conflict', *Journal of Consumer Research*, vol. 36, no. 6, April 2010, pp. 1016–1032. https://doi.org/10.1086/644761.

Lupton, D. (2014) *Digital Sociology*, London, Routledge.

Lyotard, J.F. (1984) *The Postmodern Condition: A Report on Knowledge*, trans. G. Bennington and B. Massumi, Minneapolis, MN, University of Minnesota Press.

Maclaran, P. (2012) 'Marketing and feminism in historic perspective', *Journal of Historical Research in Marketing*, vol. 4, no. 3, pp. 462–469. http://dx.doi.org/10.1108/17557501211252998.

Maclaran, P. (2015) 'Feminism's fourth wave: A research agenda for marketing and consumer research', *Journal of Marketing Management*, vol. 31, no. 15–16, pp. 1732–1738. DOI: 10.1080/0267257X.2015.1076497.

Maclaran, P., Saren, M., Goulding, C., Elliott, R. and Catterall, M. (2007) *Critical Marketing- Defining the Field*, London, Routledge.

Maguire, M. and Delahunt, B. (2017) 'Doing a thematic analysis: A practical, step-by-step guide for learning and teaching scholars', *AISHE-Journal*, vol. 8, no. 3. http://ojs.aishe.org/index.php/aishe-j/article/view/335.

Malinowski, B. (1922) *Argonauts of the Western Pacific*, London, Routledge and Kegan Paul.

Marion, G. (2006) 'Research note: Marketing ideology and criticism: Legitimacy and legitimization', *Marketing Theory*, vol. 6, no. 2, pp. 245–262.

Martin, D.M. (2004) 'Humor in middle management: Women negotiating the paradoxes of organizational life', *Journal of Applied Communication Research*, vol. 32, no. 2, pp. 147–170.

Martin, D.M., Schouten, J.W. and McAlexander, J.H. (2006) 'Claiming the throttle: Multiple femininities in a hyper-masculine subculture', *Consumption, Markets and Culture*, vol. 9, no. 3, pp. 171–205.

Mautner, G. (2016) *Discourse and Management* (with contributions from Nick Ellis, Chris Hackley, Cliff Oswick and Ruth Wodak) Palgrave Critical Management Studies, London, Palgrave Macmillan.

McAlexander, J.H., Dufault, B.L., Martin, D.M. and Schouten, J.W. (2014) 'The marketization of religion: Field, capital, and consumer identity', *Journal of Consumer Research*, vol. 41, no. 3, pp. 358–379.

McCloskey, D.N. (1983) 'The rhetoric of economics', *Journal of Economic Literature*, vol. 21, no. 2, June, pp. 481–517. www.jstor.org/stable/2724987.

McCracken, G. (1986) 'Culture and consumption: A theoretical account of the structure and movement of the cultural meaning of consumer goods', *Journal of Consumer Research*, vol. 13, no. 1, June, pp. 71–84. https://doi.org/10.1086/209048.

McCracken, G. (1989) 'Who is the celebrity endorser? Cultural foundations of the endorsement process', *Journal of Consumer Research*, vol. 16, no. 3, December, pp. 310–321. https://doi.org/10.1086/209217.

McLeod, C., O'Donohoe, S. and Townley, B. (2009) 'The elephant in the room? Class and creative careers in British advertising agencies', *Human Relations*, vol. 62, no. 7, pp. 1011–1039. www.uk.sagepub.com/hackley/SJO%20Articles%20 for%20Website/Chapter%204%20-%20McLeod%20et%20al.pdf. Accessed 23 May 2014.

McQuarrie, E.F. and Mick, D.G. (1992) 'On resonance: A critical pluralistic inquiry into advertising rhetoric', *Journal of Consumer Research*, vol. 19, no. 2, pp. 180–197. DOI: 10.1086/209295.

McQuarrie, E.F. and Mick, D.G. (1996) 'Figures of rhetoric in advertising language', *Journal of Consumer Research*, vol. 22, no. 4, pp. 424–438. DOI: 10.1086/209459.

McStay, A. (2010) 'A qualitative approach to understanding audience's perceptions of creativity in online advertising', *Qualitative Report*, vol. 15, no. 1, pp. 37–58.

Meamber, L. and Venkatesh, A. (1995) 'Discipline and practice: A postmodern critique of marketing as constituted by the work of Philip Kotler', in B. Stern and G.M. Zinkhan (eds.) *Enhancing Knowledge Development in Marketing*, vol. 6, pp. 248–253.

Merleau-Ponty, M. (1962a) *Experience and Objective Thought: The Problem of the Body*, New York, NY, Routledge.

Merleau-Ponty, M. (1962b) *Phenomenology of Perception*, London, Routledge.

Merton, R.K. (reprint 2017) *Sociology of Science and Sociology as Science*, New York, NY, Columbia University Press.

Metz, C. (1974) *Film Language: A Semiotics of the Cinema*, New York, NY, Oxford University Press.

Mick, D.G. (1986) 'Consumer research and semiotics: Exploring the morphology of signs, symbols and significance', *Journal of Consumer Research*, vol. 13, September, pp. 180–197.

Mick, D.G. (1997) 'Semiotics in marketing and consumer research: Balderdash, verity, pleas', Chapter 8 in S. Brown and D. Turley (eds.) *Consumer Research: Postcards from the Edge*, London, Routledge, pp. 249–262.

Mick, D.G. and Buhl, C. (1992) 'A meaning-based model of advertising experiences', *Journal of Consumer Research*, vol. 19, December, pp. 317–338.

Miles, C. (2013) 'Persuasion, marketing communication, and the metaphor of magic', *European Journal of Marketing*, vol. 47, no. 11/12, pp. 2002–2019.

Miles, C. (2014) 'The rhetoric of managed contagion: Metaphor and agency in the discourse of viral marketing', *Marketing Theory*, vol. 14, no. 1, pp. 3–18.

Miles, C. and Nilsson, T., (2018) 'Marketing (as) rhetoric: An introduction', *Journal of Marketing Management*, vol. 34, no. 15–16, pp. 1259–1271.

Mills, C.W. (1959) *The Sociological Imagination*. New York, NY, Oxford University Press.

Mills, S. (1997) *Discourse*, London, Routledge.

Mills, S., Patterson, A. and Quinn, L. (2015) 'Fabricating celebrity brands via scandalous narrative: Crafting, capering and commodifying the comedian, Russell Brand', *Journal of Marketing Management*, vol. 31, no. 5–6, pp. 599–615. DOI: 10.1080/0267257X.2015.1005116.

Minowa, Y., Visconti, L.M. and Maclaran, P. (2012) 'Researchers' introspection for multi-sited ethnographers: A xenoheteroglossic autoethnography', *Journal of Business Research*, vol. 65, no. 4, pp. 483–489. https://doi.org/10.1016/j.jbusres.2011.02.026

Minowa, Y., Maclaran, P. and Stevens, L. (2019) 'The Femme Fatale in Vogue: Femininity Ideologies in Fin-de-siècle America', *Journal of Macromarketing*, pp. 1–17. https://doi.org/10.1177/0276146719847748.

Moeran, B. (1996) *A Japanese Advertising Agency: An Anthropology of Media and Markets*, London, Routledge.

Moisander, J. and Valtonen, A. (2006) *Qualitative Market Research; A Cultural Approach*, London, Sage.

Morgan, G. (1992) 'Marketing discourse and practice: Towards a critical analysis', Chapter 7 in M. Alvesson and H. Willmotts (eds.) *Critical Management Studies*, London, Sage, pp. 136–158.

Morgan, G. and Smircich, L. (1980) 'The case for qualitative research', *Academy of Management Review*, vol. 5, pp. 491–500.

Moufahim, M., Humphreys, M., Mitussis, D. and Fitchett, J. (2007) 'Interpreting discourse: A critical discourse analysis of the marketing of an extreme right party', *Journal of Marketing Management*, vol. 23, no. 5–6, pp. 537–558. DOI: 10.1362/026725707X212829.

Mumby-Croft, R. and Hackley, C. (1997) 'The social construction of market entrepreneurship: A case analysis in the UK fishing industry', *Marketing Education Review*, vol. 7, no. 3, Fall, pp. 87–94.

Munro, R. (1997) 'Connection/disconnection: Theory and practice in organizational control', *British Journal of Management*, vol. 8, pp. 43–63.

Murray, J.B. and Ozanne, J.L. (1991) 'The critical imagination: Emancipatory interests in consumer research', *Journal of Consumer Research*, vol. 18, no. 2, pp. 129–144.

Murray, J.B., Ozanne, J.L. and Shapiro, J.L. (1994) 'Revitalising the critical imagination: Unleashing the crouched tiger', *Journal of Consumer Research*, vol. 21, pp. 559–565.

Nilsson, T. (2019) 'How marketers argue for business- Exploring the rhetorical nature of industrial marketing work', *Industrial Marketing Management*, vol. 80, pp. 233–241. DOI: 10.1016/j.indmarman.2018.10.004

Nilsson, Y. (2015) *Rhetorical Business: A Study of Marketing Work in the Spirit of Contradiction*, Doctoral thesis, Lund, Lund University, Department of Service Management and Service Studies, p. 205. http://lnu.diva-portal.org/smash/record.jsf?pid=diva2%3A1095759&dswid=-402.

Norris, J. and Sawyer, R.D. (2012) 'Toward a dialogic methodology', in J. Norris, R.D. Sawyer, and D.E. Lund (eds.) *Duoethnography: Dialogic Methods for Social Health and Educational Research*, Walnut Creek, CA, Left Coast Press, pp. 9–39.

Nuttall, P., Shankar, A., Beverland, M.B. and Hooper, C.S. (2011) 'Mapping the unarticulated potential of qualitative research stepping out from the shadow of quantitative studies', *Journal of Advertising Research*, vol. 51, no. 1, pp. 153–166. https://doi.org/10.2501/jar-51-1-153-166.

O'Donohoe, S. (1994) 'Advertising uses and gratifications', *European Journal of Marketing*, vol. 28, no. 8/9, pp. 52–75. DOI: 10.1108/03090569410145706.

O'Donohoe, S. (1997) 'Raiding the postmodern pantry: Advertising intertextuality and the young adult audience', *European Journal of Marketing*, vol. 3, no. 34, pp. 234–253. DOI: 10.1108/03090569710162344.

O'Guinn, T. and Faber, R.J. (1989) 'Compulsive buying: A phenomenological exploration', *Journal of Consumer Research*, vol. 16, no. 2, pp. 147–157. https://doi.org/10.1086/209204.

Olsen, B. (2003) 'The revolution in marketing intimate apparel- a narrative ethnography', in T. de Waal Malefyt and B. Moeran (eds.) *Advertising Cultures*, Oxford, Berg, pp. 113–138.

Olsen, B. (2016) 'Agency growing pains: Ethnography in the 1980s', *Journal of Business Anthropology*, vol. 5, no. 1, pp. 89–104.

Olsen, B. and Gould, S. (2008) 'Revelations of cultural consumer lovemaps in Jamaican dancehall lyrics: An ethnomusicological ethnography', *Consumption, Markets and Culture*, vol. 11, no. 4, pp. 229–257.

O'Reilly, K. (2005) *Ethnographic Methods*, London, Routledge.

O'Shaughnessy, J. (2009) *Interpretation in Social Life, Social Science, and Marketing*, London, Routledge.

O'Shaughnessy, J. and Holbrook, M. (2015) 'Understanding consumer behaviour: The linguistic turn in marketing research', in J. Sheth (ed.) *Legends in Consumer Behaviour: Morris B. Holbrook*, London, Sage.

O'Sullivan, S.R. (2016) 'The branded carnival: The dark magic of consumer excitement', *Journal of Marketing Management*, vol. 32, no. 9–10, pp. 1033–1058. DOI: 10.1080/0267257X.2016.1161656.

Ots, M. and Nyilasy, G. (2017) 'Just doing it: Theorising integrated marketing communications (IMC) practices', *European Journal of Marketing*, vol. 51, no. 3, pp. 490–510.

Parker, I. (1992) *Discourse Dynamics: Critical Analysis for Social and Individual Psychology*, London, Routledge.

Patterson, A. (2012) 'Social networkers of the world, unite and take over: A meta-introspective perspective on the Facebook brand', *Journal of Business Research*, vol. 65, no. 4, pp. 527–534.

Patterson, M. and Elliott, R. (2002) 'Negotiating masculinities: Advertising and the inversion of the male gaze', *Consumption, Markets and Culture*, vol. 21, no. 3, pp. 231–249.

Peirce, C.S. (1953–66) *Collected Papers*, C. Hartshorne, P. Weiss, and A.W. Burks (eds.), Cambridge, MA, Harvard University Press.

Peirce, C.S. (1986) 'Logic as semiotic: The theory of signs', in R.E. Innis (ed.) *Semiotics: An Introductory Reader*, London, Hutchinson.

Pelias, R.J. (2011) *Leaning: A Poetics of Personal Relations*, Walnut Creek, CA, Left Coast Press.

Peters, T. and Waterman, R. (1982) *In Search of Excellence*, New York, NY, Harper & Row.

Phillips, B.J. and McQuarrie, E.F. (2004) 'Beyond visual metaphor: A new typology of visual rhetoric in advertising', *Marketing Theory*, vol. 4, no. 1/2, pp. 113–136. DOI: 10.1177/1470593104044089.

Phillips, B.J. and McQuarrie, E.F. (eds.) (2008) *Go Figure: New Directions in Advertising Rhetoric*, New York, NY, M.E. Sharpe.

Phillips, J.M. and Reynolds, T.J. (2008) *Qualitative Market Research: An International Journal*, vol. 12, no. 1, 2009, pp. 83–99, 1352–2752. DOI 10.1108/13522750910927232

Pielichaty, H. (2015) 'Festival space: Gender, liminality and the carnivalesque', *International Journal of Event and Festival Management*, vol. 6, no. 3, pp. 235–250.

Pink, S., Horst, H., Hostel, J., Hjorth, L., Lewis, T. and Tacchi, J. (2016) *Digital Ethnography: Principles and Practice*, London, Sage.

Potter, J. and Wetherell, M. (1987) *Discourse and Social Psychology*, London, Sage.

Pratt, M.L. (1992) *Imperial Eyes: Travel Writing and Transculturation*, London, Routledge.

Preece, C., Kerrigan, F. and O'Reilly, D. (2019) 'License to assemble: Theorizing brand longevity', *Journal of Consumer Research*, vol. 46, no. 2, pp. 330–350. https://doi.org/10.1093/jcr/ucy076.

Puntoni, S., Schroeder, J. and Ritson, M. (2010) 'Meaning matters', *Journal of Advertising*, vol. 39, no. 2, pp. 51–64. DOI: 10.2753/JOA0091-3367390204.

Puntoni, S., Vanhamme, J. and Visscher, R. (2011) 'Two birds and one stone', *Journal of Advertising*, vol. 40, no. 1, pp. 25–42. DOI: 10.2753/JOA0091-3367400102.

Reed-Danahay, D.E. (1997) *Auto/Ethnography: Rewriting the Self and the Social*, Oxford, Berg.

Reynolds, T.J. and Gutman, A. (1988) 'Laddering theory: Method, analysis and interpretation', *Journal of Advertising Research*, vol. 28, no. 1, pp. 11–31.

Richardson, L. (2000) 'Writing: A method of inquiry', in N.K. Denzin and Y.S. Lincoln (eds.) *Handbook of Qualitative Research*, Thousand Oaks, CA, Sage, pp. 877–892.

Ritson, M. and Elliott, R. (1999) 'The social uses of advertising: An ethnographic study of adolescent advertising audiences', *Journal of Consumer Research*, vol. 26, no. 3, pp. 260–277.

Ritzer, G. (2000) *The McDonaldization of Society* (New Century edition), Thousand Oaks, CA, Pine Forge Press, Sage.

Roberts, M. (2015) ' "A big night out": Young people's drinking, social practice and spatial experience in the "liminoid" zones of English night-time cities', *Urban Studies*, vol. 52, no. 3, pp. 571–588.

Roberts, S. (2012) 'The reception of my self-experimentation', *Journal of Business Research*, vol. 65, no. 7, pp. 1060–1066.

Rod, M. and Ellis, N. (2014) 'Using discourse analysis in case study research in business-to-business contexts', Chapter 21 in *Advances in Business Marketing and Purchasing*, pp. 77–99. DOI: 10.1108/S1069-09642014000021003.

Rogers, C. (1945) 'The non-directive method as a technique for social research', *American Journal of Sociology*, vol. 50, pp. 279–283.

Rorty, R. (1982) *Consequences of Pragmatism*, Minneapolis, MN, University of Minnesota Press.

Roux, D. and Belk, R. (2018) 'The body as (another) place: Producing embodied heterotopias through tattooing', *Journal of Consumer Research*, ucy081. https://doi.org/10.1093/jcr/ucy081.

Russell, C.A. and Schau, H.J. (2014) 'When narrative brands end: The impact of narrative closure and consumption sociality on loss accommodation', *Journal of Consumer Research*, vol. 40, no. 6, 1 April, pp. 1039–1062. https://doi.org/10.1086/673959.

Rust, L. (1993) 'Observations: Parents and their children shopping together', *Journal of Advertising Research*, vol. 33, no. 4, July/August, pp. 65–70.

Said, E. (1978) *Orientalism*, London, Routledge and Kegan Paul.

Saldana, J. (2011) *Ethnotheatre: Research from Page to Stage*, Walnut Creek, CA, Left Coast Press.

Sartre, J.P. (1943) *Being and Nothingness*, London, Methuen (1958 edition).

Sartre, J.P. (1946) *Existentialism and Humanism*, trans. P. Mairet, London, Methuen (1990 edition).

Sartre, J.P. (1963) *Search for a Method*, New York, NY, Knopf.

Saussure, F. de (1915) *Course in General Linguistics*, trans. W. Baskin, London, Fontana (1974 edition).

Schatzki, T.R. (1996) *Social Practices: A Wittgensteinian Approach to Human Activity and the Social*, Cambridge, UK: Cambridge University Press.

Schatzki, T.R. (2002) *The Site of the Social: A Philosophical Account of the Constitution of Social Life and Change*, University Park, The Pennsylvania State University Press.

Schatzki, T.R. (2012) 'A primer on practices', in J. Higgs, R. Barnett, S. Billett, M. Hutchings, and F. Trede (eds.) *Practice-Based Education Perspectives and Strategies*, volume 6, Rotterdam, The Netherlands, Sense, pp. 13–26.

Schau, H.J., Gilly, M.C. and Wolfinbarger, M. (2009) 'Consumer identity renaissance: The resurgence of identity-inspired consumption in retirement', *Journal of Consumer Research*, vol. 36, no. 2, pp. 255–277.

Schau, H.J. and Thompson, K. (2010) 'Betwixt and between: Liminality and feminism in the twilight brand community', in M.C. Campbell, J. Inman, and R. Pieters (eds.) *NA – Advances in Consumer Research*, volume 37, Duluth, MN, Association for Consumer Research, pp. 89–93.

Schembri, S. and Latimer, L. (2016) 'Online brand communities: Constructing and co-constructing brand culture', *Journal of Marketing Management*, vol. 32, no. 7–8, pp. 628–651. DOI: 10.1080/0267257X.2015.1117518.

Schöps, J.D., Kogler, S. and Hemetsberger, A. (2019) '(De-)stabilizing the digitized fashion market on Instagram – Dynamics of visual performative assemblages', *Consumption Markets & Culture*. DOI: 10.1080/10253866.2019.1657099.

Schouten, J. (1991) 'Selves in transition: Symbolic consumption in personal rites of passage and identity reconstruction', *Journal of Consumer Research*, vol. 17, no. 4, March, pp. 412–425. https://doi.org/10.1086/208567.

Schouten, J. and McAlexander, J.H. (1995) 'Subcultures of consumption: An ethnography of the new bikers', *Journal of Consumer Research*, vol. 22, no. 1, pp. 43–61 https://doi.org/10.1086/209434.

Schroeder, J.E. (2002) *Visual Consumption*, London, Routledge.

Schroeder, J.E. and Borgerson, J.L. (2015) 'Critical visual analysis of gender: Reactions and reflections', *Journal of Marketing Management*, vol. 31, no. 15–16, pp. 1723–1731. DOI: 10.1080/0267257X.2015.1077883.

Schutz, A. (1932) *The Phenomenology of the Social World*, London, Heinemann (1967 edition).

Schwartz-Shea, P. and Yanow, D. (2012) *Interpretive Research Design*, Oxfordshire, Routledge.

Scott, L. (1990) 'Understanding jingles and needledrop: A rhetorical approach to music in advertising', *Journal of Consumer Research*, vol. 17, pp. 223–236.

Scott, L. (1994a) 'The bridge from text to mind: Adapting reader-response theory to consumer research', *Journal of Consumer Research*, vol. 21, pp. 461–480.

Scott, L. (1994b) 'Images in advertising: The need for a theory of visual rhetoric', *Journal of Consumer Research*, vol. 21, pp. 252–273.

Sebeok, T. (1991) *A Sign is Just a Sign*, Bloomington and Indianapolis, Indiana University Press.

Seregina, A. and Weijo, H.A. (2017) 'Play at any cost: How cosplayers produce and sustain their ludic communal consumption experiences', *Journal of Consumer Research*, vol. 44, no. 1, June, pp. 139–159. https://doi.org/10.1093/jcr/ucw077.

Shankar, A. (2000) 'Lost in music? Subjective personal introspection and popular music consumption', *Qualitative Market Research: An International Journal*, vol. 3, no. 1, pp. 27–37.

Shankar, A., Elliott, R. and Goulding, C. (2001) 'Understanding consumption: Contributions from a narrative perspective', *Journal of Marketing Management*, vol. 17, pp. 429–453.

Shankar, A. and Goulding, C. (2001) 'Interpretive consumer research: Two more contributions to theory and practice', *Qualitative Market Research: An International Journal*, vol. 4, no. 1, pp. 7–16.

Sherry, J.F. (1983) 'Gift giving in anthropological perspective', *Journal of Consumer Research*, vol. 10, no. 2, September, pp. 157–168. https://doi.org/10.1086/208956.

Sherry, J.F. (1991) 'Postmodern alternatives: The interpretive turn in consumer research', in T.S. Robertson and H.H. Kassarjian (eds.) *Handbook of Consumer Behaviour*, Englewood-Cliffs, NJ, Prentice-Hall, pp. 548–591.

Sherry, J.F. (1995) 'Bottomless cup, plug-in drug: A telethnography of coffee', *Visual Anthropology*, vol. 7, no. 4, pp. 351–370.

Sherry, J.F. and Camargo, G. (1987) 'May your life be marvellous': English language labelling and the semiotics of Japanese promotion', *Journal of Consumer Research*, vol. 14, September, pp. 174–188.

Sherry, J.F., McGrath, M.A. and Diamond, N. (2013) 'Discordant retail brand ideology in the *house of Barbie*', *Qualitative Marketing Research*, vol. 16, no. 1, pp. 12–37.

Sherry, J.F. and Schouten, J.W. (2002) 'A role for poetry in consumer research', *Journal of Consumer Research*, vol. 29, September, pp. 218–234.

Sinkovics, R.R., Richardson, C. and Lew, Y.K. (2015) 'Enhancing student competency and employability in international business through master's dissertations', *Journal of Teaching in International Business*, vol. 26, no. 4, pp. 293–317.

Skålén, P., Fougére, M. and Fellesson, M. (2008) *Marketing Discourse: A Critical Perspective*, London, Routledge.

Skålén, P. and Hackley, C. (2011) 'Marketing-as-practice: Introduction to the special issue', *Scandinavian Journal of Management*, vol. 27, no. 2, pp. 189–196. DOI: 10.1016/j.scaman.2011.03.004.

Smith Maguire, J. (2010) 'Provenance and the liminality of production and consumption: The case of wine promoters', *Marketing Theory*, vol. 10, no. 3, pp. 269–282.

Spicer, A., Alvesson, M. and Kärreman, D. (2009) 'Critical performativity: The unfinished business of critical management studies', *Human Relations*, vol. 62, no. 4, pp. 537–560. DOI: 10.1177/0018726708101984.

Spiggle, S. (1994) 'Analysis and interpretation of qualitative data in consumer research', *Journal of Consumer Research*, vol. 21, December, pp. 491–503.

Spradley, J. (1980) *Participant Observation*, New York, NY, Holt, Rinehart and Winston.

Stephens-Davidowitz, S. (2017) *Everybody Lies- What the Internet Can Tell Us About Who We Really Are*, London, Bloomsbury Publishing.

Stern, B.B. (1989) 'Literary criticism and consumer research: Overview and illustrative analysis', *Journal of Consumer Research*, vol. 16, pp. 34–46.

Stern, B.B. (1990) 'Literary criticism and the history of marketing thought: A new perspective on "reading" marketing theory', *Journal of the Academy of Marketing Science*, vol. 18, pp. 329–336.

Stern, B.B. (1993) 'Feminist literary criticism and the deconstruction of Ads: A postmodern view of advertising and consumer responses', *Journal of Consumer Research*, vol. 19, pp. 556–566.

Stern, B.B. and Schroeder, J. (1994) 'Interpretative methodology from art and literary criticism: A humanistic approach to advertising imagery', *European Journal of Marketing*, vol. 28, no. 8.

Stern, B.B., Thompson, C. and Arnould, E. (1998) 'Narrative analysis of marketing relationship: The consumer's perspective', *Psychology and Marketing*, vol. 15, no. 3, pp. 195–214.

Stubbs, M. (1983) *Discourse Analysis: The Sociolinguistic Analysis of Natural Language*, Oxford, Basil Blackwell.

Sturge, G. (2019) *UK Prison Population Statistics*, Briefing paper number CBP-04334, 23 July 2019, House of Commons Library.

Svensson, P. (2007) 'Producing marketing: Towards a social-phenomenology of marketing work', *Marketing Theory*, vol. 7, no. 3, pp. 271–290. https://doi.org/10.1177/1470593107080346.

Szmigin, I., Bengry-Howell, A., Griffin, C., Hackley, C. and Mistral, W. (2011) 'Social marketing, individual responsibility and the "culture of intoxication"', *European Journal of Marketing* (Q1), vol. 45, no. 5, pp. 759–779.

Szmigin, I. and Carrigan, M. (2001) 'Time, consumption and the older consumer: An interpretive study of the cognitively young', *Psychology and Marketing*, vol. 18, no. 10, pp. 1091–1116.

Tadajewski, M. (2014) 'What is critical marketing studies? Reading macro, social, and critical marketing studies', in R. Varey and M. Pirson (eds.) *Humanistic Marketing*. Humanism in Business Series, London, Palgrave Macmillan.

Tadajewski, M., Chelekis, J., DeBerry-Spence, B., Figueiredo, B., Kravets, O., Nuttavuthisit, K., Peñaloza, L. and Moisander, J. (2014) 'The discourses of marketing and development: Towards "critical transformative marketing research"', *Journal of Marketing Management*, vol. 30, no. 17–18, pp. 1728–1771. DOI: 10.1080/0267257X.2014.952660.

Tadajewski, M., Higgins, M., Denegri-Knott, J. and Varman, R. (eds.) (2019) *The Routledge Companion to Critical Marketing Studies*, London, Routledge, pp. 185–195, ISBN 9781138641402.

Tadajewski, M. and Maclaran, P. (2009) *Critical Marketing Studies*, London, Routledge.

Tanaka, K. (1994) *Advertising Language: A Pragmatic Approach to Advertisements in Britain and Japan*, London, Routledge.

Thaler, R.H. and Sunstein, C.R. (2008) *Nudge: Improving Decisions About Health, Wealth, and Happiness*, New Haven, CT, Yale University Press.

Thomas, J. (1993) *Doing Critical Ethnography*, Newbury Park, CA, Sage.

Thomas, T.C. and Epp, A.M. (2019) 'The best laid plans: Why new parents fail to habituate practices', *Journal of Consumer Research* (online early cite). https://doi.org/10.1093/jcr/ucz003.

Thompson, C.J. (1997) 'Interpreting consumers: A hermeneutical framework for deriving marketing insights from the texts of consumers' consumption stories', *Journal of Marketing Research*, vol. 34, no. 6, pp. 438–455.

Thompson, C.J. (2002) 'A re-inquiry on re-inquiries: A postmodern proposal for a critical-reflexive approach', *Journal of Consumer Research*, vol. 29, no. 1, June, pp. 142–145. https://doi.org/10.1086/339926.

Thompson, C.J. (2004) 'Marketplace mythology and discourses of power', *Journal of Consumer Research*, vol. 31, no. 1, June, pp. 162–180. https://doi.org/10.1086/383432.

Thompson, C.J. (2019) 'The "Big Data" myth and the pitfalls of "Thick Data" opportunism: On the need for a different ontology of markets and consumption', *Journal of Marketing Management*, vol. 35, no. 3–4, pp. 207–230.

Thompson, C.J. and Coskuner-Balli, G. (2007) 'Countervailing market responses to corporate co-optation and the ideological recruitment of consumption communities', *Journal of Consumer Research*, vol. 34, pp. 135–152. DOI: 10.1086/519143.

Thompson, C.J. and Haytko, D.L. (1997) 'Speaking of fashion: Consumers' uses of fashion discourses and the appropriation of countervailing cultural meanings', *Journal of Consumer Research*, vol. 24, no. 1, June, pp. 15–42. https://doi.org/10.1086/209491.

Thompson, C.J., Henry, P.C. and Bardhi, F. (2018) 'Theorizing reactive reflexivity: Lifestyle displacement and discordant performances of taste', *Journal of Consumer Research*, vol. 45, no. 3, October, pp. 571–594. https://doi.org/10.1093/jcr/ucy018.

Thompson, C.J. and Hirschman, E.C. (1995) 'Understanding the socialized body: A poststructuralist analysis of consumers' self-conceptions, body images, and self-care practices', *Journal of Consumer Research*, vol. 22, no. 2, September, pp. 139–153. https://doi.org/10.1086/209441.

Thompson, C.J., Locander, W.B. and Pollio, H.R. (1989) 'Putting consumer experience back into consumer research: The philosophy and method of existential phenomenology', *Journal of Consumer Research*, vol. 17, pp. 133–147.

Thompson, C.J., Locander, W.B. and Pollio, H.R. (1990) 'The lived meaning of free choice: An existential – Phenomenological description of everyday consumer experiences of contemporary married women', *Journal of Consumer Research*, vol. 17, December, pp. 346–361.

Thompson, C.J., Pollio, H.R. and Locander, W.B. (1994) 'The spoken and the unspoken: A hermeneutic approach to understanding the cultural viewpoints that underlie consumers' expressed meanings', *Journal of Consumer Research*, vol. 21, December, pp. 431–453.

Thompson, C.J. and Tambyah, S.K. (1999) 'Trying to be cosmopolitan', *Journal of Consumer Research*, vol. 26, no. 3, December, pp. 214–241. https://doi.org/10.1086/209560.

Thompson, C.J. and Ustunier, T. (2015) 'Women skating on the edge: Marketplace performances as ideological edgework', *Journal of Consumer Research*, vol. 42, no. 2, pp. 235–265.

Tiwsakul, R.A. and Hackley, C. (2012) 'Postmodern paradoxes in Thai-Asian consumer identity', *Journal of Business Research*, vol. 66, no. 4, pp. 490–496. www.sciencedirect.com/science/article/pii/S0148296311000609.

Tonks, D. (2002) 'Marketing as cooking: The return of the sophists', *Journal of Marketing Management*, vol. 18, pp. 803–822.

Tumbat, G. and Belk, R.W. (2011) 'Marketplace tensions in extraordinary experiences', *Journal of Consumer Research*, vol. 38, no. 1, pp. 42–63. https://doi.org/10.1086/658220.

Turner, V.W. (1967) *The Forest of Symbols: Aspects of Ndembu Ritual*, Ithaca and London, Cornell University Press.

Turner, V.W. (1969) *The Ritual Process: Structure and Anti-Structure*, New Brunswick, NJ, Transaction Publishers, Rutgers- The State University.

Turner, V.W. (1974) 'Liminal to liminoid, in play, flow, and ritual: An essay in comparative symbology', *Rice University Studies*, vol. 60, no. 3, pp. 53–92.

Turner, V.W. (1982) *From Ritual to Theatre- The Human Seriousness of Play*, New York, NY, PAJ Publications.

Turner, V.W. (1986) 'Dewey, Dilthey and Drama: An essay in the anthropology of experience', Chapter 2 in V.W. Turner and E.M. Bruner (eds.) *The Anthropology of Experience*, Chicago, University of Illinois Press.

Umiker-Sebeok, J. (ed.) (1987) *Marketing Signs: New Directions in the Study of Signs for Sale*, Berlin, Mouton.

Umiker-Sebeok, J., Cossette, C. and Bachand, D. (1988) 'Selected bibliography on the semiotics of marketing', *Semiotic Enquiry*, vol. 8, no. 3, pp. 415–423.

Üstüner, T. and Holt, D.B. (2007) 'Dominated consumer acculturation: The social construction of poor migrant women's consumer identity projects in a Turkish squatter', *Journal of Consumer Research*, vol 34, no. 1, pp. 41–56. https://doi.org/10.1086/513045.

van Dijk, T.A. (1984) *Prejudice in Discourse: An Analysis of Ethnic Prejudices in Cognition and Conversation*, Amsterdam, John Benjamins.

van Dijk, T.A. (ed.) (1985) *Handbook of Discourse Analysis*, vols. 1–4, London, Academic Press.

van Gennep, A. (1961) *The Rites of Passage*, Chicago, Chicago University Press.

van Laer, T., de Ruyter, K., Visconti, L.M. and Wetzels, M. (2014) 'The extended transportation-imagery model: A meta-analysis of the antecedents and consequences of consumers' narrative transportation', *Journal of Consumer Research*, vol. 40, no. 5, 1, pp. 797–817. https://doi.org/10.1086/673383.

van Laer, T., Edson Escalas, J., Ludwig, S. and van den Hende, E.A. (2019) 'What happens in vegas stays on tripadvisor? A theory and technique to understand narrativity in consumer reviews', *Journal of Consumer Research*, vol. 46, no. 2, August, pp. 267–285. https://doi.org/10.1093/jcr/ucy067.

van Laer, T. and Izberk-Bilgin, E. (2019) 'A discourse analysis of pilgrimage reviews', *Journal of Marketing Management*, vol. 35, no. 5–6, pp. 586–604. DOI: 10.1080/0267257X.2018.1550434.

van Laer, T., Visconti, L.M. and Feiereisen, S. (2018) 'Need for narrative', *Journal of Marketing Management*, vol. 34, no. 5–6, pp. 484–496. DOI: 10.1080/02 67257X.2018.1477817.

van Mannen, J. (ed.) (1995) *Representation in Ethnography*, Thousand Oaks, CA, Sage.

Varman, R., Saha, B. and Skålén, P. (2011) 'Market subjectivity and neoliberal governmentality in higher education', *Journal of Marketing Management*, vol. 27, no. 11–12, pp. 1163–1185. DOI: 10.1080/0267257X.2011.609134.

Venkatesh, S. (2009) *Gang Leader for a Day*, New York, NY, Penguin.

Villegas, D. (2018) 'From the self to the screen: A journey guide for auto-netnography in online communities', *Journal of Marketing Management*, vol. 34, no. 3–4, pp. 243–262. DOI: 10.1080/0267257X.2018.1443970.

vom Lehn, D. (2014) 'Timing is money: Managing the floor in sales interaction at street-market stalls', *Journal of Marketing Management*, vol. 30, no. 13–14, pp. 1448–1466. DOI: 10.1080/0267257X.2014.941378.

Wallendorf, M. and Arnould, E.J. (1988) ' "My Favorite Things": A cross-cultural inquiry into object attachment, possessiveness, and social linkage', *Journal of Consumer Research*, vol. 14, no. 4, March, pp. 531–547. https://doi.org/10. 1086/209134.

Wallendorf, M. and Brucks, M. (1993) 'Introspection in consumer research: Implementation and implications', *Journal of Consumer Research*, vol. 20, pp. 339–359.

Watson, T.J. (1994) *In Search of Management: Culture, Chaos and Control in Managerial Work*, London, Routledge.

Weinberger, M.F., Zavisca, J.R. and Silva, J.M. (2017) 'Consuming for an imagined future: Middle-class consumer lifestyle and exploratory experiences in the transition to adulthood', *Journal of Consumer Research*, vol. 44, no. 2, pp. 332–360 https://doi.org/10.1093/jcr/ucx045.

Wernick, A. (1991) *Promotional Culture: Advertising, Ideology and Symbolic Expression*, London, Newbury Park, Sage.

Wetherell, M. and Potter, J. (1992) *Mapping the Language of Racism: Discourse and the Legitimation of Exploitation*, New York, NY, Columbia University Press.

Williams Bradford, T. and Sherry, J.F. (2015) 'Domesticating public space through ritual: Tailgating as vestaval', *Journal of Consumer Research*, vol. 42, no. 1, June, pp. 130–151. https://doi.org/10.1093/jcr/ucv001.

Williamson, J. (1978) *Decoding Advertisements: Ideology and Meaning in Advertisements*, London, Marion Boyars.

Wilson, T. (2012) 'What can phenomenology offer the consumer?' *Qualitative Market Research*, vol. 15, no. 3, pp. 230–241. https://doi.org/10.1108/1352275 1211231969.

Woermann, N. (2018) 'Focusing ethnography: Theory and recommendations for effectively combining video and ethnographic research', *Journal of Marketing Management*, vol. 34, no. 5–6, pp. 459–483. DOI: 10.1080/0267257X.2018.1441174.

Wohlfeil, M., Patterson, A. and Gould, S.J. (2019) 'The allure of celebrities: Unpacking their polysemic consumer appeal', *European Journal of Marketing*. https://doi. org/10.1108/EJM-01-2017-0052.

Wohlfeil, M. and Whelan, S. (2012) ' "Saved" by Jena Malone: An introspective study of a consumer's fan relationship with an actress', *Journal of Business Research*, vol. 65, no. 4, pp. 511–519.

Woolgar, S. (1981) 'Interests and explanation in the social studies of science', *Social Studies of Science*, vol. 11, pp. 365–394.

Woolgar, S. (1988) *Science: The Very Idea*, Chichester, Ellis Horwood, London, Tavistock.

Woolgar, S. (1989) 'The ideology of representation and the role of the agent', in H. Lawson and L. Appignanesi (eds.) *Dismantling Truth: Reality in the Post-Modern World*, London, Weidenfeld and Nicolson.

Wright, S. (ed.) (1994) *Anthropology of Organisations*, London, Routledge.

Ybema, S., Keenoy, T., Oswick, C., Sabelis, I., Ellis, N. and Beverungen, A. (2009) 'Articulating identities', *Human Relations*, vol. 62, no. 3, pp. 299–322.

Yin, R.K. (2014) *Case Study Research Design and Methods* (5th edition), Thousand Oaks, CA, Sage, 282 pages.

Zeman, J.J. (1977) 'Peirce's theory of signs', in T. Sebeok (ed.) *A Perfusion of Signs*, Bloomington, IN, Indiana University Press, pp. 22–39.

Zhao, X. and Belk, R.W. (2008) 'Politicizing consumer culture: Advertising's appropriation of political ideology in China's social transition', *Journal of Consumer Research*, vol. 35, no. 2, August, pp. 231–244. https://doi.org/10.1086/588747.

Zwick, D. (2018) 'No longer violent enough? Creative destruction, innovation and the ossification of neoliberal capitalism', *Journal of Marketing Management*, vol. 34, no. 11–12, pp. 913–931. DOI: 10.1080/0267257X.2018.1536076.

Index

Note: page numbers in *italic* indicate a figure and page numbers in **bold** indicate a table on the corresponding page.

ABI-inform 45
absence, rhetoric of 188–190
abstracts 72–73
academic rigour 63
academic style of writing 61–63
access to data or interviewees 94–95
account planning 2
action-orientation 129, 222–223
adaptation of previous research 46
Adorno, T.W. 203
advertising research 2; conceptual projects 52–53; ethnography and 165–166, 171–173; focus/discussion groups in 99–103, **100**, **102**; literary theory and 184–187; postmodernist critique of 213–215; semiotics in 193–201; textual research and content analysis in 103
agency: definition of 30, 134; interpretive research paradigm and 12; situated freedom and 126–127
aims, research 73–75
algorithm-driven analytics 116–117
Alsop, C.K. 170
Althusser, L. 203
Alvesson, M. 179, 180, 204, 208, 212, 221
American University Business Schools 116
applied research tradition 163, 182
Ardley, B. 220
arguments 63–65
Aristotle 188
Arndt, J. 120, 144
Arnould, E.J. 173

Askegaard, S. 23, 145–147, 171
assemblage theory 117, 118
ATHENS 45
ATLAS 107
autoethnography 62–63, 169–171
axiology of research 123

Banister, P. 162
Bassiouni, D. 18, 31n3, 48, 177
Belk, R.W. 117, 169, 186, 195
Berger, P.L. 142
Bertrand, D. 194
bias 22, 31, 128
big data 82, 105–106, 116–117
Bloom's taxonomy 68
'blue skies' research 163
Bordieu, P. 171–172
brands, ideology and 186–187
Braun, V. *107*
British Journal of Management 2
Brown, S. 63, 157, 169–171, 187, 189, 191, 213–214
Brownlie, D. 63, 79, 180
Burrell, G. 11–12, 23, 97, 120, 122–124, 126–127, 140, 147

Camargo, G. 194
Cameron, D. 186
Campbell, C. 27
capitalist discourses 206–207
Case, P. 189
case study research 110–112
CCT *see* Consumer Culture Theory (CCT)
CDA *see* critical discourse analysis (CDA)

citation style 44–45, 57, 67–68, **68**
claims 63–65
Clarke, V. *107*, 165, 178
coding, thematic analysis and 106–108, *107*
collaborative autoethnography 169
commonalities of theoretically informed research 228–230
'common sense' understanding 79, 82, 189, 199
conceptual projects 46–47, 51–53, 57, 86
concluding comments on research 84
confirmatory research design 25, 30, 38, *39*
constitutive language 205, 217
constitutive power 131, 207–208
Consumer Culture Theory (CCT) 1, 23, 147, 160–161
Consumption 2
consumption and consumer research 2–3, 164–165; cross-disciplinarity in 26–27; death in 151; ethnography and 166–167, 174; experience and existence in 150–151; focus/discussion groups in 99–103, **100**, **102**; gender representation and 212–213; general topic areas for **15–16**, 35; ideology and 186–187; intentionality and 147–148; laddering technique in 97; meanings in 126; narrative studies in 191–193; observation in 108–109; postmodernist critique of 213–215; reflexivity in 179; representation in 179–181; semiotics and 193–201; sociological critique in 80–81
content analysis 103–105
convenience sampling 17, 30, 92, 113
conversation analysis 217, 221, 228
Cook, G. 221
correlation 92, 106, 113
critical discourse analysis (CDA) 221–222, **224**; *see also* discourse analysis (DA)
critical marketing 118
critical realism 130, 134
critical research: aims of 202–204; emancipation in 207, 217; gender studies and feminism in 212–213; ideology and 207–210; language and power in 205; managerialist

40, 217; performative 171, 218; postmodernism and 213–216; practices in 205–206, **206**; social constructionist ontology in 210–212; social critique in 206–207; subjectivities in 209, 218; *see also* power
critical thinking: functional critique 79; intellectual critique 79–80; literature review and 76–77; sociological critique 80–81; summary of 78; uncritical thinking 77–79
cross-disciplinarity 26–27
cultural studies 228

DA see discourse analysis (DA)
Danesi, M. 193
data and data gathering 30; big data 82, 105–106, 116–117; case studies 110–112; correlation 92, 106, 113; data scraping 116–117; datum/data, defined 86, 114n1; deprivation studies 110, 113; ecological validity 109, 113, 184; empirical generalisations 106, 113; ethnographic data 177–178; experiential perspective 109, 113; field notes 109–110, 113, 178; focus/discussion groups 99–101, **100**; idiographic research 92, 114; interpretive versus quantitative research 91–92; inter-subjective reliability 105, 114; longitudinal research 112, 114; 'messy' data sets 17–18, 229; multi-method approaches to 89; nomothetic research 92, 112, 114; observation 108–109, 114; phenomenological research 152–153; practice theory and 89, 114; pragmatic data gathering 90–91, *90*; primary data 9, 31, 86; research diaries 109–110; secondary data 86; textual data sets 103–106; thematic analysis and coding 106–108, *107*; theory and 88–89; transcription conventions for 97–99, 102–103, **102**, 114; universalised research 91, 114; *see also* interviews; samples
Davis, Foster 203
death, in consumer research 151
'de-centring' of knowledge 214

deconstruction, semiotic 199–200, **199**
deductive research design 47–48, 57
Deetz, S. 169, 179, 180, 204, 208
Delahunt, B. 107
Denzin, N.K. 169
deprivation studies 110, 113
depth interviews 17, 20, 30, 57; *see also* interviews
design see research design
diaries, research 109–110
digital ethnography 167–169
digitisation of data sets 105–106
direct quotes 66–68
discourse, definition of 217
discourse analysis (DA): action-orientation in 129; commonalities of theoretically informed research 229–230; critical discourse analysis (CDA) 221–222, **224**; critical qualitative research and 227–228; data-gathering approaches in 89; definition of 219–220; interpretive repertoire in 226, 231; performativity of 223, 227–228, 231; scope of 220–221; of social texts 222–223, *223*; structure, function, and variation in 222–223, *223*, 226–227, 231; themes and assumptions in 224–225, **224**; theoretical framing and 118
discursive closure 222
discussion groups see focus/discussion groups
discussion of research findings 84–85
duoethnography 169
dyadic semiotic relations 196–198, *197–198*, 201

Eagleton, T. 186, 208
Easterby-Smith, M. 178
EBSCO 45
ecological validity 109, 113, 184
Edgar, A. 207
Edwards, D. 188
EIASM Interpretive Consumer Research Conference 1
Elliott, R. 161, 165, 175, 184, 186, 220
Ellis, N. 220
Emancipation 207, 217
Emerald 45
emic approach 145, 153, 155, 159
emotional skills **29**

emphasis, research 18
empirical generalisations 106, 113
empirical research: characteristics of 9, *10*, 50–51; definition of 30, 86; empirical generalisations 106, 113; interpretive stance and 16, 115–116; method of 82–83, 86, 124
epistemology 23, 30, 82, 86
ethnodrama 169
ethnography: applied research tradition in 163, 182; autoethnography 169–171; case studies in 111; critical discourse analysis compared to 229; data-gathering approaches in 89; definition of 30, 160–161, 182; digital 167–169; experiential perspective in 162, 168, 182; features of 160–164, *162*; field notes and 178; formal versus informal data 177–178; indexicality in 174–175, 182; key elements of **174**; liminality and 164–165, 182; netnography 1, 167–169, 182; nomothetic research 163, 182; in organisational management studies 165–166; practice theory and 171–173, *172*; principles of 173–174, *173*; reflexivity and 178–179; replicability in 128; representation in research writing 179–181; styles of 175–177; video 166–167; *see also* postmodernism; poststructuralism
ethnomethodology 175, 217, 221, 228
ethnomusicological ethnography 169
etic approach 145, 159
European Journal of Marketing 1–2
existentialism 89, 144–145, 159
existential phenomenology see phenomenology
experiential perspective: definition of 113, 182; ethnography and 162, 168; liminoid experiences 164–165; phenomenology and 142, 147, 150–151; research diaries and 109
exploratory research designs: definition of 30; 'messy' data sets and 17–18; project trajectory 37–39, *38–39*; reasons for choosing 24–26, **25**

Fairclough, N. 221
Featherstone, M. 213
feminism 212–213

field notes 109–110, 113, 178
findings of research 83–84
Firat, A. 213
first chapter of research 72–73, **73**
focus/discussion groups: convening 101;
    definition of 57; principles for 99–101,
    100; qualitative data elicited through
    13, 14; recording and transcribing
    102–103, **102**; in research design 50
formal ethnographic data 177–178
Foucault, M. 220, 221–222
Four Ps 77, 79, 211
Foxall, G. 122
framing *see* theoretical framing
Frankfurt school 132, 203, 206
Fromm, E. 151
function (in discourse analysis)
    222–223, *223*, 231
functional critique *78*, 79
functionalist paradigm 12, 120,
    122–123
functional research projects 36–37,
    39–40, 57
Furusten, S. 189

Gabriel, D. 212
Garfinkel, H. 175, 217
gender studies 132, 212–213
generalisability 17, 30
generalisations, empirical 106, 113
Gergen, K. 192
Gergen, M. 192
Ghaffari, M. 119, 125, 171–172
Goldman, W. 64
Google Ngrams 105
Google Trends 82, 105–106
Gould, S. 169, 170
Grounded Theory (GT) 1, 107–108

Habermas, J. 142
Hackley, C. 166, 169, 170, 177, 184,
    187, 189, 199, 221
Hackley, R.A. 184
Harvard Business School 111
Harvard citation style 44, 45, 57, *68*
Hegel's philosophy of knowledge 142
Heidegger, M. 142
Henderson, G.R. 203, 204
hermeneutics: definition of 19, 30;
    hermeneutic circle 19–20; situated
    knowledge and objectivity 22–24,
    31, 128

Hirschman, E.C. 148, *150*, 208
Hitler, A. 197
Holbrook, M.B. 20–21, 22, 62, 115,
    150, 169–170, 189
Holt, D.B. 186, 214
Hopkinson, G. 220
Horkheimer, M. 203
'how' questions *55*–56
humanism: humanistic paradigms
    24, 30; influence of 148–150, 159;
    theoretical framing and 118
Hume, D. 116
Humphreys, A. 220
Husserl, E. 142, 147
hypotheses 16, 30
hypothetico-deductive studies 38,
    49, *57*

icons 195, 201
ideographic research 92
ideology: advertising and 186–187;
    critical research and 208–209;
    definition of 134; in management
    theory 203–204; power and 131;
    theoretical framing and 118
idiographic research 92, 114
independent student research projects
    see qualitative student research
    projects
indexes 196–197, 201
indexicality 174–175, 182
inductive ethnography 176
inductive research design 47–48, 57
informal ethnographic data 177–178
In Search of Excellence (Peters and
    Waterman) 211
Integrated Marketing Communications
    (IMC) plans 172
intellectual critique *78*, 79–80
intellectual skills **29**
intentionality 148–150, 159
interpersonal skills **29**
interpretants 196–198, *197*, *198*, 201
interpretive ethnography 176
interpretive paradigm 123
interpretive repertoire 225–226, 231
interpretive research: big data and
    116–117; characteristics of 91–92;
    critical research 202–218; criticisms
    of 12; cross-disciplinarity and 26–27;
    definition of 30; empirical knowledge
    and 115–116; hermeneutic circle and

19–20; influence of 1–3; interpretive
research paradigm 11–13; meanings
in 125–126; phenomenological
interviews and 145–146, *146*;
philosophical issues in 124–127;
power in 130–133; replicability
in 127–128, 135; research process
and 16–17; 'rich' descriptions in
124–125; theoretical framing of
88–89, 117–120, *119*, 139–141;
triangulation in 83, 87; 'two cultures'
of art and science and 21–22; validity
in 127–128; *see also* discourse
analysis (DA); ethnography
inter-subjective reliability 105, 114
intertextuality 185–186
interviews: access for 94–95;
conducting 95–97, **96**; depth 17,
20, 30, 57; objectives for 74–75;
phenomenological 145–147,
146, 153–154; pilot 94–95, 114;
recording and transcribing **98**;
sampling criteria for 92–93, *93*;
transcription of 98–99, 155; *see also*
depth interviews
introspective-praxis autoethnography 169

Jankel-Elliott, N. 161, 165, 175
Jankowicz, A.D. 70
journalism and media studies 229
Journal of Advertising 2
Journal of Business Research 2
Journal of Consumer Research 1, 150
Journal of Marketing 2
Journal of Marketing Management 2,
187

Kelly, G.A. 166
Kozinets, R.V. 167–168
Kuhn, T. 120, 134
Kunda, G. 204

laddering technique 97, 141
language: constitutive nature of
205, 217; in critical research 205;
indexicality of 175–176; social
constructionist ontology and
128–130; *see also* discourse analysis
(DA); literary theory
Leach, E. 195
Levitt, Theodore 189
Lim, M. 220

liminality 164–165, 182
liminoid experiences 164–165
Linnet, J.T. 23, 145–147, *146*, 171
literary theory: advertising research
and 184–185; icons 195, 201;
ideology 186–187; indexes 195–196,
201; narrative analysis 190–193,
190, 201; polysemy 201; relevance
of 183–184; rhetoric 187–190;
semiology 193, 201; semiosis 201;
semiotics 193–200, 201; structuralist
201; theoretical framing and 118
literature review: critical thinking and
75–77; definition of 31; educational
rationale for 18–19; importance of
26, 45; versus plagiarism 65–66;
review-based projects 9, *10*; scarcity
of published research 45–46
logical empiricism 120, 144
longitudinal research 112, 114
Loo, Benaliza 18
Luckman, T. 142
Lupton, D. 167
Lyotard, J.F. 191

Maguire, M. 107
managerialist research: critical research
202–210, **206**; critical thinking
and literature review 76–81; cross-
disciplinarity in 26–27; definition
of 217; ethnography and 165–166;
functional 40, 57; functional research
projects 36–37, 39–40, 57; general
topic areas **15–16**, 35–36; ideology
in 186–187, 203; managerial
authority, constructing 210–212;
normative 40, 57; phenomenology
and 147; representation in 180;
rhetoric in 187–190; scope of 39
marketing mix 77, 79
Marketing Theory 2
Markets and Culture 2
marking rubrics 68, **69–70**
Marlboro Man 186–187, 193
Marxist theorists 203, 208
materiality 130, 134, 172, 224–225
Mautner, G. 221
McCarthy, J.E. 77
McCloskey, D.N. 59, 190
McLeod, C. 171
meanings in research 125–126
Merleau-Ponty, M. 142

'messy' data sets 17–18, 229
meta-autoethnography 169
method of research 82–83, 86, 124
Mick, D.G. 194, 196
micro-sociology 131–132, 134
Mills, W.C. 169
Minowa, Y. 171
models 81–82
Morgan, G. 11–12, 23, 97, 120, 122–124, 126–127, 140, 147
motivation, topic selection and 40–43
Moufahim, M. 220
multi-method data gathering 89
Murray, J.B. 204

Napoleon 208
narrative analysis: definition of 201; key concepts of 190–191, **190**; marketing and consumption studies 191–193; theoretical framing and 118
narrative autoethnography 169
naturalistic research 118
netnography 1, 167–169, 182
Nilsson, T., 190
nomothetic research: case study research and 112; definition of 114, 182; ethnography and 163, 182; ideographic research compared to 92
non-response errors 17, 31
normative texts 40, 57, 80, 86
'nudge' theories of behavioural economics 117
Nvivo 105, 107
Nyilasy, G. 172

objectives, research 73–75
objectivity 22–24, 31, 128
observation 89, 108–109, 114
Olsen, B. 165, 169, 192
ontology: definition of 48–49, 134–135; realist 49, 58, 130, 135; social constructionist 48–49, 58, 116, 128–130, 135, 210–212, 224
O'Reilly, K. 161
originality of research 46–47
O'Shaughnessy, J. 20–21, 22, 115
Ots, M. 172
Ozanne, J.L. 204

paradigms *121*; definition of 31, 120, 134–135; functionalist 12, 120, 122–123; humanistic 24, 30; interpretive 11–13, 123; logical empiricist 120, 144; positivist 49, 58, 144; postmodernist 213–216; radical humanist 117, 123; radical structuralist *121*, 122–123, 127, 140, 147; relationship to theoretical tradition 139–141, *141*; sociological 120–124; see also existential phenomenology
paraphrasing 66
participant observation 9, 31, 89, 114
Patterson, M. 171, 191
Peirce, C.S. 135, 193, 196–197, 201, 229
performative research 171, 218
performativity 223, 231
phenomenology: commonalities with 229; data gathering in 89, 152–153; definition of 134–135; emic/etic approaches to 145, 153, 155, 159; existentialism and 89, 144–145, 159; experience and existence in 150–151; humanistic influences in 148–150, 159; intentionality and 147–148, 159; interview interpretation in 145–146, *146*; interview transcript analysis 155–156; major concepts of 141–143, **143**; research designs in 156–157; researcher stance in 153–154; shopping experiences and 157–158; theoretical traditions for 8, 23, 89, 118
philosophy of research: agency and situated freedom 126–127, 134; existentialism 144–145, 159; Hegel's philosophy of knowledge 142; initial considerations for 49; materiality 130, 134, 172, 224–225; meanings 125–126; power 130–133; realism 49, 130, 135; reductionism 124–125, 135; replicability and validity 127–128, 135; representation 52, 81–82, 135; research method and 124; 'rich' descriptions 124–125; social constructionist ontology 49, 58, 116, 128–130, 135, 224; see also paradigms; theoretical framing
pilot studies 94–95, 114
Pink, S. 161, 167
plagiarism 31, 46, 65–66
Plato 188

polysemy 185–186, 201, 214
positivism 49, 58, 144
postmodernism: definition of 182,
191; ethnography and 160–164;
postmodernist critique of marketing
213–215; student research projects and
215–216; theoretical framing and 118
poststructuralism 118, 182, 213, 221
Potter, J. 102, 188, 221, 225
power 130–133; constitutive 131; in
critical research 205; social critique
and 207–208; structural 130–131,
207–208, 210, 218
practical research skills 29
practice-based projects 9, 10
practice theory 89, 114, 118,
171–173, 172
pragmatic data gathering 90–91, 90
primary data 9, 31, 86
progressivism 214
project structure: abstract and chapter
one 72–73, 73; research aims and
objectives 73–75
Proquest 45
purposive criteria 92, 114

Qualitative Market Research: An
International Journal 2
qualitative student research projects:
approach to 7–8; characteristics
of 91–92; cross-disciplinarity
26–27; definition of 31; educational
rationale for 18–19; emphasis in 18;
exploratory research designs 17–18,
24–26, 25, 30; hermeneutic
circle and 19–20; interpretation and
1–3, 16–17; 'messy' data sets and
17–18; postmodernism and 215–216;
research design 47–56, 58; research
proposals 43–48, 44; scope of 39;
situated knowledge and objectivity
in 22–24, 31; skills gained through
27–29, 29; student–supervisor
relationship in 41–42, 58n1; topic
selection for 13–15, 15–16, 33–43,
34, 38–39; 'two cultures' of art and
science and 21–22; types of 9–11,
10; see also data and data gathering;
literature review; philosophy of
research; 'writing up' of research
quantitative studies: definition of 31;
exploratory research designs 17–18;

hypotheses 16, 30; interpretive
research compared to 91–92; non-
response errors 17, 31; when to use
24–26, 25; see also data and data
gathering; nomothetic research;
objectivity
quasi-ethnography 176
questions, research 54–56
Quinn, L. 220

radical humanist paradigm 117, 123
radical structuralist paradigm 121,
122–124, 127, 140, 147
randomised samples 17, 31
reader response theory 184
realism 49, 58, 130, 135
reductionism 124–125, 135
referencing style 44, 57, 67–68, 68
reflexivity in research writing 75, 86,
178–179
Reid, R. 157
relativist research 83
reliability, inter-subjective 114
replicability of research 127–128, 135
replication crisis 128
replication studies 38, 58
report structure 71–72, 72
representation in research 52,
81–82, 135
representative samples 17, 31, 100,
114, 135
research aims and objectives 74–75
research design: conceptual 51–53, 57,
86; deductive 47–48, 57; definition of
58; empirical 50–51; 'how' questions
55–56; inductive 47–48, 57; research
philosophy 48–49; 'what' questions
54–55; 'why' questions 55–56; see
also phenomenology
research diaries 110
research philosophy see philosophy of
research
research proposals 43–48, 44
research topics see topic selection
review-based projects see literature
review
rhetoric: of absence 188–190; in
organisational and academic practice
187–188
'rich' descriptions 13, 124–125
rigour, academic 63
Ritson, M. 165, 184, 220

Roberts, M. 164, 171
robust arguments 63
Rogers, Carl 149, 153
Rorty, R. 230
*Routledge Interpretive Marketing
    Research* series 2
rubrics, marking 68, **69–70**
Rust, L. 176

samples: convenience 17, 30, 92, 113;
    criteria for 92–93, *93*; definition of
    32; purposive 114; randomised 17,
    31; representative 17, 31, 100, 114,
    135
Saren, M. 79
Sartre, J.P. 142, 169
Saussure, F. de 193
scepticism 80
scholarship, standards of 68–71, **69–70**
Schroeder, J.E. 148, 184–185, 229
Schutz, A. 142
scope of research 39, 220–221
secondary data 86
Sedgwick, P. 208
semiology 193, 201
semiosis 192–201, 229
semiotics 201; communication
    codes in 129; definition of 135;
    discourse analysis and 221; dyadic
    and triadic semiotic relations
    196–198, *197–198*, 201; origins
    and scope of 193–195; philosophy
    of 229; practical 198–200; semiotic
    deconstruction 199–200, **199**; themes
    and concepts of 195–196, **195**;
    theoretical framing and 118
Sherry, J.F. 169, 194
signs 192–196, 201; see also semiotics
situated freedom 126–127
situated knowledge 22–24
Skålén, P. 221
Skoda motor cars 197–198
Snow, C.P. 21
social constructionist ontology: critical
    research and 210–212; critiques of
    224; definition of 58, 135; language
    and 128–130; realist ontology versus
    48–49, 116
social critique 206–207
social phenomenology 118
sociological critique *78*, 80–81
sociological paradigms see paradigms

sociology 228
sociopoetics 169
Spradley, J. 178
standards of scholarship 68–71,
    69–70
statistical tests 24
Stephens-Davidowitz, S. 105, 117
Stern, B.B. 148, 184–185, 204, 221
structuralist approach: definition of
    201; radical structuralist paradigm
    121, 122–123, 127, 140, 147
structural power 130–131, 207, 210,
    218
structure: discourse analysis 222–223,
    223, 231; project 72–75; report
    71–72, **71–72**
student research projects see qualitative
    student research projects
student–supervisor relationship 41–42,
    58n1
Subjective Personal Introspection (SPI)
    63, 118, 169–170
subjectivities 207–208, *209*, 218
sub-text 227–228
supervisors for research 41–42, 58n1
Svensson, P. 166, 221
swastika, symbolism of 197
symbols 195–197, 201
Szmigin, I. **102**

Tanaka, K. 194
Tate, S.A. 212
teleethnography 169
textual research 103–106
thematic analysis 106–108, *107*
theoretical framing: benefits of
    117–120, *119*; data gathering
    and 88–89; practice theory and
    171–173, *172*; purpose of 139–141;
    see also paradigms; philosophy of
    research
theories 81–82
third person, writing in 62–63, 179
Thompson, C.J. 22, 23, 117, 144, *146*
thoroughness of scholarship 70–71
titles of research projects 40–41
Tiwsakul, A. 170
tone of writing 61–63
Tonks, D. 187
topic selection: changes of topic 42–43;
    checklist for **34**; exploratory project
    trajectory 37–39, *38–39*; general

topic areas 13–15, **15–16**; initial
considerations for 33–37; relevance
of topic 36–37; scope of 39; student
motivation and 40–43; working titles
40–41
transcription conventions: definition
of 114; for focus/discussion groups
102–103, **102**; for interviews 97–99;
transcript analysis and 155–156
transcription of interviews **98**
transparency 84
A Treatise on Human Understanding
(Hume) 116
triadic semiotic relations 196–198,
197–198, 201
triangulation 83, 87
Turner, Victor 164–165, 182

uncritical thinking 77–79, *78*
universalised research 91, 114
Üstüner, Tuba 214

validity of research 127–128
van Gennep, A. 164
van Laer, T. 192
variability of texts 222–223, *223*,
226–227, 231
Venkatesh, A. 163, 213
Viagra 192
video ethnography 166–167
Villegas, D. 168

Wernick, A. 195, 196
Wetherell, M. **102**, 221, 225
'what' questions 54–55
Whelan, S. 171
'why' questions 55–56
Williamson, J. 194
Willmott, H. 204
Wohlfeil, M. 171
working titles for research projects
40–41
'writing up' of research: academic
writing tone 61–63; claims and
arguments 63–65; concluding
comments 84; critical thinking
in 75–80; direct quotes 66–68;
discussion 84–85; findings 83–84;
method section 82–83, 86; models
81–82; normative texts 40, 57, 80,
86; plagiarism 31, 46, 65–67; project
structure 72–75; referencing style
44, 57, 67–68, **68**; reflexivity 75, 86,
178–179; report structure 71–72,
71–72; representation 179–181;
research process and 59–61; standards
of scholarship 68–71, **69–70**; theories
81–82; triangulation 83, 87

Ybema, S., 220
Yin, R.K. 110

Zhao, X. 186

Lightning Source UK Ltd.
Milton Keynes UK
UKHW022214150121
377144UK00003B/43